MW00334085

CHOOSING THE BEST SELF-PUBLISHING COMPANIES AND SERVICES 2018

JIM GIAMMATTEO

JOHN DOPPLER

Series Editor
ORNA ROSS

Choosing the Best Self-Publishing Companies and Services 2018

An Alliance of Independent Authors Guide: Successful Self-Publishing Series Book 2

Copyright © 2017 Jim Giammatteo, John Doppler, Orna Ross, The Alliance of Independent Authors

All rights reserved

ISBN ebook: 978-1-909888-41-8

ISBN POD Edition: 978-1-909888-42-5

Published by Font Publications, London, UK

Category: Writing, Publishing

No parts of this publication may be reproduced, stored in a retrieval system, or transmitted in any form or by any means, electronic, mechanical, photocopying, recording, or otherwise, without the prior written permission of the copyright owner. This book is sold subject to the condition that it shall not, by way of trade or otherwise, be lent, re-sold, hired out, or otherwise circulated without the publisher's prior consent in any form of binding or cover other than that in which it is published and without a similar condition including this condition being imposed on the subsequent purchaser. Under no circumstances may any part of this book be photocopied for resale.

The assessments in this book are the opinions of the Watchdog Desk of the Alliance of Independent Authors.

Cover Art: © Dmitri Malinovski

Cover Design: Andrew Brown at Design for Writers

Editorial: Brett Hardman, Margaret Hunter

Formatting and Interior Design: Margaret Hunter at Daisy Editorial

10 9 8 7 6 5 4 3 2 1

CONTENTS

PART X
SERVICE RATINGS

PART XI
APPENDICES

PART I
INTRODUCTION

WRITER BEWARE!

BY VICTORIA STRAUSS

The new viability of self-publishing has attracted legions of authors, creating an intensely crowded marketplace where it's harder than ever to stand out. More and more self-publishers are choosing to invest in editing, design, cover art, even publicity. In response, a whole industry has sprung up around self-publishing. And that's where a problem begins to arise. Because when demand is high, scammers and schemers inevitably show up to take advantage.

The Alliance of Independent Authors (ALLi) and Writer Beware have tracked the amazing growth of these schemes and scams over the past few years. From "editing services" that do little more than run manuscripts through spelling and grammar checks, to overpriced designers and artists and formatting services, to bogus publicists who charge a premium for junk-mail "marketing," to predatory self-publishing services that advertise themselves misleadingly and engage in relentless upselling, self-publishers face a wide array of dangers.

Lack of competence is also a big problem. There are skilled providers for every step of the self-publishing process, but there are also many people offering services—often for a lot of money—that they aren't qualified to deliver. These people may not be scammers; in fact, they may have the best of intentions. But goodwill is not a substitute for experience. For most writers, the difference between a scammer and an amateur is negligible: either way, they wind up with a smaller bank account and an inferior product.

Yet another challenge: navigating the enormous amount of propaganda and proselytizing. Whether to self-publish or publish traditionally is currently the most polarized area of discussion in all of publishing.

Self-publishing evangelists compare traditional publishers to lumbering dinosaurs, incapable of adapting to a changing world. Self-publishing, they say, is the only worthwhile path to freedom and success. Traditional publishing evangelists characterize self-publishing as nothing more than a titanic slush pile, and declare that real credibility is reserved for books that carry the logo of a traditional publishing house.

Neither of these views reflects reality, though each holds a grain of truth. In this contentious debate, it's hard to find anyone who hasn't taken a side—which can make things difficult for writers who are searching for unbiased information.

How, then, to make your way in this complicated, confusing new realm? This guide is an excellent place to start. It gives you the skills and information you need to comparison shop among self-publishing providers and platforms. And if you are planning on successfully self-publishing, comparison shopping is essential.

There are scores of self-publishing services offering a range of prices—from free to five figures—and features. Only by comparing one with another and getting to know what's possible can you be sure to find the best match for your needs and goals.

Be educated. A good knowledge base is your best defense against schemes and scams. Take the time to learn about self-publishing before jumping into it. The informative articles in the guide can help, as can ALLi's Self-Publishing Advice Centre (selfpublishingadvice.org)—and be sure you have a good understanding of trade-publishing as well (see **Part Two**).

Authors these days have the luxury of choosing their path to publication, and both self- and trade-publishing offer their own sets of advantages and challenges. Unless you understand the whole range of options available to you, you can't truly make an informed decision about which way to go.

Be social. Hang out with other self-publishers—you'll learn a lot from both their successes and their mistakes. ALLi's member forum is invaluable, and the active Kindle boards are a treasure trove of information on every conceivable aspect of self-publishing.

Be smart. For any person or service you're thinking of hiring, check references, credentials, and reputations.

Don't take anything at face value. Another great resource is the Bewares, Recommendations, and Background Check forum of the Absolute Write Water Cooler, which has hundreds of discussion threads on agents, editors, self-publishing services, and more. You can also contact ALLi or Writer Beware; if we've received any reports of problems with a particular service, we'll let you know.

Be hyperskeptical. Self-publishing is one way to build a writing career, but it is not the only way, or the right way for all. There is no "best" method of publishing, only the method that's right for you and your book. Be wary of anyone who tells you otherwise.

Successful self-publishing is hard work. Be prepared to get out of it what you put into it. Good luck!

WELCOME TO THE INDIE AUTHOR MOVEMENT

BY ORNA ROSS

Congratulations! You want to know more about self-publishing services so that must mean you've written a book. Your first perhaps? Or maybe you're moving from trade-publishing to self-publishing, or you've self-published already and now want to explore new services that will expand your reach?

Whatever your circumstances as a writer, thanks to the digital revolution, putting a book out is getting easier all the time. But publishing well—presenting an author's words in a way that makes them valuable to readers and reaching as many readers as possible—is as hard as ever. Good publishing is seven processes done well. Each has its own set of challenges and requirements to be met:

1. Editing (content, copy/line editing, proofreading)
2. Design (ebook and print cover design)
3. Production (manuscript conversion, ebook and print layout/formatting, audiobook production)
4. Distribution
5. Marketing
6. Promotion
7. Rights licensing.

The new self-publisher is, therefore, embarking on a steep learning curve. Almost immediately, questions start to arise. Who are my readers? Family and friends, or wider? What services and supports do I need? How much will it cost me? How much can I make? Can I *really* go it alone? What will other people think?

Starting out, many writers type "self-publishing" into a Google search and instantly find themselves drowning in results, bogged down in jargon, or confused by who does what and who serves whom. The answers to their questions are in there somewhere but framed in a hundred different ways by a thousand different people.

Soon, instead of clarity, the writer emerges with a whole new suite of questions. How much should an editor cost? How do I protect my copyright? What is an ISBN? Do I need one? How do I get one? Is it worth paying for promotion?

No wonder aspiring authors feel overwhelmed. They are adrift in an unregulated market: on one hand creative, innovative, and exciting; on another, idiosyncratic, illogical, and incoherent. Some services are run by people who are knowledgeable, dedicated, helpful, and fair; others are clueless, greedy, callous, and manipulative.

Writers must make their self-publishing choices in an environment where the same service can cost $500 or $15,000 depending on where you shop; where companies understate the challenges of writing and publishing well and overstate the value of ineffective services, particularly around marketing and promotion; where one large operation with many imprints (notably Author Solutions) dominates the information stream, including Google ads/search, and traps unwary writers into thinking they are trade-publishers, offering kudos and investment.

As Victoria Strauss points out in her introduction, tyro self-publishers can easily fall victim to literary fraud, scams, and misleading practices, duped by the pretense that their book is being "published," while in reality it is only being printed or formatted. This is production, not publishing and, as we have seen, production is just one of those key seven stages in the publishing process.

Alliance of Independent Authors (ALLi)

One of our daily jobs at ALLi is to help our members, and the wider indie community, navigate what Victoria calls the "shark-infested waters" of the self-publishing sector. This function is overseen by our Watchdog Desk, headed up by John Doppler, one of the co-authors of this book, and Philip Lynch, ALLi's Resources Director, supported by Giacomo (Jim) Giammatteo, the other co-author, and community voices like David Gaughran, Dan Holloway, Mick Rooney, Helen Sedwick, Victoria Strauss, and Mark Williams, and our Author Members.

From the outset, our organization has also offered a Partner Membership to self-publishing companies and freelancers who offer good services, creative solutions, and decent business practices to authors, and are willing to sign up to our Code of Standards (see **Appendices**).

Partner Members can be individuals or organizations, and they range from huge companies like Amazon KDP and Apple iBooks to family businesses and individual freelance editors and designers. Many of them are writers themselves, or otherwise embedded in the writing and publishing community, and we are delighted to connect them to our Author Members.

We also maintain a growing ALLi database of questionable publishers, editors, services, literary agents, contests, review sites and magazines, publicity and marketing firms, and other companies whose practices do not conform to our Code of Standards.

This archive is assembled using feedback from our members, our Watchdog Desk and other associates, and affiliated research, enabling our members to separate the best from the rest.

This book—the only serially updated guide to the global self-publishing services industry—is designed to convey the benefit of that information to our members and to other authors contemplating, or already enjoying, self-publishing.

We explore this rapidly growing sector with the aim of

demystifying it and providing self-publishers with the necessary tools to choose the best services for them.

DEFINING OUR TERMS

In the latter decades of the 20th century, that dim and distant time before the internet when books were distributed almost exclusively through bookstores, authors funding publication of their own books were said to be "vanity publishing."

The divide seemed simple. If *they* were paying, you had a publisher; if *you* were paying, you were vain, and you had a vanity publisher. Actually, it never was that clear-cut. Even in the relatively closed system of late 20th-century publishing, many great books were self-published before being picked up by the trade.

If your book was good enough, the implication went, then it would have found a proper publisher, one willing to invest in it. If you hadn't managed to do that, you were most probably vainly deluded about your own ability as a writer. You needed, at best, to rewrite and improve or, preferably, give up and go away.

The vanity accusation was a good way of keeping authors feeling insecure, and in some quarters, the stigma from that time lingers still.

That this assumption was deeply wrong has been revealed by the new technologies and platforms that have expanded possibilities in the self-publishing sector. Manuscripts from aspiring writers that would be relegated to what trade-publishers (charmingly) call "the slush pile" are now finding engaged readers and avid fans.

Now, approaching the end of the second decade of the 21st century, there is a plethora of choices, and the problem for the author is not a tight, closed system but a confusing, perhaps even overwhelming, cornucopia of options.

The publishing industry is now made up of two broad streams. The first is what used to be called just "publishing" and which we at ALLi now call "trade-publishing," where a company owned by anyone other than the author of the book invests in the tasks of publication like design, editorial, marketing, and publicity.

The second revenue stream is "author-publishing," most commonly called "self-publishing," where the author of the book funds publication.

This self-publishing sector breaks down into three separate streams:

- Poor assisted services/self-publishing packages to be avoided (often still called "vanity presses" or "vanity publishers").
- Services and freelance operators hired directly by authors who upload their own books directly to commission-based platforms like KDP or IngramSpark (maximizes profit, but requires authors to source and manage their book's production and promotion).
- Good assisted services/self-publishing packages that provide packages which include some, or all, of the seven processes of publishing (for those who want a higher level of support or who value time more than money).

The option to take a more independent route, by employing your own editors and designers and, perhaps, a publicist to assist with social media or other campaigns, and uploading your files directly to online retailers like Amazon, Apple, and Ingram, and distributors like

PublishDrive and Draft2Digital, is the one taken by most of our members who make a living from their work.

Some choose to upload only to Amazon to benefit from the advantages available to them if they go exclusive.

Going direct means making choices all along the way that maximize your creative and commercial advantage, drawing together online tools and creative collaborators to supplement your own competencies and self-taught skills, and getting stuck into hands-on book preparation and production: learning by doing.

First time out, it takes the author on a steep learning curve, which is why some people like to break themselves in gently by starting with the support of a full-service package.

A one-stop publishing package is generally an expensive option and often, depending on the contract offered by your service, may limit your opportunities and your control (see **Part Five**).

The first half of this book will help you to make this big decision and to appraise any service, whether large or small, package, or single function.

HOW TO READ THIS BOOK

B eginning with an overview of the current publishing and self-publishing industry, this book defines the questions we all need to ask of ourselves and of any services we are considering when setting out. In deciding which route you'll take, you are doing much more than simply choosing a service; you are adopting a method and a process.

The second half of this book offers a comparative sample of the most significant service providers, analyzed in depth. To evaluate these players, we've used recommendations from our members, warnings from our Watchdog Desk, other community word-of-mouth advice, and in-depth research.

We tell you what these service providers do and don't do, what they charge, and for what. We outline what to look out for when trying to compare one service with another in a landscape where they don't all offer the same thing. How do you compare an apple with an orange with a banana with a cabbage? We've done our best. Offerings have been categorized, prices examined, royalty structures broken down, terms and conditions trawled, phone calls made, small print scrutinized, and claims checked against the experience of real-life authors who have actually used these services.

Our aim is to demonstrate the options you are likely to encounter. We'll show you which services are doing a good job, and why you might avoid others. Most importantly, in an industry where things are changing so rapidly, we aim to provide the criteria by which you can evaluate any self-publishing service yourself.

Using these examples, we show you the good and bad signs to look for and the questions to ask. And throughout, we show you case studies of members who have made numerous publication choices.

Other things you should know about this book:

- This book is designed to grow and change based on developments in the industry and reader feedback, and it is updated regularly by our Watchdog team.
- All our Watchdog team and advisors are independent authors themselves, who dedicate much time and attention to keeping unsuspecting authors out of the hands of poor services.
- Our ratings build on the work of Jim Giammatteo, who has done the nitty-gritty work of breaking down the detail and comparing terms, royalty splits, etc. across the board.
- We don't always agree on everything, but we all agree on what makes a good service and how services can improve.

And we all believe passionately in the creative power and potential of self-publishing and author collaboration and connection.

The aim of our guide is to give you all the information you need to make informed decisions for yourself about which pathway is best for each of your books, whether DIY author-publishing, assisted self-publishing, trade-publishing, or a combination.

And having decided, you'll know how to make the most of the opportunities each particular pathway offers and how not to get snared in other people's priorities along the way.

It's called independence, and that's the attitude we're here to foster in the writing community. At ALLi, we encourage our members to be proud of their indie status, and to carry that pride into all ventures, negotiations, collaborations, and partnerships, not only in the interests of our own success, but to further the empowerment of all writers, everywhere.

Writers are banding together and supporting each other to catch and build this new wave of author empowerment.

We are telling each other about good services (that help us sell good books) and how they differ from vanity outfits (that sell shoddy author services). We are showing each other how to do the tasks we need to do, with minimum outlay of time and money, and sharing the techniques and tools, the news and views that empower each of us to write and publish well. This is the indie author movement, and all of us at ALLi are proud to be here, doing what we can to support it.

The shift in power toward the author makes many people uncomfortable, including many writers themselves. With the control and freedom delivered by self-publishing comes responsibility, and that can be daunting. Often, it is in trying to avoid this responsibility that writers hire second-rate or problematic services. The danger is that the fear factor—nervousness, anxiety, dismissing all trade-publishers as the enemy, undervaluing our indie achievements, not preparing for effective negotiations—could see us selling ourselves short. This is where the independent author mindset comes in.

WHAT IS AN INDIE AUTHOR?

BY ORNA ROSS

At ALLi, we use the terms "author-publishing" and "indie authors" to distinguish those writers who earn, or aim to earn, their living from writing from those who are writing a book for family, friends, or personal community.

The latter is also, of course, a noble endeavor and, somewhat ironically, even as we see some author-publishers failing to sell, one from which unexpected bestsellers sometimes spring. The creative industries are never predictable.

But "self" publishing is a misnomer for the proactive indie author. It implies that we do it all alone when, actually, everyone needs help to write and publish well. "Independent" too is a relative term; a good book is always a team effort. "Indie," an abbreviation of "independent," is an inclusive umbrella term at ALLi.

Some of our members are fiercely autonomous, as DIY as it's possible to be, actively advocating the self-publishing route for all and envisaging the imminent end of trade-publishing as we know it. While these members of the community tend to be more vocal, many members are actually happy to collaborate with a publishing service where that seems advantageous, some working with paid services, others with trade-publishers.

For ALLi, being an indie author does not mean that you have to be wedded to self-publishing in every situation. Some people use the term "hybrid author" to describe a writer who publishes books through both trade and self-publishing platforms. At ALLi, we believe the term "indie author" adequately—and best—describes such a writer.

What, then, marks out an "indie" from other authors? For ALLi, you are an independent author if these points apply to you:

- You have self-published at least one book.
- You see yourself as the creative director of your books, from conception to completion through marketing, promotion, and beyond.
- You expect that status as creative director to be acknowledged in any partnership you negotiate, whether a paid author service, or in a deal with a trade-publisher or agent.
- You only work with paid services that acknowledge you as the rights holder. If dealing with an offer from a trade-publisher, you expect a higher royalty rate and advance than an author who doesn't have an established readership.
- You recognize that you are central to a revolutionary shift in publishing, which needs to move from seeing the author purely as a resource (in the new parlance, "content provider") to respecting the author as the creative director with much to offer in each step of the publishing process.
- You are proud of your indie status and carry that self-respect into all your ventures, negotiations, and collaborations, for your own benefit and to benefit all writers.

As a guiding principle, and recognizing that we are always going to be constrained to varying degrees by time and money, we advise all members to make their writing available wherever people might find and enjoy it, whether that's different retailers, different regions, or in different formats. The more retailers and regions and formats you're in, the stronger your foundation for consistent, long-term income.

It *is* possible to find your way through the glut of self-publishing services. It's about knowing the kind of book you want to write, the kind of reader it's aimed at, and the kind of writer you want to be. It's about understanding that there are parts of this job that nobody can do for you and other parts where partnership is not only possible, but necessary. The mix will vary from book to book and author to author, but we are all, however independent minded, in the collaboration business.

What self-publishing doesn't do is absolve us of the responsibility of learning our craft and our art. Writing can be both, as we know, but what is not often acknowledged is that so, too, can publishing.

In setting out to choose a self-publishing service, you are setting off on the adventure of a lifetime. Self-publishing a book is an intensely creative experience. As somebody who spent 20 years in traditional media and publishing before getting involved in this movement, I found that self-publishing changed everything for me as a writer.

I am overjoyed to be here for this revolution in the literary world, to witness the changes it is igniting in the community of writers and readers—the most important, because most influential, human community.

So yes, you can take creative hold of this fragmented and incoherent marketplace and find the perfect place within it for you and your books. We have thousands of members and subscribers who are doing just that. With knowledge and dedication, they are immensely enriching their own lives and the lives of their readers, and of the literary, cultural, and creative industries.

Read on to find out how to join them.

PART II

THE PUBLISHING INDUSTRY

FIRST: THINK DIGITAL

The first thing you need to know is that when you go independent, you go digital. As readers and writers, we tend to think first about print books selling through bookstores, but digital publishing—ebooks, audiobooks, and print-on-demand (POD) books—delivers too many advantages for us to favor consignment print and bookstore distribution (the traditional model favored by trade-publishing).

WHY DIGITAL?

Digital Self-Publishing Levels the Playing Field

When readers search for, find, and buy books on the internet, how the book was published is irrelevant. A self-published book has a page on Amazon or Kobo or iBooks that's just as much a selling opportunity as the pages for books from the big trade-publishers, and if your book is well written, edited, and designed, the reader won't know the difference. "Being able to compete head-to-head like this is unprecedented and a fantastic opportunity for all of us who publish books," says ALLi advisor and self-publishing guru Joel Friedlander. "This creates an environment in which it's your own passion, your own persistence, and your own promotional creativity that will sell your book. That's great, because all those things are within your power."

Digital Self-Publishing Delivers Global Readership

Back in the late 19th century, when publishers in the US and UK divided up the copyright world, book rights were tightly controlled within geographic areas. A book published in the US, for example, was not freely for sale in the UK or Australia. Now POD books, ebooks, books as apps, and online bookstores are changing all that.

You press "Publish" today in Canada, and you can be read in Japan tomorrow. This greatly increases the potential readership for a title that might have struggled to sell enough numbers at national level. Thus, many niche markets and more literary and midlist writers can now flourish.

Digital Self-Publishing Pays Better Royalties

An indie author can receive as much as a 70 percent royalty from an ebook self-published with Amazon, iBooks, or Kobo, compared with 10 percent or less from a book sold through trade-publishing.

Digital Self-Publishing Gives Readers a Point-of-Purchase at the Moment of Discovery

In the old way, a reader read about a book in the review pages, or heard about it on the radio, or was recommended it by a friend. They wrote down the author and title and went to the bookstore and asked for it, and maybe it was in stock. Now a reader can buy your book online at the moment they discover they want it. It can be theirs at— literally—the touch of a button in that vital instant known by salespeople as the "desire-to-act" moment.

Digital Self-Publishing Keeps Books in Publication

There's no such thing as "out of print" with digital and no such thing as "returns." In the old publishing system, most new books got a few weeks around publication time to make their name. Now, indie authors are like Bob Dylan, on a never-ending tour. There's no reason why you can't be promoting in 20 years' time a book you publish today, if you want.

Digital Self-Publishing Allows Authors to Set Prices Directly

In trade-publishing, authors have no control over the pricing of their books. In indie self-publishing, the ability to manipulate price at the touch of a button, and to give away free books, delivers a competitive advantage.

Digital Self-Publishing Allows for Changes and Revisions

Trade print publishing takes months, or sometimes years, to fix errors. Publishers print revisions only after a print run has sold. All the major self-publishing services allow you to revise your book whenever you want, in both ebook and POD versions.

Digital Self-Publishing is Flexible and Nimble

Aside from exceptional bulk sales, trade-publishing sells to retailers, not readers. A self-publisher can make any kind of deal with any group or organization and set up any collaborations and partnerships that suit them and their books.

Digital Self-Publishing Delivers Great Analytics

In the trade system, an author gets a six-monthly or yearly royalty statement that is often complex and incomprehensible. Ask a trade author how many copies a book has sold, and the answer will probably be that they don't actually know. Online ebook and POD sellers provide near real-time sales figures, so you can get immediate insights into the usefulness of marketing and promotion efforts, or experiments with pricing. Amazon's Author Central also provides access to BookScan, which delivers point-of-sale retail information for print books.

Digital Self-Publishing's Economies Allow Writers to Afford Tools and Talent

A lot of editors, proofreaders, designers, and other pros have gone into the freelance marketplace, and many indie authors are now hiring editors who used to be employed by large publishing houses. New technologies make publishing easier and cheaper all the time. So every talent and tool you need to build a wonderful book is now available to you, at a reasonable price.

Digital Self-Publishing Gives Creative Freedom

In the old trade-publishing system, only the most successful celebrity authors had control of, or even input into, matters of design and title or, sometimes, even subject matter and treatment. As a self-publisher, you decide what's going to be in your book, how long it will be, how it will look, what it will be called. That level of control and responsibility is an exhilarating, sometimes scary, experience.

Digital Self-Publishing Encourages New Literary Forms

This creative freedom, together with new technologies, is giving rise to new literary forms: books as apps, Kindle Singles, novellas, multimedia books, books as online courses, cell-phone novels, and many more. And one of the least discussed benefits of ebooks— hidden away beneath chatter about their effect on publishers' bottom line—is that they allow stories to be exactly as long as they want to be. And it seems many of them want to be between 10,000 and 35,000 words long. This has the makings of a whole new genre in both fiction and nonfiction.

Taken together, these changes are remaking authorship. Self-publishing now offers real creative and commercial opportunities.

This doesn't mean that clicking that "Self-Publish Your Book Now" ad you saw on Google is a good idea. First you need a clear understanding of how the self-publishing marketplace operates.

SELF-PUBLISHING SERVICES

Ebook Retailers

These are the large online bookstores that have their own self-publishing platforms. They present the resulting self-published titles side by side with books supplied to the store by trade-publishers.

The largest is Amazon, which has three self-publishing systems attached: the KDP platform for ebooks (and in the early stages of testing, print books); CreateSpace for print books; and ACX for audiobooks. Others of note are the iBooks store, with self-publishing platform iTunes Connect; Barnes and Noble (B&N), which owns self-publishing platform NOOK; and the Kobo store, which sells self-published books created in Kobo Writing Life.

Also in this group is Google Play, the search behemoth's self-publishing platform. Not currently recommended by ALLi due to complexities concerning pricing, it has been closed to new writers since 2015.

These stores account for the vast majority of ebooks sold.

Distributors

There are so many online stores around the world now selling ebooks, it would be impossible for an indie to find and supply them all. Distributors get your book into bookshops, particularly the online retailers, but in some cases also the physical stores.

The best distributors offer what contracts refer to as a "nonexclusive" clause: they allow you to pick and choose, so you can go direct to stores like Amazon, but also use their services to take you into other, less accessible, stores.

The best-known distributor is Smashwords, which was the first in the field, founded by our distribution advisor, Mark Coker, in 2008.

Other major and growing players are Ingram, Bertram, and Gardners for print books; and Draft2Digital for ebooks.

IngramSpark is unique in providing a one-stop platform for both ebook and print book stores.

PublishDrive, from Hungary, is worth watching for the large number of international stores it supplies.

Many time-pressed indies use one distributor to take their books everywhere. It was this impulse that led to the foundation of Draft2Digital. "I am that lazy author," says founder Aaron Pogue. "I don't want to have to deal with lots of outlets. I just want to upload the book once and have done with it, so I can keep my time for writing."

While ALLi's advice is to publish directly to major retailers like Amazon, Apple iBooks, Kobo, and Ingram rather than through an intermediary service, distributors may present a convenient alternative at the cost of some control and revenue.

Assisted Self-Publishing

Assisted self-publishing services offer publishing support—production, design, editorial, and marketing—for an upfront fee, and sometimes also a sales commission on each book sold. Contracts, rights, costs, editing standards, quality of production, promotion, and marketing vary widely in this sector, which is also home to most of the problematic vanity publishing operations.

There are two broad categories of assisted self-publisher.

Assisted Self-Publishing with Full-Service Packages

These companies offer a complete author service, from manuscript through design, formatting, production, final proof, print, and distribution to a network of tens of thousands of retailers.

Assisted Self-Publishing with à la Carte Services

Some services—like CreateSpace and Matador—offer a basic publishing package, supplemented by a menu of services like manuscript critique, editing, design, print and production, marketing, and promotion that can be added on a pick-and-mix basis.

I am a debut fantasy author who decided to self-publish using a package provider. The whole experience was an overpriced shambles. The communication from my publisher was appalling. They were very attentive when trying to get me to sign up, but once paid, the service was woeful. It would take days for a response from emails, and messages left by voicemail were never returned.

Add to that, once the book was finally published (the only thing I was happy with), book shops struggled to get any answer from them, with regard to ordering stock for book-signing events. They even tried to then publish my book in e-format, when I asked them not to (as I was doing it myself through the KDP platform) and it took many weeks for them to remove the product.

I am pleased that I self-published my novel, but the experience for me was one of stress and frustration. I thought that writing the novel was the hardest part. For me, it turned out to be the easiest step in the whole process. I have learned the hard way, but I am now intending to release my forthcoming novels myself, keeping a firm and solid grip on my destiny.

— ANTHONY LAVISHER

On the other hand, historical novelist Alison Morton was very pleased with her experience.

I'm with Adam Smith on division of labor; I did not want to spend my time learning a whole new skill set which may or may not be up to the highest possible industry standards when others, professionals, could do it for me. I weighed up all the information, advice, and research, and decided I wanted a complete package: a single point of contact, a coordinated service.

SilverWood Books seemed to me to stand out well above the others: ethical, book-oriented, realistic, as well as happy to answer all my intrusive questions in a professional and businesslike way.

I send them a copyedited MS Word file, which they turn into a beautiful paperback and ebook: formatting/typesetting and interior design, compilation of front and back matter, bespoke cover to my specification, all filing/registration fees, ISBN allocation, Nielsen enhanced listing, preorder, and Look Inside on Amazon, PDF ARC, proofs, POD setup, digital archive fee, ebook formatting for different retailers, legal deposit, bookseller information sheet, print ordering, quality control checks, and project management.

Also, a lot of advice, handholding, and 24-hour or less response, an author book promotion toolbox, author community and events, plus links into the publishing industry, e.g. representation/exhibiting at the London Book Fair.

Apart from the confidence of having a competent services provider, I also gain time—time to write. I'm sure one reason why I've been able to turn out a substantial series of top-quality, full-length books in a relatively short space of time is due to contracting a publishing services provider to do the production work for me.

— ALISON MORTON

The best assisted publishing companies are clear about what they are delivering and what you're paying for. In the less reputable companies, you will receive countless emails and phone calls about "must-have services" if your book is to compete. You will find more discussion of assisted self-publishing companies in the sections on Vanity Publishers and Author Solutions, below.

Agent-Assisted Self-Publishing (AASP)

AASP can take many different forms. At one end of the scale, it means an agency encouraging an author to upload their backlist and showing them how, without taking any payment. Agents do so on the basis that they are the author's representative, and self-publishing titles often give a revenue boost to the author's trade-published titles that they represent.

At the other end are the many agents now uploading files to Amazon in an account under their own name, and then collecting 15 percent of the sales revenue.

Some agents are actively seeking unpublished writers to "assist" in this way; some even call for the author to finance editing, cover design, marketing, etc., while the file gets uploaded in the agent's name and account.

Some authors believe, and some are even being persuaded, that choosing this route and paying that 15 percent will smooth a pathway to trade-publication.

Few of these deals are good for authors, who lose their ability to directly manage their books indefinitely (e.g. pricing, distribution, and the ability to transfer to another service provider), not to mention losing 15 percent of their sales revenue. And if they ever want to leave an agent who holds the identifiers for their book, such as Amazon's standard identification number (ASIN) or the International Standard Book Number (ISBN), the author will have to re-upload their books under accounts in their own name, which will cause them to lose their hard-earned position in retailers' sales charts.

"For those looking to traditionally publish, don't get roped into thinking that if an agent helps you self-publish, you'll have a better chance at reaching traditional publishers with your next manuscript," says Melissa Foster of Fostering Success, who some years ago was lured by precisely such a promise.

What I've learned is that it's essentially a way for agents to stay afloat in a changing publishing environment... by trying to recoup income from self-publishing sales of manuscripts they were unable to sell [to trade-publishers].

What has become a 'standard' of AASP equates to self-publishing: authors handling and paying for all of the work for their titles— formatting, editing, cover design, and marketing—but with the agent managing the digital dashboards and receiving 15 percent of income for the life of the book. If they cannot sell the work [to a trade-publisher], then capturing income by taking 15 percent of your hard-earned self-publishing revenue should not be an option—unless they are securing a marketing deal for you elsewhere.

While it may feel great to have an agent 'on your side,' digital dashboard management can be taught to you in seven minutes, without any loss in revenue. This is not a model I will be pursuing again.

— MELISSA FOSTER

At ALLi, we advise that authors do the same due diligence as with any self-publishing service. Take time to understand what you are giving up in order to be agent assisted, and what you stand to gain.

Securing certain marketing deals can require an agent's collaboration. Amazon KDP's White Glove Program (WGP) helps out agented authors and gives a book some promotion in return for a period of exclusivity. In such cases, the agent often earns 15 percent of your income for the life of your book, long after your WGP contract is over. While WGP can be very helpful, we suggest that authors negotiate a shorter term for the revenue split.

The key considerations when it comes to AASP are as follows:

1. Who holds the rights and for how long? Always ask about reversion, and beware of early termination fees in contracts.

2. What is the commission split? With Kobo, Apple iBooks, and some KDP territories, the maximum author commission is 70 percent. No digital publisher or literary agency can get you more than that. If you question closely, you may find they are using the same platforms and giving you less, a percentage of their receipts, and sometimes minus their costs. So what are they offering in return for this lesser commission? Ask specifically about production and marketing support.

3. What marketing support is provided? Marketing is the only commercial reason you may want to go with an agency or digital publisher. It is crucial to ask what marketing they'll be doing that you can't do for yourself. If it's Facebook ads, who's in charge of that? What about reviews? Blog tours? Is their proposed support ongoing, as digital marketing needs to be? If their marketing support consists only of training you to manage your social media, that's not marketing, that's training. Do you really want to sign away your rights when instead you could invest in a short-term course and learn to do it yourself?

Other Assisted Publishing

AASP is just one form of partnership-publishing. There are many others emerging in the shifting landscape. Also called "shared publishing," "hybrid publishing," "subsidized publishing," or "joint ventures," partnership-publishing requires that both parties invest time and money, sharing the tasks and the risks.

Such publishing contracts generally stipulate little or no advance but a much larger percentage of royalties, sometimes up to 50 percent. This is far beyond the average 10 percent given by a trade-publisher's contract, where the publisher assumes the entire financial risk.

Authors must be especially wary when considering partnership-publishing ventures, as vanity presses will often co-opt terms like "hybrid publishing" or "subsidized publishing" to whitewash substandard service or predatory behavior.

At ALLi, we stress that in any legitimate publishing arrangement, money flows to the author. A scheme in which the author provides most of the publication costs upfront violates that core maxim. An unscrupulous "partner" publisher has little incentive to contribute to the marketing of a book if it's already made a profit on author fees. That's not to say that partnership-publishing is inherently bad. There are cost-sharing arrangements where both the author and the publisher profit, but the prevalence of bad contract terms and vanity presses masquerading as partnership-publishing demands extreme caution when you meet this term.

Trade-publishers are beginning to embrace partnership-publishing, especially digital-only imprints. For example, Random House has introduced Hydra (SF/fantasy), Alibi (mysteries and thrillers), and Flirt (new adult); and Little, Brown UK has Blackfriars. Macmillan New Writing, Harlequin, Thomas Nelson, and other such publishers with a strong online presence are exploring these author-publisher partnerships as well. But again, the main value in these partnerships to authors seems to be the validation from an outsider. In terms of creative freedom and control, a lot can be lost.

It seems to me that digital imprints require authors to embrace the limitations of digital publishing, without providing any of the offsetting advantages available to self-publishers, like control over format and pricing, and the freedom of not being tied to a restrictive contract. Meanwhile, the publisher can push books into a growing marketplace at a much lower cost than with a conventional imprint, and reap the profits.

— Victoria Strauss

As with AASP, keep in mind the three key considerations:

1. Who holds the rights and for how long?
2. What is the commission split, and what support are they offering in return for your reduced commission?
3. Marketing, marketing, marketing.

Distribution for self-publishers who go direct is second to none. Production can be cheaply outsourced or easily done with the correct software. The commercial reason to go with a digital publisher is marketing, so ensure what you're getting is worthwhile. Don't be led into making a mistake through a need for validation, a lack of clarity about who is doing what, or sheer tiredness at the end of the writing and editing process.

Author Collectives and Cooperatives

Indie author collectives range from informal, online sharing groups to organized purchasing pools who band together to buy services as a group. ALLi itself is a collective, though not a publishing one. All such groups provide a network and support system for like-minded authors, and offer many advantages.

A cooperative goes one step further. By hosting readings and tour stops, and providing critique and commentary on each other's work, a cooperative does much of the work traditionally left up to marketing teams, writers' groups, or individual writers. It can also, through sharing social media tasks and marketing projects, etc., ease some of the financial burden and time-consuming work needed for indie authors to promote themselves. An example is Triskele Books, as one of its founding writers, Gillian Hamer, explains:

The motivation behind the birth of Triskele Books came after a series of online conversations over a few months. We'd known each other online for about six years, and although we lived in different countries, we were all firm friends, comfortably part of a closed critique group, Writing Asylum.

It became clear we'd all reached a similar level with our writing: of a publishable standard or not far away. Liza and I both had agents who were putting a lot of time and effort into not getting deals, while Jill banged her head against the agent wall, facing excuses from 'the economy' to 'the writing's too cerebral.' Traditional publishing seemed to think we were too risky.

That's where the idea started. If Jill wanted to be cerebral, I wanted to cross genres between crime and paranormal, and Liza to tell the story she wanted to tell about revolutionary France, then we'd have to go indie.

— GILLIAN HAMER

"Independent but Also as Part of a Team of Six"

A collective can provide the best of both worlds: a sense of unity and connection without giving up autonomy. Generally, all writers retain rights to their own work and make their own decisions about formatting and marketing. Some collectives incorporate, some start publishing other authors' books (see below); others have no plans to do that, ever.

Crowdsourced/Collaborative Publishing

Crowdsourcing means using communities of people to create an object, reach a goal, or fund an idea. Crowds can be virtual or physical, but primarily, with today's technology and the global platforms it enables, crowdsourcing is mainly a digital phenomenon, and has never been easier or more popular.

Crowdsourcing websites such as Fiverr, CrowdSpring, and PeoplePerHour can be employed to find professionals from almost all industries, forging new relationships and fan bases, and achieving goals. And authors are coming together around individual projects. Some ways that crowd power and collaboration can work are explained below.

Co-Editing

This is a concept that is becoming increasingly popular. Authors can now use their fans, or chosen beta readers ("beta" is borrowed from the gaming/computer industry's term "beta testing", trialing machinery, software, or other products, in the final stages of its development with a party unconnected with it). Authors' beta readers give feedback on final drafts. This helps authors refine and polish their books, before investing in a professional editor.

Co-Design

Authors can now source items like book covers, artwork, merchandise, websites—any sort of design—using websites such as CrowdSpring. Websites like this bring together the crowd, in this case a swarm of over 100,000 professional and semiprofessional designers from around the world, and provide a platform on which people in need of design work can post projects. There are others such as DesignCrowd and PeoplePerHour, who also offer freelancers for administration, tech, and other functions an author may need.

Co-Writing

Crowdwriting websites like WattPad allow writers to write in public, chapter by chapter, and get live feedback on what they've written. People who comment can offer suggestions and join the writer in deciding the direction of their work. Authors are also increasingly writing in other writer's "worlds," especially in certain genres like fantasy and thrillers. And collaborations are widespread among indie authors. One cool example: in March 2017, four authors met for the first time at Chicago Union station and boarded an Amtrak train for

New Orleans. "On the (bumpy, noisy, sleepless) journey south, we plotted a story, then wrote for a week in New Orleans while having some adventures in the area," says one of the four, JF Penn (known to many indies as the author advice guru, and ALLi Author Enterprise Advisor, Joanna Penn) who put *Demon Hunters* together with co-writers Zach Bohannon, Lindsay Buroker and J Thorn.

Co-Marketing

J Thorn is now becoming known for co-writing and co-publishing arrangements.

Where I started with the collaborations was around the marketing side. Reaching out to people and saying, 'Hey, we're all writing in this same genre. Why don't we box up our books and put them out there and we'll all promote them together.' I think that's where it started and I think for people who are considering collaborating, that's a great place to start because the creative process is messy to begin with, and when you involve other people, it's even messier.

It's great, but it's messy and I think if you don't have any sort of practice at that give and take of collaboration, the marketing is the easiest way to get going on that.

— J Thorn

Crowdfunding

Crowdfunding allows creators to post public projects, to which people can donate money in return for "rewards," and the pleasure of being involved. Ben Galley, ALLi's crowdfunding advisor, is a fan of crowd power.

My books are epic fantasy, a genre with a lot of passion in its fans. That lends itself well to graphic treatment, and it was a dream of mine to turn my first book into a graphic novel, and I chose to not only find a designer through crowdsourcing, but also to finance the entire project using crowdfunding. To me it was a chance to connect on a deeper level with my friends, and add value to the project.

The campaign closed with $8,471.68 raised. It's given me immense pleasure to see my project successful, to see my fans so invested in my concept, and to have instigated such a symbiotic experience.

— BEN GALLEY

See also Orna Ross's 2015 campaign to raise money to make a special edition print book in replica of an 1897 first edition, as a tribute to WB Yeats: ornaross.com/secret-rose.

Authors Publishing Authors

"I see a model like TV writing, where indie authors have a story runner and then episode writers," says Bob Mayer of his Cool Gus imprint, which he says is one of the most successful author-publishing partnerships, with sales ranking in the top 1 percent and numerous titles in the top 100 in their genres on Kindle, NOOK, iBooks, and other ebook platforms. "I work with my wife, Jen Talty, in that mode, and she works with other authors including number-one *New York Times* bestsellers."

In this model, Jen acts as creative authority with a broad scope, while Bob and the other authors develop their stories within the broad framework.

Jen calls it "streaming." The author gives her what they have and then she gives them options. The author gets to pick and choose what they want to use or not. With her streaming, I can write four times faster. And better.

I've done a NY Times *bestselling collaboration in traditional publishing and understand the extreme difficulties in doing this in a creative field, but with the right people, it can work very effectively. It requires a high level of trust and a sound business plan.*

— Bob Mayer

If you're considering collaborating with another writer, ask the same questions you would ask of any publisher, including the key questions around rights, commissions and royalties, and marketing.

Trade-Publishing

Many people forget that trade-publishing is an author service too. Activist indie authors first used the term "traditional publishing" for this sector and the most agitative activists favor "legacy publishing," expressing the belief that the combined effect of technology and entrepreneurial authors means publishing as we used to know it is on the way out.

At ALLi, we believe that as long as writers need validation and support, they will always be interested in somebody who will invest in them and their books.

Writing is hard. Publishing is hard too, in a different way, and many writers, poorly skilled at business, marketing, and promotion, welcome the idea of handing it all over. In some cases, it makes commercial and creative sense for an indie to bring in a publisher. We have a number of members who choose to self-publish some titles, and trade-publish others. Or to use a trade-publisher for their print edition while reserving audiobook and ebook rights for themselves. The biggest, and still the best-known, deal of this sort was Simon & Schuster's acquisition of the print rights to Hugh Howey's *Wool* series in 2013. At the time, the publisher said: "This is a modern twist on the old paperback license."

It makes total sense for an author to hold onto their more lucrative ebook and audiobook rights, and many of our members are making smaller deals and hooking up with small independent presses to do mutually advantageous projects.

So no, trade-publishing isn't going anywhere, but its practices and mindsets have been given a big shakeup by the new technologies and the way many savvy, highly motivated writers have responded to self-publishing opportunities.

Authors need to know they have many options for how they can reach readers now, and they should meet publishers and agents as potential business partners. Of course, we are delighted when somebody wants to invest money in our work, but that doesn't mean all their suggestions are going to be right.

Everybody must do what is best for the book, and in the case of creative differences, the author is the creative director with the final say and the power to walk away and try a different route.

TRADE-PUBLISHING IS AN AUTHOR SERVICE TOO

In trade-publishing, people talk about the Big Five (formerly the Big Six until Random House and Penguin merged in June 2013). This is a nickname for the five major global publishing conglomerates: Hachette, Harper Collins, Macmillan, Penguin Random House, and Simon & Schuster.

Getting published by a trade-publisher is still the goal of many authors, as it is perceived to have some advantages over smaller independent presses or self-publishing. At ALLi, however, we are seeing a growing number of members abandon trade-publishing to publish their own work, lured by the greater creative freedom and potential income.

The advantage of having a trade-publisher is that somebody else is investing in your book and believes in it, and in you. That validation and support means a great deal to some authors and may also (and should) be financially represented by an advance on royalties (though advance payments are dwindling and in many cases disappearing in the current publishing climate).

For those who want the services, and validation, of a trade-publisher, the entry bar is high, as the publishing houses (and the literary agents who supply authors for them) receive many more submissions than they can accept.

If you do find a publisher who wants to publish your book, you will trade some creative control over how your book is packaged and marketed and a sizable chunk of your potential income in return for their investment. Trade-publishers typically pay 25 percent or less to the author from ebook income, and 10 percent or less of income from a print book, while self-publishing platforms pay up to 70 percent.

Services you receive from a trade-publisher, in return for this reduced royalty income, include editorial, production, and promotion. A good publisher will offer multiple rounds of editing, including copy-editing and proofreading, along with book design and digital formatting, and for some books, significant marketing and publicity support.

If you self-publish, these services are still essential and cost considerable money and time to manage.

While self-publishing platforms make your book available on wholesale lists so book buyers who become aware of it can carry it, trade-publishers have sales agents who will represent your book to a variety of different bookselling outlets, from online retailers to physical bookshops to specialty stores. Your book will also be represented in the publisher's seasonal catalogue and via wholesale distributors.

You'll also get a baseline amount of book marketing and book publicity. Contrary to many authors' impressions, only a small percentage of books from a trade-publisher get a big marketing or publicity budget. These days much depends on the author's own platform, how hard an author works to get the word out, and the interest of the booksellers or the media in the particular genre and title.

While ebooks and POD are wonderful for direct selling to readers, trade-publishing still works best for bookstores. If you want your books carried in bricks-and-mortar chain stores, or an airport bookstore, a trade deal helps a lot (though again, these things are being increasingly done by indies).

Many indie authors would welcome from a trade-publisher a fair deal that would take them into bookstores. Such fair deals are not yet easily had. We regularly hear from successful indies who are offered contract terms from trade-publishers that are no better than those offered to new, unknown writers without readership or author platform. These publishers are interested in the author's following and success but don't adjust their terms and contract to appropriately acknowledge it.

Most often, the figures just don't add up to a workable deal. ALLi members regularly receive such offers. Although the publisher might be a good fit, and both sides want it to work, agreement can't be reached—the publisher can't offer terms that compete with self-publishing.

Indies who want to go the trade-publishing route need to think very carefully about what value is actually being added through all seven stages of the publishing process. We also hear about literary agents who try to take a proportion of authors' self-published income, though they have done nothing to earn it. Careful attention needs to be paid to what a publisher or agent can bring to each format: ebook, print book, audiobook. For indies, it often makes sense to begin negotiations by offering print rights only. (See more on this below.)

As with all services, vigilance and an understanding of your own writing goals are essential. At the beginning of the 20th century, the publishing industry carved up territorial copyright between the US and UK, and delivered royalty incomes, terms, and conditions that were favorable to publishers and unfavorable to writers. As a result, for most of that century, the typical income for a professional author was one-third below the national wage or worse, in most countries.

Now, at the beginning of the 21st century, we are at a turning point. In this critical time of flux, when so many things are being reconfigured, how independent authors position ourselves when the trade-publishers and their agents come calling—as they surely will when we self-publish well—is critical. It has implications for all indies, and for the future of all writers and publishers.

Unless we want self-published books to just become the new slush pile, a way for trade-publishers to find tried-and-true prospects who have already done the hard work of finding readers, we must appreciate what the power shifts in this rapidly changing publishing landscape mean for independent authors.

"I began my career with a hardcover, pre-empt, dream-come-true debut novel, to be published by a major NYC publisher—until they pulled the book, 90 days before publication date because of cover-art problems," says CJ Lyons, an author who moved from trade- to self-publishing and now publishes both ways.

After my dream debut vanished, I kept writing, and another NYC publisher asked me to create a new series for them... only problem was that my fun, sexy beach reads were shelved literally to the left of Moby Dick *and were released only once a year. In response to my fans begging for more reads faster, I turned to self-publishing, mainly as a marketing tool, until a year later, when I realized I was paying the bills with my self-published ebooks!*

Since then I've embraced this renaissance in publishing as a way for writers to make a living wage and readers to find the books they want as fast as they want, and I've gone on to sell over three million books, as well as signing to work with two traditional NYC publishers to open up new markets for my work.

— CJ LYONS

PART III

WHAT HELP DO I NEED?

THE VALUE OF ASSISTANCE

I t is a good idea to ask yourself why you want assistance with your book.

Maybe you just don't want to do it all yourself. You want a service that will take away the tasks you don't want to do, just like a publisher would, leaving you free to write. That's a valid reason, but before you make the decision, make sure that's what you'll be getting. Ensure you know not just what you're paying your assisted service to do (you'll find help with that below) but also what they actually can and cannot do and, crucially, what the picture would look like if you were to take an alternative route.

Too often, authors choose package services because they're seduced by advertising, or they think it's the only way to self-publish, or they are frightened by the tech talk and don't realize that when you get beyond the jargon of file names and formatting, it is no more complicated to upload and produce an ebook or POD manuscript than to produce a manuscript with Microsoft Word (some would say less so).

In the chapter on going direct (**Part Five**), there are strong arguments for the value of control. There are also, however, situations where a writer has more money than time and is happy to hand over the publishing tasks. If you can afford it, having a reputable company hold your hand through the process can be comforting and make things easier to negotiate, especially first time out.

There are good assisted publishing services and choosing one is an important decision—with expensive consequences if you get it wrong —so as with any serious investment, you need to shop around before you buy. Ask the right questions, know the depth and quality of service you are getting, and educate yourself on the alternative options. Do your research. Understand why you're going to extra expense. Understand what they are charging you for, and how much money they are taking—not just in the upfront payment, but farther ahead too, in the form of royalties.

Also, when choosing, take note of the service's intent. It is in this end of the self-publishing market that we find most of the rogue providers.

THE SEVEN STAGES OF PUBLISHING

BY ORNA ROSS

W hether you are going to go direct, hire a complete package service, or something in between, before deciding on a service, you need to understand the seven stages of publishing, and what services are available for each. This will allow you to ascertain precisely what you can do for yourself, with help from friends, family, and author community support, and what services you want to buy.

WRITING

There are seven stages to the writing process, too. In writing, five of these come before you get into self-editing; what I call the Clarification Stage. At that point, having done as much editing as you can yourself, you bring in others. But that gives five whole writing stages where you must do most of the work yourself.

You can feel very much alone through those first five stages, which are:

1. **Intention:** When you decide what you are going to write about and the form: book, article, poem, short story.
2. **Incubation:** When you germinate the idea, making notes.
3. **Investigation:** When you research the idea, making more notes.
4. **Composition:** When you compose the first draft.
5. **Amplification:** When you deepen your ideas and improve the shape of your manuscript.

There are some writing services that aim to support you through those stages, keeping you writing, assessing your work, and offering tools and services that may help you through.

Coaching and Mentoring

One-on-one time with a writing coach can be a helpful tool in the early stages of writing. It's important to find the right mentor who understands your project and your needs, and has a compatible work style and ethic.

Depending on what you need, a mentor can act as a sounding board to help work through plot and characterization issues; help find the best structure, style, and tone; or even give you writing assignments to get your brain working though writer's block. It's a versatile tool because it's a creative relationship that takes on the needs of each individual project.

Manuscript Appraisal

Manuscript appraisal is a good tool to use when you're not sure if you've gone in the right direction. Having someone look at your manuscript objectively offers a writer not only an idea of how readers will receive the book but also concrete information about stylistic choices, plot, and characterization.

The major difference between an appraisal and an actual edit is that the end product of an appraisal is a report that details the general workings of the manuscript. The assessor leaves the author to consider the feedback and make any applicable changes. The report discusses structure, plot development, story pacing, and characterization for fiction; structure, pacing, and samples and examples for nonfiction. And for both, these reports discuss reader engagement, tone, and overall strengths and weaknesses.

Book Doctors

There are many different circumstances where it can be beneficial to have a book doctor. They work with writers to take existing material and drastically reshape it into a workable manuscript. It's different from a structural or developmental edit because the book doctor will not only identify problem areas, but will implement the solution, which can result in them rewriting portions of the manuscript. A good book doctor will make the process a collaboration, so at the end of the day, the author still feels ownership of that project.

Be aware that there is some overlap of terms between book doctoring, manuscript appraisal, and content editing. Always check to be sure of what you're getting.

Ghostwriting

Ghostwriting happens when, for whatever reason, a client is unable to write their project. A ghostwriter will step in and complete the writing, but it's still a creative collaboration. The client and ghostwriter work together on structure, voice, plot, etc., but the ghostwriter, although their name may never appear on the cover, is the sole content creator.

Writing Tools

There are lots of different writing software programs on the market now but the industry standard for word processing remains Microsoft Word, and having access to and a basic understanding of Word is important to smoothly go through the editing process with others.

So even if you use other software like Scrivener or Apple's Pages, you will probably end up having to export into Word for various reasons.

Other useful tools that aren't exactly writing software come from the productivity people 80 PCT. The Freedom tool restricts access to the internet, and Anti-Social restricts access to certain websites, so you can focus on writing. These are so useful that many members thank the software in their acknowledgments, for helping to make the book possible.

Another useful writing tool you might like to consider is a

dictation tool that turns your speech into text. I use Dragon Naturally Speaking from Nuance.

A Note on Editing and Self-Editing

Editing is a stage in both the writing process and the publishing process. It's important not to confuse the Clarification Stage of the writing process, during which you'll do loads of self-editing, with the editing that will be done later by another: beta readers, copy-editors, line editors, and proofreaders.

Self-editing is what *you* do, as you write the book and as you work with writing services to improve it. Then, when you have done all you can do, when you can't see another improvement that can be made, you bring in an editor.

Both of these editing phases are essential; one is not a substitute for the other.

EDITING

Every writer needs at least one editor. We do not see our own work clearly, and a fresh set of eyes is essential to catch mistakes and oversights in our manuscripts, no matter how perfect we think they are. The best writers in the world are edited into publication; it is a mistake for indie authors to believe we can DIY this. Usually, it's what we don't know we don't know that lets our books down.

Editing ourselves to some degree is, of course, necessary, and the sixth stage of the writing process. But going over and over our manuscript in the effort to avoid hiring an editor is a waste of valuable writing time (and can actually be a sophisticated form of creative resistance, stopping us from moving briskly through the publication of the current book and onto the next).

Investing time in finding the right editor and investing money in the proper service is vital. A good editor is actually invaluable. In the early stages, in addition to adding ideas, asking open questions, and suggesting solutions, they will appreciate and reinforce your creative intentions.

Worthwhile editing services will add to the professional look and quality of your book, bring major problems to your attention, and help you with problem areas you have identified. But not all editing is the same, and as you progress through the process of writing, you'll need different levels and types of editing.

It's important to understand what type of editing you need and to base price and time expectations accordingly. For example, content editing can be more time-consuming than a proofread, and prices will be reflective of that.

Content Editing

As you shape up your first draft and need a first reader, or if you are in need of guidance for a widespread problem around pacing, plotting, or character development in later drafts, then content editing is what you're looking for. (This can also be called book doctoring, manuscript appraisal, developmental editing, substantive editing, and many other names, as people use all these terms differently. Do check).

Whatever it's called, this is a down-and-deep look at the manuscript, and is likely to call for major rewrites. At the point of needing this editing service, you are still several passes away from being ready to publish. This level may identify outstanding grammar and punctuation errors, but is more focused on the big picture.

Copy-Editing/Line Editing

Once you are satisfied that you have a solid manuscript and are finished making major changes, you can move on to copy-editing/line editing. At this stage, editors will be doing a thorough scrub of the manuscript, looking for things like:

- consistency, grammatical errors, style
- factual errors (especially important in nonfiction books)
- fluidity of language—overuse—aesthetics, like the overuse of certain words, phrases, hyphens, or fragmented sentences
- linguistic efficiency.

This phase of editing leaves you with a clean manuscript.

Proofreading

The final step in any professionally produced manuscript is proofreading. When your manuscript has gone through its final edits, design, and layout, a proofread will find any final errors that have slipped through the cracks. Originally, proofreading meant reading the physical page proofs, to make sure that everything was ready for print. Now it is your opportunity to check for any final problems and oversights and catch any grammatical errors or errors that may have been accidentally introduced during a previous round of corrections.

Jim Giammatteo on the Importance of Editing

I try to avoid blanket statements, but when it comes to editing a book, I feel comfortable saying that every author needs some kind of editor. Maybe you don't need a development editor, and maybe you and a few associates can handle proofreading, but I haven't found anyone yet who could do their own copy-editing. Copy-editors send their own work to other copy-editors. We do our best to evaluate editing services based on what we can see. As an example, if a service is under consideration for an ALLi Partner Membership, we'll ask members if anyone has used the company's services, and what their experience was. We also check the company's website. If I look at a website for an editing service and I see errors, I would have a difficult time recommending them. And we always dig deeper than the website testimonials.

Some writers are very kind. They tell me an editing service is great, without having checked the work after getting it back. Kind, yes, but smart enough to be an author-publisher? Not so.

Many editors charge by the word, or page. Some will only provide a quote after reviewing a sample of the work. I use a proofreader who charges by the number of mistakes. I like this method. If my work is good, with few mistakes, it means I pay less.

I believe it's imperative that you and the editor determine upfront if you are compatible. The best way to do that is for you to submit a sample of your work and they provide a sample of their editing. This is more difficult with a content/developmental editor, so a conversation on the phone, and/or references, might be better.

In this book, we don't evaluate package services based on their editing skills, as it would have been far too time-consuming but, where appropriate, we make comments if we feel the pricing is too high. That leaves it up to you to determine if you want to proceed.

COVER DESIGN

Your book's cover is its first impression with readers. A cover that looks good, represents your story, and is of a professional quality will help your book be appealing to your audience and stand up next to trade-published books in its category. Finding a cover design artist who is willing to work with you to ensure that these three criteria are met is important.

Design services can vary widely in price, and more expensive does not always mean better. It's important to have done some research around what you want and what's currently working well in your genre. Do you want a specific look that brands all your books? Similar covers for particular series? Imagery that matches other covers in your genre? Or do you want to be more creative, and do something different?

Investigate the requirements of the services you'll use. For example, online retailers such as Amazon display tiny thumbnail images of your cover. If your cover image is unrecognizable at this small size, you will lose potential sales.

These technical considerations may affect your choice of subject or presentation on the cover. Identify your goals and requirements before approaching a designer and deepening the conversation.

Whether you choose to get a cover image from a design service or design your own cover, you should familiarize yourself with issues around copyrights and licensing for any images/fonts used. We have more information available in the Author Advice Centre (**selfpublishingadvice.org**). Also check out *The Self-publisher's Legal Handbook*, by our legal advisor, Helen Sedwick.

If you go through a service, be sure you know before paying or signing anything who owns the rights and how the cover can be used by both parties.

Selecting a Cover Designer

When choosing a designer, look at their catalogue of covers. Do they all look similar regardless of genre? Do they reuse the same image on more than one cover? Is there diversity in fonts and layouts? Would you pick up any of these books at a bookstore or click their thumbnails on a retailer's website?

Designing Your Own Cover

Countless authors have produced their own covers, only to find that the glowing praise of friends and relatives is not reflected in the book's sales.

The sins of the amateur designer are numerous: poor composition, disregard for the conventions of genre, inappropriate font choices, illegible text at reduced sizes, cluttered design without a strong focus, and a multitude of technical errors specific to online retailers.

Cover design is best left to those who possess both an extensive background in graphic design and a thorough understanding of ebook and POD cover requirements.

Jim Giammatteo on the Importance of Cover Design

If you are one of the lucky people who has the talent to design and create your own covers, then you are ahead of the game. But remember, a book's cover is one of the most important parts of promotion. Despite what many people think, books really are judged by their covers. So before you decide to undertake this task yourself, make sure you have the skills.

Gather opinions on your design from lots of people—friends, fellow authors, and readers. Don't fall into the trap of putting a book out because you like the cover. Verify that others like it too. And don't stop at confirmation that someone likes it. Make sure your cover does its job. A cover must be appealing and intriguing enough to make a reader want to stop what they're doing and look further.

One thing I do when seeking opinions is only show the cover in the size it would appear online in stores like Amazon, Apple, Barnes & Noble, etc. That's where most potential readers will see it, so it's more important that it looks good in thumbnail size than in full print size.

PRODUCTION

Production can be a daunting task for a first-time self-publishing author. Once you get past the jargon, though, some simple tools and services can make it a much more manageable task. Depending on what your goals are, the worth of production services varies. The first time, it helps to have someone there who will take the lead on the process and help you understand each step, but you may find that it's more fitting for you to do it yourself in the future.

Alternatively, you may not have the time or desire to do hands-on book production. (See Part Five: **Going Direct** and David Gaughran's essay **The Value of Control** before deciding.)

Manuscript Conversion

Manuscript conversion is simply taking one form of your manuscript —be it in DOC/DOCX, RTF, PDF, or even a physical copy of a backlist title—and making it into another format that is ready to be uploaded as an ebook or POD file. Kindle, for example, will allow you to upload a variety of file types, but will then convert the document to a MOBI file that is compatible with Kindle e-readers.

With the exception of converting a physical book into an editable file, manuscript conversion is fairly easy with the right tools. With word processing programs like Scrivener, it is possible to easily import a DOC/DOCX file—or write in the program—and save it as any of the major file types needed for various publishing platforms. Scrivener is handy for self-publishers because as well as being an excellent writing software, it also takes care of formatting with minimal effort or knowledge needed.

Ebook and Print Layout and Formatting

There are several programs available to help authors format and lay out their books for a variety of purposes. Their prices can range widely, so it's important to know what you need for your particular projects and goals. If you write crime thrillers, you're not likely to need a program with functionality for designing pages with lots of graphics, so something like Scrivener is adequate.

If you write something like cookbooks, children's, or other illustrated books though, something like Adobe InDesign, though more expensive, is the better investment for you.

When considering services, make sure that they have the ability to produce the layout and format you need. Because production can be intimidating, it's a step in publishing where writers can be easily taken advantage of. Be sure that you look at the fine print and consider the questions put forth in this book. Services that can't give you a clear price, and reasons for the price, should be passed over in favor of providers who have a reputation for transparency and can show professional-quality products that fit your project's specifications.

Layout and formatting are not as easy as they sound. Assuming you plan on offering both ebook and print book versions, that means you have to produce the book in several different formats: MOBI, EPUB, and PDF. Not only do you have to ensure the accuracy of these files, you have to also ensure that each file works on as many devices as you can test: Android phones and tablets, iPhones and iPads, computers, Kindles, NOOKs, Kobo readers, etc.

— JIM GIAMMATTEO

And you also have to make sure it looks good in print. And then, of course, there's audio.

Check out the Partner Member services in the ALLi searchable database in the Member Zone. Ask for the names of other books the person providing the service has worked on, look those books up, and see what you think of the work.

Audiobook Production

It is difficult to match the level of professional audio production at home. ACX is a service provided through Amazon that helps authors connect with narrators and producers to achieve a high quality in audiobooks. See ACX in **Self-Publishing's Big Five** in Part Six for more details.

DISTRIBUTION

Distribution refers to the process and logistics of actually getting your book to the consumer. There's a myriad of services and platforms, from Amazon to Ingram to iBooks, that help you put your work in the hands of readers. Each one has pros and cons, depending on your needs.

Are you looking for accessibility, discoverability, user-friendliness, and international markets or a smaller distribution, say on Amazon only, to get sales rolling?

Are you willing to commit to being exclusive to one platform (for instance, with Kindle only), and if so, for how long?

Are you looking to sell ebooks only, or do you want to make print books available too? If you do, do you want to push for shelf space in physical bookstores?

Will you want your book to be available in libraries? Will you sacrifice any royalties for that discoverability?

Later in this book, we'll examine the most popular ebook distribution platforms in detail, as well as the two big POD platforms, CreateSpace and IngramSpark.

For now, it's helpful to have a general understanding of the types of distribution available to authors.

What is a Distributor?

A distributor, in its most general sense, is any company that provides products to retailers or libraries instead of directly to consumers.

Many companies acts as both publishers and distributors, producing books as well as making them available to various retail venues. The majority of these distributors are actually wholesalers, passive suppliers who only respond to book orders, as opposed to active distributors who have a sales team dedicated to placing books with retailers.

We'll cover this important distinction in more detail in **Agreements with Wholesalers and Distributors**.

What is an Aggregator?

An aggregator is a service that provides books to multiple distributors, giving authors access to potentially thousands of retailers from a single point of entry.

However, the distinction between a passive wholesaler and an active, sales-oriented distributor is significant here. Employing an aggregator who boasts of "tens of thousands" of retailers and libraries in their distribution network will not ensure that your book is carried by those retailers; it only ensures that a retailer who *asks to purchase that book* has the option to do so.

Making your book known to these retailers—and the readers they service—is the goal of the next stage of publishing: marketing and promotion.

MARKETING AND PROMOTION

Book Promotion

Boosting sales and increasing visibility and discoverability through promotions are time-honored traditions in virtually every market. Utilizing limited-time markdowns, free-download days, and giveaways can boost your revenue and bring in new readers, who will possibly buy other titles now or in the future.

The efficacy of any given promotional strategy can't be guaranteed, but when used wisely, they can reap great benefits for an author. For example, it may seem counterintuitive to give a book away for free to raise revenue, but if you are releasing a new book in a series, having a period of free downloads for the first book can bring in new readers who would otherwise not have purchased the new book.

Self-published authors struggle with marketing and promotion more than any other area. To assess marketing and promotional services, you can use the techniques outlined in the next chapter, **How to Evaluate Self-Publishing Services**.

Book Marketing

Book marketing goes well beyond limited-time promotions and looks at the full scope of what we at ALLi think of as Reaching Readers. Anything that gives readers information about you or your books, gets readers interested in you, and attracts notice is marketing. As with any aspect of publishing, you can go direct and/or work with a service to help connect consumers with your book.

When you put together a marketing plan, you want to keep in mind what existing platforms you might already have. A dedicated following from previous books? An author website? An engaged social media following? Contacts with press or reader blogs?

Also look at what areas you can improve to help bolster sales and visibility. Marketing means looking at how you're getting readers to discover you and your work. Will you be a part of a library program that doesn't necessarily boost sales, but boosts discoverability? Can you write guest blog entries for blogs that would appeal to your target market? Are you signed up for social networking sites like Twitter and using an Author Page on Facebook?

Not every marketing tactic is right for every writer or market, so when you create your marketing plan—or buy the service from a third party—do check out what other successful authors in your field are doing, and also what they've tried and left behind.

Traditional PR

As the old saying goes, "If it ain't broke, don't fix it." And that goes for PR. Targeted, personal press releases, interviews, and reviews in print publications are still valid ways of reaching readers. The mode may have changed—reaching out independently as opposed to through an agent or publisher—but the goal is still the same: get the word about your work out to prospective readers.

Whereas promotions focus on limited-time sales opportunities for readers, discounting, and suchlike, PR is more front end and related to peers, looking to gain reviews, blog tours, and book signings, together with ongoing efforts like social media engagement.

It's important to have a good plan of how to bring your book out with a bang, but also to schedule time to do ongoing marketing that will keep readers interested.

An author's appeal is rarely just their books; it's also their life, character, habits, process. In an atmosphere where consumers are constantly bombarded with advertisements, if you only pop up when you want them to buy your books, you'll be out of sight—and out of mind—before you can say "My new book..."

As self-published authors are more and more in control of our own publishing and marketing processes, it's important to find a balance that also facilitates our privacy and time to continue writing. Readers don't need to know every time you eat eggs Benedict, but they should definitely want to know when your latest novel's cover is in from the designer.

If it all seems too overwhelming or like a part of the process you'd rather take a back seat on, a myriad of services are available to help you. Keep your eye out for providers who don't seem like they can produce the results they guarantee (see below). It's important to find a service provider with whom you work well and who understands your needs, and is realistic about what you can expect.

Facebook Ads

It seems almost too easy to be true. Everyone who's anyone has a Facebook account, and using that is a great way to access a massive international audience. Setting up a Facebook Author Page should be a priority for two reasons:

1. It's the easiest way to connect with readers and direct them to various projects with more frequency than a newsletter, and it allows them to share that with others—widening your reach with minimal effort.
2. You can place highly targeted ads and control them.

> Facebook's advertising program has taken targeted
> marketing to a new level. You can specify the frequency
> with which your ads appear, the times of day, the
> geographic regions, and the demographics of your
> audience. You can tailor your marketing push to any budget.

The format is user friendly, but it does change frequently. As Facebook's understanding of how users interact with ads and the site as a whole expands, the marketing changes to be more effective for users, and more lucrative for Facebook.

Analytics are available to help users understand how their ads are being viewed, shared, and clicked, and what the reach is. If you choose to, you can "boost" your ad for an additional fee, and the level of the boost is dependent on how much extra you want to pay. Facebook on its own is a helpful tool, and its easy-to-use interface makes it a natural go-to for a limited-time promotion or in-person event. Combined with Facebook ads, many authors are finding it's a game-changer.

ALLi member Mark Dawson offers a comprehensive online course on Facebook advertising for authors, as well as free content to improve your social media marketing. You can sign up at selfpublishingformula.com.

Promotions

Promotions should be used in conjunction with a well-thought-out marketing plan aimed at increasing three key areas: discoverability, which is crucial to gaining new readers; availability, which means ensuring your work is accessible to your audience; and sales, which includes not only increasing the sales of the title on promotion but also of any other titles you may have.

There's an endless array of services available to help authors promote their books but, like the other services covered in this book, not all are equal. Many providers don't have a record of success (walk away), are so expensive that the cost outweighs the benefit (walk away), and are geared more to selling you services than selling your book to readers (walk away). But there are many that are worth the investment. Amazon has several promotional services to offer authors that are detailed in the next chapter.

Ebook Discovery Services

BookBub is considered the gold standard for ebook discovery services due to its massive audience, and sterling track record of boosting sales and attracting new readers to your books.

Because of that success, BookBub commands a higher price than most ebook discovery services (the median price is $238 to promote a free book, and $1,198 to promote a book priced at $2.99).

It's also more difficult to secure a slot in the mailings. To be considered for a BookBub promotion, your book must be full-length and error-free; free, or discounted by more than 50 percent; and it must not be available at a lower price within 90 days.

If that describes your project, you can create an account to submit your book for consideration. An editorial team reviews submissions, and if you're accepted, you'll schedule a limited-time promotion on your selected retailers and pay. Once BookBub verifies you've discounted the book on the retailer website, it'll run your ad.

It's definitely a more difficult process to go through than many other promotions, but the targeted marketing approach and reputation for promoting only the highest-quality books make it, in most cases, a worthwhile investment of time and money.

BookBub's competitors vary tremendously in price and quality, but a few stand out as worthwhile alternatives. ALLi's Watchdog Desk publishes a detailed comparison of these services in our Self-Publishing Advice Centre: selfpublishingadvice.org.

RIGHTS LICENSING

It's easy to upload a book to a POD platform or an ebook platform and think that's it. But each book actually represents several sets of rights: print, digital, audio, film, foreign, etc. It's important to understand who owns the rights, for how long, and why.

A discussion of rights could fill a book itself, and indeed does! See Orna Ross and Helen Sedwick's *How Authors Sell Publishing Rights*. However, for the purposes of this book, a brief summary will suffice.

When you "sell" your work to a publisher, what you're actually doing is licensing them to publish your work in exchange for an advance and royalties. In most cases, this primary right being licensed is the right to publish your work in a specific medium (e.g. print) and region (e.g. North America).

Subsidiary rights (sometimes known as "sub rights") are everything else. Common subsidiary rights include:

- Ebook rights (the right to publish the work as digital text)
- Audio recording rights (the right to publish the work as an audiobook)
- Mass-market paperback rights (the right to reprint the book in paperback after a hardcover edition is released)

- Translation rights (the right to translate and sell the book in other languages)
- Commercial rights (the right to sell merchandise based on the book and its characters)
- Dramatic rights (the right to adapt and perform the work for film, television, and stage)
- Anthology rights (the right to publish your work as part of a collection).

As you might imagine, subsidiary rights can be valuable commodities. JK Rowling wisely retained her subsidiary rights for the Harry Potter series, and in 1999 just the film rights for the first four books netted her approximately $2,000,000.

It is imperative that you understand the value of subsidiary rights, and know what you're signing away in a contract.

As a self-publisher, if you've followed the advice in this book, all of your rights belong to you. This gives you a tremendous advantage over trade-published authors whose publishers are not using their rights.

Some self-publishing services (and all trade-publishers) aim to retain rights for a certain period of time in exchange for marketing or promotional services. If you choose to go this path of assisted publishing, it is of the utmost importance for you to completely understand the rights implications.

What, if anything, are they giving you as compensation? In trade-publishing, it should be an advance and royalties; if a service wants you to give them the rights to your material, but is also asking for payment, it's a strong indication that it may not be working with your best interests in mind.

As a self-publisher, there are two major resources to consider if you want to take full advantage of your book's subsidiary rights. PubMatch and IPR License are services that aim to harness new technologies in the selling of rights. (ALLi members have the benefit of our arrangements with both. Check the Member Zone, Discounts & Deals, for the latest update.)

Both are easy to use, internationally available, and make licensing your book easier than it has ever been in the past. But please note that does not mean it is easy. Ever.

If you decide to go this route, be prepared to invest considerable time and administration to rights management.

PubMatch

PubMatch is a partnership between Publishers Weekly (PW) and the Combined Book Exhibit family of companies, which aims to create an international business atmosphere to facilitate rights deals throughout the year. Although PW is based in the US, it does have international clout and connections, and PubMatch is now linked with the London Book Fair.

The PubMatch website boasts bold infographics explaining how rights break down and which countries offer the most promise.

It offers ways to post your book for publishers and agents to find, as well as various ways to seek out potential business partners accepting titles. The service is geared not only toward writers, but also toward publishers looking for talent and easy ways to connect for rights transactions, as well as toward agents and artistic service providers.

IPR License

According to London-based IPR's website, it is an international platform "on which to list and license literary rights. The platform offers the opportunity to monetize or find the best new content in a global marketplace. It also acts as a copyright hub, making it easier to locate copyright holders to clear permission for use of their work."

IPR has a massive global network that is used by all levels of publishers from self-publishers to major publishing houses. The TradeRights marketplace is a partnership between Copyright Clearance Center and Frankfurt Book Festival. That deals solely with literary rights, whereas PubMatch also facilitates artists and is geared toward opening new avenues for rights holders to market their licenses worldwide.

See more about the licensing of rights in the section **Choosing a Rights Service**.

PART IV

HOW TO EVALUATE SELF-PUBLISHING SERVICES

HOW WE RATE SERVICES

At ALLi, we have evaluated hundreds of self-publishing services and vendors. These ratings (which appear at the end of this book and in our online version) offer a means of swiftly weeding out the bad operators, and identifying the good ones.

We also offer Partner Memberships to exemplary services. Partner Members are carefully vetted against a panel of 25 criteria, and are regularly reviewed to ensure they are providing high-quality services to authors.

Finally, we perform in-depth comparisons of some of the most popular services to help authors find the best fit for their needs.

Although these rating methodologies vary in their level of scrutiny, each type of assessment hinges on adherence to the ALLi Code of Standards. It's our guidepost when evaluating services, and your first line of defense against unscrupulous operators.

The ALLi Code of Standards

Services that adhere to the eight principles of our Code of Standards are likely to offer a positive experience to their clients. Services that fail to live up to any one of these standards do not have the author's best interests at heart, and should be avoided.

Integrity

We recognize that Partner Membership of ALLi means our primary aim is to enable authors to effectively publish and sell books. We follow through on all promised services and fully honor all advertisements and publication agreement terms. We never spam, oversell, or harass authors to buy our services or sell a dream to the uninitiated.

Integrity is the most critical aspect of a client–vendor relationship, and it's often the hardest one to evaluate. Companies may offer much, but once the contract is signed and the client's payment is in hand, they may fail to deliver on their promises.

This is where customer reviews prove to be a precious source of information, especially word of mouth from trusted colleagues. If you're relying on anonymous customer reviews, view them with restraint. Whether named or anonymous, while one negative review may be a fluke, an impossible-to-please client, or even someone with a personal grudge, numerous complaints from multiple sources indicate a pervasive problem.

Services that rely on spam, high-pressure sales tactics, or inflated promises should also be regarded with caution. These are the hallmarks of trying to find a client for a product, rather than trying to find the right service for the client. Integrity demands that the service provider works to the benefit of the author. One that's more concerned with meeting a sales quota than with serving your needs has abandoned that principle.

Value

We add value to each publication commensurate with the fee charged, relieving authors of key publishing tasks, enhancing readability, design, or discoverability.

Price and value are related but separate issues. One provider may have reasonable pricing, but still deliver poor value, either failing to honor the promises made or bringing useless services that don't benefit the author. Another may have higher-than-average pricing but deliver exceptional value for that fee. (Don't assume that higher pricing means better service, however. In the majority of cases, it does not.)

The best way to appraise the value of a service is to examine the end result. If it's providing editing, are clients' books well edited? If it's publishing to retailers, are the sales pages professional and error-free? If the provider specializes in marketing and publicity, can you see evidence of their footprint on the landscape of the internet?

When the results of the service are not easily gauged, as with certain PR services, customer reviews are again a useful guide. If the typical customer is disappointed with the results, chances are you will be too.

Pricing

Our price quotations are accurate, transparent, and complete. Pricing is in line with market norms.

Pricing should be clearly and fully disclosed, with no hidden fees. Reputable service providers inform their clients; they do not hide vital information from them, especially key information like pricing.

Pricing that is drastically different from market norms—above or below typical pricing—is another red flag. Grossly inflated pricing is rarely justified by the quality of the services rendered. In the other direction, pricing that seems too good to be true usually is.

When comparing prices to determine the market norms, be sure to measure against known, reputable providers with a proven track record. Predatory operators often have higher visibility than the legitimate ones, so comparing the first results you find on Google may yield highly inflated averages.

Clarity

We make clear what we can and cannot do for the self-publishing writer and how our service compares to others.

Service providers must be clear about what services they are providing, and how those services will benefit the author. Too many self-publishing services rely on vague descriptions of services and even more vague promises of success. This can lead to confusion and open the door to deceptive practices.

When evaluating a provider, learn to slice through the marketing fluff and look for concrete statements about how it operates. If you can't find any, or the provider seems evasive about the process, that's a danger sign.

Examples of Concrete Statements:

- "We distribute your book through Amazon, Barnes & Noble, Apple, and Google Play, and internationally through Ingram's global network."
- "We guarantee 1,000 hits to your Amazon sales page, independently tracked, or your money back."
- "Our Silver Package includes professional cover design and copyediting up to 70,000 words."

Examples of Meaningless Fluff:

- "We distribute your book worldwide." (To what countries? Through what networks?)
- "We will promote your book to our thousands of Facebook and Twitter followers." (How many? Do those followers actually see and interact with the page? Are those followers interested in a book like yours, or are they just other authors promoting their own books?)
- "We take care of everything!" (What, exactly, and how?)

Partnership

We involve authors in planning and decision-making for key aspects of the publication process, from titles and cover design to sales and marketing strategies.

ALLi characterizes indie authors as creative directors of their books who expect that status to be reflected in any partnership.

Service providers that respect indie authors recognize their role in supporting the author's creative vision. That attitude tends to shine through in their marketing materials and direct communications: "How can we help you succeed?" as opposed to "You need our services." "Here's what we offer," rather than "This is what you need to do."

After the contract is signed, the author should remain an active participant, not a helpless passenger.

Service

We are accountable for our work. We keep authors informed each step of the way and provide good customer service and follow-up.

Good service incorporates all of the other principles in the Code of Standards, but centers on one key concept: accountability. Accountable providers' representatives treat the client as their personal responsibility. They treat the client as a person and not a commodity or case number. When a problem arises, they take steps to correct it, and they follow up to ensure that the client is happy.

But service is most obvious when it's missing. That lack of accountability ripples through every aspect of a provider's operation and every item in the Code of Standards, so those with poor service tend to be flooded with a wide variety of complaints.

Communication

We provide helpful and timely information to authors at all stages of publication, and beyond, and facilitate authors to get any ancillary information we cannot provide.

Communication overlaps with several of the principles in the Code of Standards because it's paramount at all stages of the author–vendor relationship. Correspondingly, it's one of the most common reasons for customer dissatisfaction.

Poor communication can stem from several causes. The vendor might be understaffed and too busy to answer questions. They might not respect the client. Or they might be actively concealing information.

Each of these is a recipe for a disastrous business relationship. If you see complaints about a provider's communication, be wary, particularly if the breakdown seems to happen after the contract is signed.

Remember: You have a right to full and accurate information from a prospective service provider before you enter into any agreement. Pricing, options, and process should all be discussed openly, and these discussions should never be conditional on signing the contract.

You have a right to know what's in the contract you're signing, in clear, easily understood language. Ask to see a typical contract before entering into negotiations. Any unpleasant surprises buried in the contract are a bright red flag that should put you on highest alert.

You have a right to know how your money is being spent, and what actions are being taken on your behalf. When a service provider condescends to a client by saying, "Just let us do our thing," or "It's complicated," it is no longer treating the author as a partner and an equal.

You have a right to regular, timely updates on a project's status. Lack of communication in this area is a frequent cause of customer dissatisfaction—and with good reason.

Community

We have a long-term commitment to author-publishing and support the empowerment of self-publishing authors.

Most reputable service providers are active within the author communities they serve. They show their support for indie authors by catering to the specific needs of self-publishers, by listening to authors, and by joining and supporting professional groups.

However, some providers position themselves in opposition to a community. They pander to disgruntled authors by proclaiming contempt for traditional publishing or prey on insecurities by insisting that authors can't succeed without their help.

Neither attitude reflects the reality of indie authors. No author exists in a vacuum. We are all part of the publishing industry, a larger community that includes self-publishers, traditionally published authors, hybrid authors, service providers, professional organizations, and more.

A service provider that relies on needlessly divisive tactics is not working to empower authors, but is working to isolate them. This type of manipulation should be regarded with suspicion.

WHAT TO LOOK FOR IN ASSISTED SELF-PUBLISHING SERVICES

In addition to compliance with our Code of Standards, there are specific issues we look out for when evaluating a potential Partner Member for ALLi. These areas deserve extra scrutiny when considering any self-publishing service.

1. Nonexclusive Contract with Clear Terminology

Never sign a contract with a publishing service unless you have fully read and understand what you are signing. Some providers issue a physical contract, while others will request a click to a "terms of service" document online.

As an author looking for a service, you should receive a contract that refers to an agreed set of services: some combination of editing, design, formatting, print, distribution, marketing, and promotion. You should not be assigning secondary publication rights, copyright, or subsidiary rights (film, TV, translation, etc.) to the provider.

Be wary of providers using terminology in a contract like "We, the publisher."

A reputable service will also include a clause outlining cessation of the agreement and the period of time (e.g. 30–60 days), and means by which this should be executed by either party.

If you start to read the terms of the contract and they appear unclear, or there is an overuse of legal terminology, it may be an indicator that the contract is not author friendly and was drawn up solely to protect the rights of the provider in the event of legal action.

If you are unsure about the contract, or any terms, always request clarification. If your service is cagey about answering direct questions, take your business elsewhere.

2. Clear Breakdown of Fees

Understand whether quoted discounts or royalties on book sales are offered based on the retail price of a book or on the net receipts (the money the service collects).

Ascertain what the print-only cost of a book is, and what price the provider charges to offer books directly to you.

Knowing these crucial details allows you to work out what kind of markup the provider is placing on books sold directly to you "at cost." If it's difficult to elicit this information, then it's likely the provider has something to hide and wishes to confuse and complicate the process. Take your business elsewhere.

3. Multiformat Availability

Look for a service that offers the whole gamut of print options, other formats, and distribution platforms. Few services have the resources to print in-house, but they should have external print partnerships or affiliate agreements to deliver customer requirements.

If your provider cannot offer a hardback print edition, an offset print run, an EPUB or MOBI format, or the option of a full-color interior, it's likely the service has limited print resources (possibly only a POD facility) and few or no distribution programs in place. Take your business elsewhere.

4. A Book-Centric Attitude

Your service should be reader and book-centric and not author- or service-centric. Look for these signs of quality:

- Books are prominently displayed on the service provider's website.
- Books are sold in an online bookstore, with clear buy links and biographical details.
- Books are of professional quality, particularly cover design, paper quality, format, and internal layout.
- Book launches and author events are promoted on the website and externally. Service and author social network links are prominently displayed on the website. Links and listings to articles on self-publishing specifically as well as the general book industry.
- Official logos as proof of membership in publishing associations and connection to reputable industry guides.

No sign of books? Take your business elsewhere.

5. Ownership of Book Files

If you paid for the editing, formatting, and conversion of your manuscript to a digital format, you should own it. A good provider will allow that. Always seek clarity on this key question before you enter the production process. If it's not forthcoming, take your business elsewhere.

6. Access or Referral to Editing Professionals and Services

A package self-publishing service should offer access to professional editors (named and listed) and any other pre- and post-production services required. If the provider does not offer such information, it may be a clear sign that it accepts anything for production "as is," no matter how poor the quality.

Be wary of a provider that will not give the name of a specific publishing professional or the name of an affiliate service it uses.

A good service will always advise you on what work is required to improve your book. You should also be free to work with any other external service or professional you wish in conjunction with your chosen service.

Never accept the line, "Oh, we only accept books using our editing/design services." If the provider cannot be flexible, then take your business elsewhere.

7. ISBN Ownership Facility

A good service will always offer you the option of using your own ISBNs and publishing imprint name. Do not let the provider insist you use its assigned ISBN. By doing this, you give up the right to be identified as the publisher of your book.

There is nothing inherently wrong with using an assigned ISBN from a provider so long as you understand that you, the author, will not be the "publisher of record" and cannot take the edition of your book "as is" to another service, without first changing the book files and logos and reregistering the new edition with your own ISBN and publishing imprint.

There may also be additional issues with copyright on the cover images used. And you can't use a CreateSpace ISBN to distribute on Ingram, for example.

Contact the ISBN issuing agency in your country (Bowker in the US; Nielsen in the UK) to request and purchase a block of ISBNs yourself, before contracting a service.

8. Agreements with Wholesalers and Distributors

It's important as a self-publisher to understand the difference between a wholesaler and a distributor.

A wholesaler is a company with a warehouse and a vast database of listed books—some physically housed there as well as "available" on a database inventory for purchase and shipment to booksellers.

A distributor has a team of sales representatives operating on behalf of a list of client publishers, dedicated to selling "their" catalogue of books to buyers in bookstores.

A wholesaler reacts to book orders from the trade, whereas a distributor is proactive about selling its clients' books to the trade. So, a self-publishing service listing books with a wholesaler won't, in and of itself, sell a single book.

Few self-publishing services have book distribution deals in place, despite the claims you may hear. They depend on online print book sales through vendors like Amazon and Barnes & Noble, and ebook sales through platforms like Apple's iBookstore and Amazon's Kindle Store—both functions you can easily and cheaply organize for yourself. They are rarely successful in getting print books onto the shelves of physical bookstores, either major chains or independent stores. Those that do achieve it by having small niche distribution deals, often direct, and combined with considerable input and promotion by authors and their social networks. If any provider is promising you this service, read the small print. Ask how it will deliver this distribution.

Many self-publishing services, including Amazon, use Ingram for print (and, since the advent of Spark, for ebooks too), as this gets print books listed in the Ingram book catalogue. Ingram, the largest book wholesaler in the US, also operates as a distributor for many large and independent publishers.

In the UK, Gardners is the largest wholesaler of books, and Bertrams is another UK wholesaler offering distribution services.

However hard a service works to support and promote a book, its primary revenue comes from providing solutions to an author's needs. Most providers are not Macmillan or Random House. The best may have the success and penetration of a small independent press publisher, but most are little more than printers.

If that's what you find, you should take your business elsewhere.

9. Strong Presence on Social Networks

Up until a few years ago we wouldn't have listed this one. Now, social media serves two fundamental functions—as a necessary promotional tool for the service's authors and books, and for public transparency of the service itself.

Social networking is an important tool in the arsenal of a self-published author. It is fertile ground to grow contacts, reach like-minded people, and promote fan bases and brand following. It can be a red flag when we don't see a provider on any social network, but it's not necessarily a negative. It might suggest that the provider has limited staff resources, or that it doesn't understand the importance of social media, or it might suggest that it's hiding from public exposure and criticism. Before deciding, you'll have to dig deeper, and if necessary, take your business elsewhere.

10. Transparency of Staff Skill Set

Too many self-publishing services are opaque about the number of staff members, and about skill sets and experience in publishing, editing, design, and marketing.

Too many are one- or two-person bands, claiming to be much more. We've no problem with small operators—many of our most valued Partner Members are sole proprietors—so long as there is no misrepresentation, and the service can deliver what it promises. If you suspect otherwise, take your business elsewhere.

11. Marketing and Promotional Support

The reason most authors choose a self-publishing service is that they are daunted by the thought of marketing and promoting their books. Yet for many services, marketing is just leaflets, business cards, a website, or showing an author how to set up a social media account.

Good marketing and promotion require the service to work with the author to bring ideas and suggestions, as well as being willing to take the author's ideas on board. Planning and implementation of a strategy and launch should take place over a period of several months, and it should do something that works for books in that particular genre.

The service should not just be using the author's own provided contact list. It should also bring a press and bloggers list and other tools and resources. A "press release" should see the provider sending targeted information to particular journalists and bloggers, not a blanket, standard email.

Printed bookmarks, posters, and business cards are not marketing services; they are materials.

Another red flag is expensive display advertising in magazines like *Kirkus* and *Publisher's Weekly*. Readers do not read these magazines, and those who do—librarians and book industry people—generally make buying decisions based on the editorial, not the ads. Be very wary of such packages unless you have a clear underlying strategy that includes them.

If this is all that is being offered by your service, you are effectively on your own when it comes to marketing and promoting your book. Take your business elsewhere.

12. Communication

Communication is the biggest complaint we hear from authors who contact us about problems with a provider. "If they had at least told me" is a common feeling. Poor self-publishing services often have high staff turnover because interns or part-timers are employed to fill gaps, and authors get moved from one person to another, with little satisfaction from anyone.

Your service should listen to you and identify your needs. Both of you should agree on your book's requirements, and you should never feel that you are being sold services you don't need. Ask about communication systems and who's in charge if something goes wrong.

If your provider doesn't have the ability to work well with you, communicate and update you in a timely fashion, and keep to deadlines, then—yes—take your business elsewhere.

TEN QUESTIONS TO ASK SERVICE PROVIDERS

W hen choosing a service provider, ask these questions.

1. What Rights Am I Encumbering?

When a right is licensed to another entity, it is *encumbered*; its use becomes restricted by the other party, and potentially less valuable because of that restriction. Understand the consequences of encumbering rights, even if the license you're granting is nonexclusive and time limited. Limit the license to what is appropriate for the payment you are receiving. If you are paying for the service outright, ensure you retain all rights. For more on rights, see our guidebook *How Authors Sell Publishing Rights*.

2. Where Will My Book Be Distributed and Sold?

Ask for a list. Ask what distribution means in this instance. Will somebody be engaging with booksellers on your behalf, or are you just going to be placed on a database or website along with hundreds of thousands of others, with no discoverability service built in?

3. Is Your Service Exclusive or Nonexclusive?

Digital publishing services marketed directly to authors almost always operate on a nonexclusive basis. That means you can use the service to sell your ebook while simultaneously selling your ebook in other venues.

There are three notable exceptions to this, all big players:

- You need an Apple computer to create ebooks with Apple's iBooks Author tool. It's a proprietary format. No other device aside from an iPad or iPhone can view an ebook created by the Apple iBooks Author tool.
- Ebooks enrolled in Amazon's optional KDP Select program, which gives better royalty terms in some areas and allows your book to be lent to Amazon Prime readers through Amazon's "library," are exclusive to Amazon for the period of enrollment. This 90-day term of enrollment is renewed automatically unless the author leaves the program.
- Audible, the audiobooks distributor, reduces royalties for those who choose the nonexclusive option.

4. Who Owns the File after Publication?

ALLi's line on this is simple: If you have paid for conversion and formatting services, you should own the file. Steer clear of services that don't facilitate this.

5. Can I Make Changes to My Book after It Goes on Sale?

Most direct retailers like Kobo and KDP (ebook) and CreateSpace (print book) allow you to upload new and revised files as often as you like. Smashwords, and Draft2Digital are the only distributors to allow this. Other multichannel distributors, like BookBaby and Ingram, charge fees to make changes.

6. Do I Set My Own Prices?

While some services have restrictions (e.g. Amazon won't allow prices below $0.99), standard practice is to let authors set their own pricing. Amazon also guarantees its customers (readers) that they won't find your book at a lower price elsewhere, so if you reduce your price elsewhere, Amazon may price match at its discretion.

Some authors who want to use "permafree" books as a marketing tool use this to their advantage, making their ebook available for free elsewhere, knowing Amazon may then match the price to free. This has proven trickier in recent years, as Amazon has shown increasing reluctance to price match certain titles. Amazon generally looks to major retailers for its price matching, and may ignore pricing on some distributors.

7. Is Payment an Upfront Fee or a Percentage of Sales or Both?

This is one of the most important clauses in your contract.

Giving up a percentage of sales can ease the financial burden on cash-strapped authors, and ensures that the service provider has an incentive to see your book succeed. However, the cumulative cost of that percentage of sales will likely outweigh the value of the service in the long term.

Paying in advance means you won't have an ongoing deduction from your sales, but requires caution: once the service provider has your money in hand, will it remain dedicated to the success of your book?

The ideal payment arrangement will likely depend on your sales expectations and your immediate budget.

8. How Is My Royalty Calculated?

While different services have different models, the fees should be transparent and upfront. For example:

KDP, Barnes & Noble's NOOK Press, and Apple's iBooks are all free to use until the point of sale. They make their money by taking a cut of your payment for each sale made, from 30 percent upwards. Depending on your pricing, it may be more.

The Smashwords service is similarly free to use and it distributes to all major ebook retailers except Amazon. Smashwords pays you 85 percent of your list price on sales directly through the Smashwords site, minus PayPal transaction fees. It pays between 38 and 60 percent of list price, depending on the retailer and region. (See **In-Depth Reviews** for details.)

BookBaby and other distributors charge fees upfront. You earn "100 percent net" from these services, but that number can be misleading, as "net" may include any number of fees and deductions from your sales.

Always read the royalty terms carefully. Many companies are less than transparent in the figures they offer. For example, a service from Author Solutions called Booktango claims to offer free e-publishing services plus 100 percent royalties, but that's only if the sale is made on its own site. Even then, there's a 30 percent "bookstore fee." Ultimately, you're receiving 70 percent, not 100 percent.

Do the math. If, like many writers, numbers make your head spin, get somebody to help.

9. Are There Any Extra Fees or Charges I Should Know About?

There are instances in which you might end up paying more than standard rates for conversion or formatting, such as if your book is longer than average, if you have a lot of charts, tables, or images requiring formatting, and so on. Make sure no unpleasant things— such as hidden fees or rights grabs—are lurking in the terms of agreement or the contracts. Highlight any potential issues at quotation stage so there are no nasty surprises.

10. Where's the Value?

"Your publishing partner should add value to your manuscript," says ALLi's Author Advice Centre's editor, Debbie Young, who worked with SilverWood Books for her first publication.

You may have only one book to publish, but they will probably have published hundreds, amassing a wealth of experience that will fill them with ideas for enhancements you would not have thought of. A professional and experienced company will offer a coherent set of services that makes your book the best it can be.

— DEBBIE YOUNG

PERFORMING YOUR OWN EVALUATIONS

With the rapid growth and evolution of the self-publishing industry, the number of providers serving authors has grown as well. At ALLi, we aim to identify many of the worst predatory operators, and shine a spotlight on some of the best author-centric services, but new providers appear each week. The number of service providers rapidly outpaces any watchdog's ability to review.

Just as indie authors must learn aspects of publishing, distribution, and marketing, so they must also learn to appraise potential service providers to protect themselves from exploitation.

We've examined the ALLi Code of Standards and how it can help you identify predatory schemes. But how can authors know if providers are actually in line with those standards?

View Provider Websites Critically

A prospective service provider's website is a good place to start your research, but always remember that the website is a marketing tool under the provider's exclusive control, designed to present it in the best possible light. It should be viewed with a healthy dose of skepticism.

However, the *manner* in which that information is presented may prove even more useful than the information itself.

Is the website professionally designed, with well-edited copy? A provider that can't be bothered (or doesn't know how) to present its offering professionally is likely to cut corners on your work as well.

Is information about pricing and services presented clearly, upfront, and without evasion? A provider that doesn't disclose pricing or is vague about the services provided may be trying to conceal vital information from you, and that's not a good sign for future relations.

Does the marketing pitch rely on intimidation, or attempt to belittle you or prey on your insecurities? Does it falsely claim that the provider's services are the only path to success? Does it drip with contempt at a particular sector of the publishing industry, either indie or traditional? These are all signs of a predatory provider that tears authors down rather than building them up and supporting them. That behavior reveals a fundamental lack of respect that will characterize your entire relationship with the provider.

Examine the Provider's Work

If possible, look up examples of the service provider's work. If it provides cover art, are the designs eye-catching and unique, or are they repetitive templates? If it provides editing, is the book interior free of errors? If it provides marketing and publicity, is the book easily found outside of the provider's website?

Don't rely on the carefully selected examples spotlighted by the service provider. You'll want to see a random sampling of its work.

Listen to Your Fellow Authors

When shopping for a service provider, the recommendations of trusted friends and colleagues are invaluable. Each person in your circle of friends is one node in a much, much larger network, so by asking for recommendations, you're not only tapping into their personal experience, but the experiences of their friends and colleagues. Take advantage of the power of that network.

Author groups on social media are another powerful resource. If you're not a member of a group that includes seasoned, professional authors, you're missing out on a priceless source of information.

Seek Out Complaints

It's somewhat counterintuitive, but complaints can be one of the best indicators of a provider's quality of service. Glowing reviews may be solicited by the provider itself, or posted by naive clients unaware that they're being exploited.

Complaints, on the other hand, are a glimpse behind the polished façade that the provider presents. In particular, you should watch for the following.

Quantity of complaints: Dissatisfied customers are an inevitable part of doing business. At some point in the lifecycle of any business, something will go wrong, and a customer will be unhappy. These isolated negative reviews should not be an automatic disqualifier when evaluating a service provider, but when the number of complaints is substantial, there is a problem with the way that provider is serving its clients.

Consistency of complaints: Watch for recurring themes in complaints, especially issues concerning hidden fees, poor customer service, worthless services, or services not delivered.

These patterns may reveal incompetence or predatory behavior. Communication is particularly important, as predatory providers tend to shower new clients with attention until they've got the client's money in hand. Then the communication abruptly dries up, and the client is relegated to voicemail limbo while the next victim is being courted.

Reactions to complaints: Be on the lookout for threatening, blame-shifting, rude, or litigious responses by the provider's representatives. This is a bright red danger sign that signals an abusive, unprofessional operation.

Consult the Watchdogs

Author watchdogs like Victoria Strauss of *Writer Beware!*, David Gaughran, and ALLi review many of the big service providers. Even if they haven't performed an in-depth review of the ones you're considering, you may find useful background about their behavior among the wealth of information they've gathered.

You may also learn valuable information from consumer advocates, but beware: all watchdogs are not equal.

The Better Business Bureau (BBB) is one glaring example of a consumer watchdog that has failed its mission. The BBB offers paid "accreditation" that places a rating from "A+" to "F" on the provider's listing. The very practice of soliciting money from the providers it is supposed to monitor is troubling. Even more troubling is the fact that providers notorious for their predatory behavior were inexplicably awarded A+ ratings after paying for accreditation.

Despite these ethical and practical concerns, the BBB does have its uses. Consumers often leave reviews and complaints on the BBB website, and if you disregard the BBB's assessment of whether the issue was "resolved" or not, these can offer insights into the customer experience and dangerous patterns of behavior by the service provider.

SELF-PUBLISHING SERVICES TO BEWARE OF

The value-added service—a bonus or add-on service that complements a primary purchase—is a sales tactic we see every day:

"Your hotel stay includes free Wi-Fi and a continental breakfast."

"If you upgrade to the Deluxe package, the five-year extended warranty is included automatically."

"Would you like fries with that for just a dollar more?"

At their best, these offerings provide a welcome bargain. But at their worst, they can be used to deceive and defraud consumers.

Car dealerships are notorious for inflating the price on a car with high-profit, low-value extras. They'll offer floor mats, car alarms, upgraded upholstery, extended dealer warranties, clear coat, rustproofing (the car isn't rustproof already?), tinted windows, vehicle ID number etching, cruise control, GPS, the "deluxe" stereo system… and suddenly, that $30,000 retail price has nearly doubled.

These costs are often bundled into a package that makes it hard to determine the value of the individual components. What's presented as a convenience may actually be predatory pricing hidden under a mountain of fluff. To determine if you're getting a good deal on a

package, you'll need to separate that fluff from the services of
real value.

Beware of Costly Add-Ons

The following services are commonly used to pad self-publishing
packages, either as an add-on service or as a bundled feature with
questionable value to the author.

Please note that these services are not inherently bad. However,
they deserve extra scrutiny when their price tag is concealed among
other bundled services.

Copyright Registration and LCCN

Copyright registrations in the US and the UK are simple and
inexpensive. In the US, where copyright registration is a prerequisite
for filing suit against infringing parties, the process can be completed
online in about five minutes, at a cost of $35.

Similarly, obtaining a Library of Congress Control Number
(LCCN) is as simple as opening a free account and submitting your
book's information. There is no cost, and you'll receive your LCCN
within a few days.

There is no credible reason for an author to pay $100 or more for
these simple procedures.

Press Releases

To be successful, a press release must have an engaging headline, a
unique angle, and informative, well-crafted content. It should be part
of an intelligent marketing strategy, and it must be targeted to the
right journalists at the right venues. There is an art to writing
effective press releases.

With that in mind, consider these press release headlines churned
out by one provider as part of its publishing packages:

A Breathtaking Thriller that Delves into the Mayhem and Enigma of
Deceit and Evil
A Breathtaking Thriller that Delves into the Mayhem and Enigma of
Deceit and Love
A Breathtaking Thriller That Delves Into the Mayhem and Enigma of
Deceit and Faith
A Breathtaking Thriller that Delves into the Mayhem and Enigma of
Deceit and Murder
A Breathtaking Thriller that Delves into the Mayhem and Enigma of
War and Government

A fill-in-the-blanks approach like this ensures that your press release will be ignored. (To add insult to injury, more than a third of the text of each press release above was dedicated to promoting the publishing service.)

If you choose to purchase a press release as part of a package, be sure the provider is qualified to handle your publicity. Investigate its past work, and use Google search on titles it represents to see if the press releases were actually picked up by media outlets. Verify that the press releases are unique and tailored to the individual work.

If the provider doesn't have a solid PR track record, then its press release may be a breathtaking waste of money that delves into the mayhem of deceit and exploitation.

Inclusion in Catalogues

Catalogues from obscure publishers flood the market today. When mass-mailed to retailers, libraries, or journalists, these unsolicited catalogues are destined for the trash heap.

Don't waste good money on dumpster lining.

Publicity and PR Campaigns

An effective PR campaign is carefully targeted and multifaceted. Unfortunately, some assisted self-publishing services take a quantity-over-quality approach, blindly spewing out the aforementioned press releases and catalogues to every agent, publisher, or media outlet they can find. Professionals despise this kind of shotgun approach and tend to delete them on sight. And obviously, those communications do no good if they go directly into a wastebasket or spam folder.

Before considering a paid publicity campaign—and they're not cheap—find out exactly what you're paying for. How, exactly, will it promote your brand?

Look for independent evidence of the provider's successful campaigns. Are clients being featured on radio and TV segments? Are they being covered by journalists? Or is there no trace of those authors outside of the provider's website?

If there's scant evidence that these campaigns are working, you're not likely to be the exception to that rule.

Complimentary Copies

Complimentary copies of your book are nice to have, but weigh their value against the price you're paying for the whole package.

In the continental US, ten copies of a 240-page book will cost approximately $48 on CreateSpace. That's a tiny percentage of the cost of some assisted publishing packages, so keep the relative benefit of this perk in perspective. In these instances, the term "complimentary" just means the cost of the books has been factored into the price of the package already.

Retailer Previews

Google Preview, Amazon's Look Inside the Book feature, and other retailer previews are free benefits available to any author publishing on those platforms. Needless to say, if service providers try to take credit for that feature as a value-added service they are providing, they are not being entirely honest.

Retailer previews are standard features provided free of charge, so scratch this one off any list of supposed benefits a service provider offers.

Closed Awards and Recognition Programs

These are a common ploy among the larger vanity press schemes. By purchasing a package, you become eligible for an award or "recognition program." It's essentially a pay-to-play contest that's only open to the small subset of authors who have coughed up several hundred dollars to that vendor. The award itself carries little significance for the average reader, and so the contest provides more benefit to the seller than to the author.

Accounting

Proper accounting is not a feature; it's a requirement for any reputable service. If a provider lists accounting as an added benefit, cast a skeptical eye on that claim. If it charges you a fee to access an accounting dashboard, turn and walk away.

Proofs

Does the provider expect you to accept its work without your review or approval? Not if it's a reputable company. Digital previews and proof copies are a requirement for any service that prepares your books, not a benefit that sets it apart.

Social Media Promotion

Social media can be an excellent channel for promotion, but there's more to it than simply churning out ads. Be wary of service providers who promise social media promotion but who lack the audience and engagement to make it work.

For example, a provider claims it will increase your exposure by promoting your book to its Facebook fans. On inspection, the

Facebook page has just under 1,000 fans after three years of operation —an unimpressive number for a provider that offers social media services. Worse, each post is an advertisement that has at most one or two likes.

If the provider can't successfully promote its own products and services, how will it promote yours? If it can't hold the interest of people who have explicitly liked its page, how will it gain the attention of an audience that doesn't know you?

Author Page on the Service Provider's Website

Unless the provider attracts massive traffic, a page on its website— even one that's prominently featured—is not a valuable offering. Beware of claims of improved exposure without solid numbers to back them up.

One word of warning about metrics: don't be misled by the term "hits" when a provider describes its web traffic. A "hit" is simply a request for one element on a page: an image, a video, a script file, a font, etc. A single visit to one page may generate dozens of hits. Providers that describe their web traffic in terms of hits may be trying to deceive you, or they may be genuinely unaware of the uselessness of that metric.

Either one is cause for concern.

Reviews

Due to widespread author dissatisfaction, high cost, and a lack of tangible results, editorial reviews in general are considered to be a poor investment, even when purchased from a respected source such as Kirkus. When purchased from a provider that carries no name recognition among readers, they are no more credible than your Aunt Becky's glowing praise.

If you do opt to purchase an editorial review, either à la carte or as part of a package, be sure the reviewer has credibility and name recognition. If the provider is reselling a review from a third-party service like Kirkus, comparison shop to see if it is gouging with huge markups. Unscrupulous providers often resell reviews at astronomical markups, sometimes as much as 700 percent over Kirkus's already steep pricing.

Hidden inflated pricing is everywhere. To remove the confusion from comparison shopping, seek à la carte services or service packages whose components can be broken down into discrete prices. If that's not possible, approach any of the services above with a healthy measure of caution.

VANITY PUBLISHERS

As venerable trade-publishers, long-established agents, and new digital-only imprints all get involved in providing self-publishing services, intent becomes the core criterion.

ALLi's definition of a vanity publisher is one that engages in misleading or, in the worst cases, outright deceptive practices, with the intention not of bringing books to readers but of extracting as much money as possible from the authors.

They sell a dream, presenting expensive services in a manner that exploits new authors' hopes for their work. They exaggerate and blur lines, so that naive authors believe they have been published, when all that has happened is their book has been printed, at far more cost than they would have paid their local printer.

Like bad used-car sales staff, these publishers fail to point to the scratches on the body (the flaws in the book) or the cracked chassis (the lack of real distribution or marketing services in their offering).

We regularly hear of naive or uninformed authors who are left with a basement, attic, or garage full of books they have no hope of selling. Such operations, some charging four- or five-digit fees, proliferate on the internet and have the highest number of self-published titles each year. The worst services are outright unethical.

ALLi knows of services that have used false addresses in affluent areas to reel in the unwary author; services where the personnel use false names and aliases; services that take a fee and an exclusivity license, not allowing the author to publish elsewhere; services that require the author to purchase a substantial number of copies of the book; and a great many services that trade on misleading promises and vague language.

The worst of these operators will do anything to get the author to pay for services, and often shoddy services at that. Work that hasn't been read is lauded; the "gatekeeping" of trade-publishers is demonized; a veil of complexity is thrown over the publishing process; and sales reps bombard the prospective customer with emails and phone calls that urge them to do the right thing by their book.

GOOD SIGNS AND WARNING BELLS

Here are some things to watch out for, good and bad, when choosing a service provider.

GOOD SIGNS

Information Upfront

A sign of a good provider is that it provides all the information upfront, and in plain, jargon-free English. You shouldn't have to root out information in the backend of an FAQ page. You should be clearly told what the service does, how it's done, and what it costs.

Competitive Pricing

Low cost is always attractive when combined with high quality. As an author starting out, the trick is to aim high, in terms of publishing standards, but keep your costs to a minimum.

Realistic Empathy

The provider makes every effort to understand your book, your ambitions, your abilities, and your budget, while also giving you a reality check regarding commercial viability.

Track Record

There is nothing more valuable than the experience of another author whom you trust. Not that you believe everything somebody else says, but there's nothing like personal testimonial. The service should be happy to put you in touch with previous clients so that you can gain firsthand references. It's a good idea to contact some of the authors directly, too. Authors usually have fan websites and personal blogs and will be far more candid about their experiences and success with a publishing service if you contact them privately. Seek out recommendations and advice from your friends and author community. If a provider you're looking at keeps getting glowing recommendations, then it deserves consideration.

Good Team

Staff should be tactful and pleasant. You should get a sense of teamwork, with everyone behind your project.

Good Clear Contract

You should see a formal contract, clearly worded in terms you can understand. The copyright should remain with you, the author; you should not be tied in for any fixed time period; you should not be bound to exclusivity.

Contacts and Connections

The provider should have established relationships within the distribution chain from top to bottom (distributors, wholesalers, retailers, readers) and an online shop. It should also be able, and willing, to direct you to other distribution channels.

No Stings in the Tail

A lot of money can be made from authors after they publish. A common way to do this is to charge correction or alteration fees, which means if you find an error in your book and want to change it, you'll be charged.

Correction fees are standard—even some of the best providers charge them—but it's how much they charge that separates the good from the bad.

(This is one feature of IngramSpark that we at ALLi don't love, and though we appreciate very much that the company has waived change fees for our members, we look forward to the day all authors can make the changes they need to make.)

There can be other charges too, such as customer service charges, annual fees, and others.

WARNING BELLS

Providers Who Ask for Your Rights, and Charge You for Them

There are some providers who will ask for terms of up to three or five years, plus exclusivity, and still charge you for a publishing package. In the publishing business, an author expects compensation for the giving up of rights. This compensation generally comes in the form of a royalty payment on each copy sold and an advance on royalties, to tide the author over while the book is made and distributed.

The advance and the royalty are an exchange for the author

handing over to the publishing house the right to print, copy, publish, and sell the work. No provider should take your rights and not offer compensation in return.

Providers Who Act like Car Sales Staff

This is a common occurrence in the self-publishing world, especially with certain package providers. After contacting the provider, an author can be bombarded with emails and phone calls urging authors to publish. In our opinion, this is poor form. Authors should be given facts and left to decide, not sales pitches that lack necessary information. In our experience, this is usually practiced by providers whose interests lie with quick sales and conveyor-belt-style profit models, rather than the value for the author.

High Prices

Always assess what you are paying for, and what it will take to recoup. Many providers will fill out their packages with things an author does not need. Business cards, for instance, can bump up the price. Offering "copyright registration" is another area that can make an author think they're getting a good deal, when this is technically automatic. High prices drop authors in debt, and it can take years to break even.

Representatives

Beware the title "representative." In the publishing world, and in other industries, representatives sell something to you. So, if a self-publishing service talks of putting you through to a representative, or "your rep," put the phone down and move on.

Any Sort of Vagueness

When you need all the information at hand to make an informed decision, you don't want to be trawling through dozens of pages to get at it, or sending emails to slow customer service departments. Providers that offer comprehensive information upfront are the best ones to deal with.

Hidden Charges of Any Kind, or Constrictive Royalties

When you know that KDP and Kobo and iBooks do not charge service fees, give authors access to so many readers, and provide up to a 70 percent royalty rate (in the author's favor), it really does put other providers into perspective. Look deep for costs such as revision charges, annual fees, renewal fees, or down payments, and also for low royalties and commissions. With today's technology, aspects such as unit price and running costs have been driven down, so there is no excuse for providers masking their own profit with high administration fees and manufacturing costs that all bite into your profit.

DOS & DON'TS

DO:

- Find out how the publishing business works.
- Talk to other authors, and take your time.
- Ignore the provider's own "author testimonials." Instead, contact an author from its bookstore page who is not mentioned in a testimonial.
- Ensure you know all your options.
- Evaluate quality. Order a couple of the service's books in the format you're planning to use, so you can assess physical quality and order fulfillment.
- Investigate reputations. Do a web search on the service's name plus "complaint" and "scam."
- Purchase your own ISBNs.
- Refer to reliable and established writing organizations and bodies like your local writers' representative body, ALLi, Writer Beware, and the Independent Publishing Magazine.
- Follow ALLi's Self-Publishing Advice Blog and those of our

advisors, such as Joel Friedlander, Joanna Penn, and Jane
Friedman.

- Talk to successful self-published authors.
- Look for flexibility and a best match for your needs.
- Compare services and pricing.
- Look carefully at any contracts and terms of service.
- If considering an assisted service, choose one that offers all
  formats, non-exclusivity, and doesn't push add-ons.
- Know your own creative intentions, and be realistic.

DON'T:

- Open your wallet until you are sure the publishing step
  you're about to take is the right one for you and your book.
- Assume or take things on trust.
- Restrict yourself to what you find through Google search.
- Accept the first provider you find.
- Purchase rigid all-in-one packages.
- Choose a POD-only provider without understanding the
  limitations of print-on-demand.
- Pay your POD publishers hefty fees for Kindle and/or iPad
  conversions as an additional fee-based service.
- Think you're "published" by Penguin or Simon & Schuster
  if you purchase an Author Solutions package.
- Rely on online testimonials and company sales reps.
- Pay before understanding what services you are getting.
- Sign anything without reading the fine print.
- Choose a self-publishing service that pretends to be a trade-
  publisher, or pretends it can do more for your book than is
  actually possible.

AUTHOR SOLUTIONS

When it comes to author services, one company tends to get particular attention due to its size, global reach, and the support of Penguin Random House, a major trade-publishing brand name. Author Solutions (ASI) is the umbrella name for a controversial company distrusted by many savvy self-publishers.

Tragically, despite innumerable complaints, multiple class-action lawsuits, and constant rebuke by author watchdogs, ASI is often the first port of call for uninformed writers seeking a publishing service. Novice authors are lured in by ASI's aggressive marketing and omnipresent advertisements. Because they do not research the company's background, many prove to be easy prey.

Even those aware of ASI's reputation need to be vigilant: There is no publishing house called "Author Solutions." It trades under a variety of imprints, including AuthorHive, Xlibris, iUniverse, Trafford, Abbott Press, Balboa, AuthorHouse US & UK, Booktango, FuseFrame, iUniverse, Inspiring Voices, Legacy Keepers, Archway, LifeRich, Partridge, Palibrio (the Spanish language imprint), Pitchfest, Author Learning Center (a "membership" option that serves as a funnel for the paid imprints), Publish in the USA, WestBow, and WordClay.

Some of these imprints are more author-centric than others, but none follows what ALLi promotes as best practice, or fully abides by our Code of Standards. In our opinion, most fall at the first clause: "We follow through on all promised services and fully honor all advertisements and publication agreement terms. We never spam, oversell, or harass authors to buy our services or sell a dream to the uninitiated."

We have tried to discuss this with ASI but with unsatisfactory response (see below).

Bloggers Emily Suess and David Gaughran, our watchdogs Jim Giammatteo, John Doppler, Philip Lynch, Mick Rooney, Orna Ross, and Victoria Strauss have all expressed concern over ASI's treatment of authors. In the USA, where the parent company is located, more than one class action has been taken against ASI and its former parent company, Penguin Random House.

The authors in one of these suits alleged breach of contract, unjust enrichment and various violations of the California Business and Professional Code, and of New York General Business Law. Ultimately, Penguin Random House was dismissed from the case, along with some—but not all—of the claims against ASI. The case was settled in August 2015 and discontinued, but not before revealing that only one-third of ASI's revenue comes from selling books to readers. Two-thirds of its revenue comes from selling services to authors.

The terms of the settlement were not released.

AUTHORHOUSE CORRESPONDENCE

Below is some email correspondence received by our Watchdog Desk about AuthorHouse, an Author Solutions (ASI) imprint. We are grateful to the author who gave permission for us to reprint this correspondence (complete with errors). Author name, book title, and other small details have been omitted or changed to protect author identity.

From the Author to ALLi:

At the beginning of this year AuthorHouse were trying to persuade me to pay for a screen write for xxxxx, a book they had published. I thought it was a scam and said so despite the amazing number of times a consultant tried to persuade me. Now his boss has found and liked xxxx [another of the author's books] so I was treated to an hour of hard sell. I said I would have to get my family to review and could not just talk to them, I needed something in writing to explain.

So they sent the enclosed email. Despite the number of books I've written, at my age (85) I am not able to get out and physically sell so as I am a pensioner and not wealthy, I cannot throw money away on a pipe dream.

...

Is this film suggestion a scam? Should I be tempted? Your knowledge of the publishing industry is invaluable. Could I ask your advice please?

Excerpts from the Letter to the Author, from AuthorHouse

Month/date, 2015 Author Name, Book Title

Good Day!

I trust that this email finds you well. First of all, I would like to thank you for taking the call earlier and it was my pleasure to speak about your book. ...

I hope you agree with me on this that the book's potential is not just limited to publishing retail industry but even more to Hollywood movie industry. ...

I know that this book needs this big push so that we could help you with your book's success. That is the reason why we are doing this. We have carefully analyzed each marketing avenue and we are confident that this would surely provide your book the best possible way to be noticed not just by ordinary person, not just by highly interested individuals but even for those who are decision makers and major executives in the movie industry.

I am suggesting that we do these to create huge and essential noise for your book. Let us win the attention of the major movie companies We are not just helping with you by planning out the marketing strategy but on the investment needed as well.

As promised, I am sending you detailed plan of the extensive marketing we are willing to provide you and your book.

COMPLETE MARKETING SETUP FOR YOUR BOOK TARGETING HOLLYWOOD DECISION MAKERS

TRANSFORMATION OF THE BOOK TO A COMPLETE MOVIE/MARKET READY PROJECT

PROFESSIONAL REPRESENTATION TO A+ HOLLYWOOD COMPANIES

PROFESSIONAL RECOMMENDATION TO HOLLYWOOD EXECUTIVES AND DECISION MAKERS

...

With Hollywood Director's Cut package you can seize the initiative with a compelling bundle of services designed to turn heads and get a few crucial nods from film and TV executives in the highly competitive entertainment industry, including:

AuthorHouse will match you with a top Screenwriter from our community of screenwriters that best fits your book's genre

A professional Screenwriter to provide a thorough three to five-page outline detailing the plan to adapt your book's manuscript into a film and/or television screenplay

The Hollywood Treatment will be placed into our Hollywood Database where movie and television writers, agents, directors and producers have access to the information

The Screenwriter waives all rights to ownership of the treatment; you maintain full ownership Registration of your Treatment into the Library of Congress

I highly recommend that we give your book this rare opportunity be represented well in the industry. I have seen a lot of good titles failed to thrive in this industry not because it was not good enough but simply because the authors fail to see the potential of the book and this is the one thing that I want to prevent. You, of all people, know the value of your book. And your book deserves this huge marketing exposure. The Books-to Screen Hollywood program is by far the most unique and powerful marketing tool the company has introduced to it's authors. I suggest you take this campaign.

Proposed Price:

Hollywood Treatment: PRICE £2,599 Your Price: £1,299.00

...

Timing? Never been better, it is the best time to make them see the true essence of your work. Also, movie companies now is in very much in dire need of new concepts, that is the main reason why they are now turning their focus on self publishing authors.

...

I know how important this project of yours is to you and I would like to tap in these important people to have the book be taken seriously. Not to mention that it will be our company doing the job of an agent for you and the leg work as well, without asking any cut from it. Thus, you will enjoy full control and registration under your name and 100% revenue going your way.

All for the best,

RONALD REESE

Senior Marketing Consultant AuthorHouseUK

ALLi urges authors to be vigilant and to put services under a microscope before parting with money. Compare what you're getting with offerings from providers that get a good rating in this guide, like KDP, Kobo, Draft2Digital, Smashwords, CreateSpace, and IngramSpark. Analyze what any service could cost elsewhere, or if you handled it yourself.

Talk to other authors, and don't be lured by false or vague half-promises. Under such scrutiny, more often than not, the price tag for a publishing package quickly goes from being good value to looking very extortionate indeed.

BEWARE THE BRANDS

Vanity Presses Powered by Author Solutions

- Abbot Press (Writers' Digest/F+W Media)
- Archway (for Simon & Schuster)
- Balboa Press (Hay House)
- Dellarte Press (Harlequin)
- Partridge (for Penguin)
- WestBow (for Thomas Nelson/HarperCollins)

Customer Service/Marketing Packages by Author Solutions

- BookCountry
- Lulu

Conferences/Festivals Supported by Author Solutions

- Bay Area Book Festival
- LA Times Festival of Books
- Miami Book Fair International
- Toronto Word on the Street
- Tucson Festival of Books

Companies that Run Author Solutions Ads

- London Review of Books

- Guardian Weekly
- Library Journal
- Kirkus
- Publishers Weekly
- New York Review of Books
- Readers' Digest
- ForeWord
- Clarion
- The New York Times

In the next chapter we look at the seven stages of publishing, what services you must have to publish well, and why you might consider the alternative option of skipping the intermediaries and going direct to retailers and distributors yourself.

PART V

GOING DIRECT

THE VALUE OF CONTROL

BY DAVID GAUGHRAN

I make a living from book sales, despite being a slow writer, working in less popular genres, and not coming from traditional publishing armed with a backlist ready to upload. What I did have in my favor was a lot of time on my hands. I was able to carefully analyze what the biggest sellers had done to increase their sales and then experiment with adapting those approaches to my own books. After some years of doing this, it's clear to me that the key advantage of self-publishing is control.

If you self-publish, you get to pick yourself instead of waiting (maybe forever) to be picked. You get to choose an appropriate cover for your book, not one foisted on you by a publisher anxious to move onto the next batch of titles. And you get to set a price that will encourage readers to take a chance on an unknown author, instead of being overpriced and ignored. Control is also important in other fundamental ways that won't be obvious until you start self-publishing and trying to reach readers.

Marketing

It's obvious from talking to prospective self-publishers that marketing is the task that causes the most stress and trepidation. Of course, scammy operators know this. They prey on these fears by offering a series of magic bullets at exorbitant prices. And they don't work.

At all!

I can prove this. Take the vanity press of your choice. Search for the publisher name on Amazon. Check the ranking of the book that comes up first (that should be the one selling best). See how poorly it's doing? Read the stories of successful self-publishers. Notice how none of them have used a vanity press. Notice how none of them recommend the kind of marketing being sold by the vanity presses (such as spamming millions of people who don't care about your book or buying YouTube advertising packages). That should tell you something.

At this stage, I've tried almost everything in terms of marketing and can draw clear lines between what's effective and what isn't when it comes to promoting books. And I think I can put your mind at ease. Out of all the marketing tools at your disposal, the ones that tend to take up too much time, cost a lot of money, or make you feel uncomfortable tend to be the least effective.

So what is effective? In proof of the ultimate serendipity of the universe, the tools that actually shift books in meaningful numbers won't cost too much, eat into your writing time, or make you feel like a slimy huckster.

The stuff that is actually proven to work includes things like running a limited-time $0.99 sale, especially in conjunction with a reasonably priced ad on a reputable reader site. Other powerful promotional tools don't even cost anything, such as building a mailing list of readers that are genuinely interested in your work. Or making the first book in your series cheap or free. Or getting together with a group of authors in the same genre to cross-promote your books.

You can find plenty of information online about these marketing techniques, but the important thing to note for now is that you will not be able to use them if you go with a vanity press or other self-publishing service that doesn't give you control of your book's product page at the various retailers.

Losing Control

In the rest of this book, you will have been given innumerable reasons to avoid vanity presses like AuthorHouse, Xlibris, iUniverse, Trafford, Balboa Press, Archway, Westbow, Abbot Press, and Booktango. I want to give you a few more reasons. When you sign up with a self-publishing "service" like this, you lose control in the following ways.

Incorrect Categories

You won't be able to directly control which category your book appears in on the various retailers. This is crucial for both discoverability and visibility. All the retailers have a huge variety of virtual shelves your book can appear on, and these can be quite granular. In a physical bookstore, books tend to be divided up into quite general categories like self-help, romance, science fiction, and thrillers. Online retailers like Amazon have much more specific categories like post-apocalyptic science fiction or political thrillers. And they give you the ability to place each book on several such virtual shelves.

Getting on the right virtual shelf is incredibly important. You need your book to appear to readers who are interested in it. There is zero value in your epic space opera series appearing to readers searching for inspirational Christian romance. And the only way to ensure your book will appear on the right shelf on Amazon is by uploading directly to Kindle Direct Publishing (KDP). If you use an intermediary service, there is a strong likelihood that you won't get in the most appropriate granular subcategory for your book, and a reasonable chance you will get put in either a useless general category like fiction or on the wrong shelf altogether.

Changing Price

Many vanity presses don't let you change your book's price at all, and others charge a fee for any such price changes. Even when you can change price, it can take days or weeks to take effect. But when you are running a limited-time sale you need to be able to change your price within hours, not days. The only way to control price in this manner is to upload directly to Amazon's KDP.

Measuring Success

All the major ebook retailers (Amazon, Barnes & Noble, Apple, and Kobo) provide up-to-date sales figures in your account interface. This is crucial for measuring the effectiveness of any marketing. These near-live sales figures allow you to know what works and what doesn't, and the results can often be counterintuitive. For example, I learned that being interviewed in the *Sunday Times* shifts fewer books than taking out a $20 ad with a small reader site. It's nice to appear in a newspaper, of course, but knowing the precise value of that exposure shows me what kind of attention I should actively pursue.

If you use a vanity press or self-publishing service to publish your books, you won't have up-to-date sales figures at all. You will be flying blind, unable to measure the effectiveness of your marketing efforts. Without this data, you won't be able to know what was a waste of time and money, and what's worth trying again.

Keeping Control

There's a simple way to keep control of all this stuff and give your book the best possible chance of success, and the best thing about it is it won't cost you a penny. Uploading to Amazon is free, until the point that you make a sale. Uploading to Kobo is free. And instead of paying a fee or percentage to access those marketplaces, you will keep all your royalties.

Getting into Apple necessitates owning a Mac (and the process can be daunting) and there are many other retailers, but you can have access to them by using a reputable distributor like Smashwords or Draft2Digital. These services don't charge upfront fees and only take a small percentage of your royalties at the point of sale.

Don't fall for the vanity-press propaganda. It's not "easier" to pay a lump sum and have someone take care of all this for you; it will end up causing far more heartache in the end when they publish your book in a substandard way. Worst of all, you won't be able to use the proven marketing techniques of successful self-publishers.

Your book deserves better. You deserve better. Keep control.

WHAT TO LOOK FOR IN A DIRECT DISTRIBUTOR

I f you value time more than money, you may want to go with one distributor only. New distributors emerge all the time. At the time of this writing, Smashwords, Draft2Digital, and PublishDrive are ALLi Partner Members, as is IngramSpark. IngramSpark is unique in allowing for a single upload for both ebook and print book (pbook).

There are a few different ways you can approach these distributors, and use them separately or together, in combination with each other and various retailers.

If you want to maximize commercial benefit, ALLi's current advice is to go direct to:

- Amazon: ACX, CreateSpace, KDP
- Apple iBooks
- Kobo
- IngramSpark (for print, see below)
- NOOK

and use distributors for the rest. We go into more detail on the various choices for ebooks, print books, and audiobooks below in **Part Seven** and **Part Eight**.

When analyzing any distributor, look for:

- **Cost effectiveness:** See our reviews to help you know the real costs of a particular service and how to analyze good value for money.
- **Ease of use:** It should be quick and easy to publish and distribute digital files.
- **Reputation:** The service should be known and have a good reputation with other authors.
- **Reliability:** The service needs to be reliable in terms of delivering content to readers.
- **Security:** Protection of content and assuring the delivery to the right set of end users is essential, as is a secure commerce platform.

STAYING EXCLUSIVE VS. GOING WIDE

O ne of the most common questions we're asked through our Ask ALLi program is: Should I put my book in KDP Select and go exclusive to Amazon?

Here's what Amazon says about why you should opt for this program:

Earn Higher Royalties

Earn your share of the KDP Select Global Fund when customers read your books from Kindle Unlimited and the Kindle Owners' Lending Library. Plus, earn 70 percent royalty for sales to customers in Japan, India, Brazil and Mexico.

Maximize Your Book's Potential

Choose between two great promotional tools: Kindle Countdown Deals, time-bound promotional discounting for your book while earning royalties, or Free Book Promotion where readers worldwide can get your book free for a limited time.

Reach a New Audience

Help readers discover your books by making them available through Kindle Unlimited in the US, UK, Germany, Italy, Spain, France, Brazil,

Mexico, Canada and India and the Kindle Owners' Lending Library (KOLL) in the US, UK, Germany, France and Japan.

The Drawbacks

The first rule of investment is to diversify. Monopolies are never good, and you don't want to be dependent on any single income stream for your bread and butter.

Indie authors rightly love Amazon, but once you have more than two books, it really does make sense to think about going wide. ALLi's advice is to have your books as widely available as possible, in as many formats as possible.

In a post on exclusivity and Amazon, our distribution advisor, Mark Coker, founder of Smashwords, says, "It can take years to build readership at a retailer. Authors who cycle their books in and out of KDP Select (Amazon's exclusivity program) will have a more difficult time building readership at Amazon's competitors."

And then there's the global growth of book buying on other platforms. Amazon may be the biggest player in the US and the UK, but there are other retail stores and devices that dominate in other countries.

In Germany, which many experts agree is the next big market for ebooks, Amazon has 40 percent of the market. Apple iBooks and Tolino (an ebook reader with associated stores run by a group of German publishers) have the rest.

Sales in Canada come mostly from Kobo for most of our members, and both Kobo and iBooks have expanded into more than 70 countries. Joanna Penn, ALLi's enterprise advisor, agrees.

I'm 40, and I am not just building for the next year, I'm building for the rest of my life and hopefully leaving something for my family when I'm gone. As Amazon continue to rise and rise, we see the push back of many different industries against their domination. Who knows what the next five years will hold?

One of the best things about being an indie is personal choice, but, of course, this can make it harder as well. We can't tell you what to do with your books, but here is what I (Joanna) do myself.

For anyone with one book and no platform, exclusivity seems to be the best way to get your book moving, at least in the initial period. I helped my Dad self-publish his historical thriller, Nada, last year, and put that in KDP Select. There was no point in going with the other platforms when the majority of his sales would be Amazon, and he had no intention of doing any ongoing marketing for the book. Free books allowed us to get the sales started and get some reviews.

For translations, in a new market, with little ability to do other forms of marketing, exclusivity is also a good idea. I'm using KDP Select for my Spanish and Italian books, and the free promo days have enabled us to get the algorithms moving and get some reviews.

For an established series that you are building over time, using more than one site is my personal choice. The compound effect will mean that over time, as I add books onto the platforms, and reach readers one by one, my sales will grow on the other sites. I also like spreading my income streams so I am not dependent on one platform for my livelihood. That's why the vast majority of my English language fiction and nonfiction is on all the major platforms.

Trying new things is important! For this year's NaNoWriMo, I'll be writing a standalone novella that I will put on KDP Select in order to try out Kindle Unlimited. As a reader, I love the idea of KU. I already utilize borrows on Prime, and I consume a lot of books. I also love to play with the available options we have.

— JOANNA PENN

In summary, with multiple books, you can adopt multiple strategies. For the one-book author, KDP Select may well be the best option.

A NOTE ON ISBNS

To keep track of your book through complex distribution chains, the books industry uses ISBNs (International Standard Book Numbers). This is a controversial topic in the indie community, with opponents objecting to the cost of ISBNs, and proponents arguing that this identification and cataloging is a necessary part of professional book production.

ALLi advice is to purchase your own ISBNs, so that you are identified by all possible interested parties—bookstores, libraries, catalogues—as the publisher of your book, now and in the future. Here, ALLi Member Karen Myers makes the case.

Karen Myers on ISBNs

I write for many reasons, but one of them is to communicate with someone else. I'm sure that resonates with many writers. Right behind that is the sense that I am joining that long river of communication that is the world of books, a stream that has flowed for hundreds of years, and I want my little drops to join in and make that stream just a little larger. Maybe I will communicate with someone who finds my work decades after my own death.

If you want your work to survive and be part of that river, you have to treat what you're making as an honest-to-God book that could live forever, not just a document that gets thrown up in digital form somewhere and makes you a little money.

Using ISBNs to Future-Proof Your Books

My name is my brand. My books belong to me, and my stamp upon them is an ISBN, a unique and universal identifier that will bring them out of darkness to anyone's search, years from now and in databases I cannot envision. It doesn't matter whether the book is printed or in digital form; that's just a detail. I would no more omit my ISBN from a book I've written than I would take away my name.

I've heard people comment, well, you don't need an ISBN to publish an ebook at this site or that, and that's a true statement. But when you're caught up in the here and now of the latest development in the explosion that is new indie publishing, it's easy to lose perspective.

Consider the following situation:

I publish a book, digital only. I don't bother with an ISBN. I distribute it on Amazon, which assigns it an ASIN, an Amazon product code. I distribute it on Barnes & Noble, which assigns it a B&N product code.

I distribute it on Kobo, which assigns it an ISBN owned by Kobo, so my book will appear to be published by Kobo, not me.

I distribute it on Smashwords, which assigns it an ISBN owned by Smashwords, so my book will appear to be published by Smashwords, not me.

With the exception of Smashwords, none of these identifiers appears within the ebook itself.

And now, let 20 years go by... Barnes & Noble and Smashwords are out of business. Amazon changes its product code conventions and no longer uses ASINs. There is no searchable database made available by Amazon for the old ASINs. Kobo, which owns the ISBN it provided, controls what the Bowker Books In Print or successor databases contain and updates the information about your book in ways you would not approve of, and since you have no ISBN of your own, that's the only record of your book in Books In Print. Someone who chanced across a reference to your book based on an old copy from Barnes & Noble can't find it because the B&N identifier is no longer alive, and may or may not connect it with a Kobo record in Books In Print, which has a completely different identifier.

Does this seem like a good thing to you?

We forget how shallow the history of digital technology is, and if we're not in the information technology industry (I am), we have a natural human tendency to think that whatever's available today will always be available. But the real world is limited by money and time, and databases, formats, and standards evolve or die on a daily basis. The older standards are the most stable, and the standards for books, embodied by ISBNs, are as stable as anything we have, because books have been around longer as cultural and commercial objects than any other medium.

When I publish a book, and it's usually in both print and digital form, I always use my own ISBN and control all the Books In Print data about the book. I use a different ISBN (as required) for the print and digital editions. I have my doubts that the current practical divide of the digital format between MOBI and EPUB will last, and so I use a single ISBN for both of my digital format editions, since the standards haven't quite settled in this area, and Bowker permits it.

Think in the long term. Buy a batch of ISBNs (much cheaper in bulk), use them, and help your books speak to other generations for as long as they have anything to say.

For more of Karen's insights into publishing, visit her website at hollowlands.com.

PART VI

SELF-PUBLISHING'S BIG FIVE

PUBLISHING THROUGH AMAZON

I f you can read it, Amazon has a publishing platform for it. The biggest online retailer in the world is also the company that kicked off the self-publishing revolution back in 2009 with the introduction of Kindle Direct Publishing (KDP). As such, it is the first port of call for any independent author who wants to sell books. But with Singles, Scouts, Selects, Subscriptions... it can get a tad confusing, especially for newcomers.

This chapter covers Amazon's ebook publishing platforms and programs, together with ways to promote your book in the world's largest bookstore.

Amazon is constantly introducing new innovations and also regularly changing terms and conditions, so do check directly with its own advice pages, the Kindleboards (the advice forum), and the ALLi Self-Publishing Advice blog for the latest updates.

Publishing Programs

- Kindle Direct Publishing (KDP)
- Kindle Scout

- Kindle Singles
- Kindle Owners' Lending Library (KOLL)
- Kindle Unlimited (KU)
- Kindle Worlds (KW)
- Prime Reading

Promotion Tools

- KDP Select
- Amazon Advertising
- Amazon Giveaways

AMAZON DIGITAL PLATFORMS

Kindle Direct Publishing (KDP)

K DP is the virtual granddaddy of Amazon DIY platforms, established in 2007 for independent authors who want to publish in ebook format. The service is free until you sell a book, then a percentage is deducted from revenue (30+ percent, depending on a variety of factors, most notably KDP Select, detailed below).

You need an Amazon account to get started, and you can upload your manuscript in most formats and then convert the file to Amazon's own MOBI format using the tools provided on the platform. Or you can upload MOBI direct.

You can preview a copy of the finished ebook and make subsequent changes before publishing.

Indie authors receive royalties of 35–70 percent of the sale price, depending on a variety of factors: the price of the book, the territories in which it is published, and whether you will publish exclusively on Amazon. You don't need an ISBN for ebooks; Amazon will assign its own identifier, the ASIN (Amazon Standard Identification Number), but this is only recognized within the Amazon ecosystem. If you want your book recognized by all retailers, libraries, physical bookshops, and other books professionals, ALLi recommends you purchase your own ISBNs and allocate one to each format your book appears in. This makes you, not Amazon, the publisher of record.

How to: First, ensure your book is formatted to the platform specifications. Once you're ready to begin, log in to your account, go to your bookshelf, and click the Add New Title button. Then, complete the fields in Step 1 (Your Book) and Step 2 (Rights & Pricing), and you'll be ready to publish.

Pros: Amazon provides a fantastic platform to indie authors through KDP, giving your ebook a huge, global reach.

Cons: Incentives to publish exclusively with Amazon mean lower royalties are being paid in many territories to those who publish elsewhere. Not well established in all territories as yet.

Joanna Penn: I find KDP, CreateSpace, and ACX absolutely brilliant and wouldn't be a full-time author-entrepreneur without them. The reporting and analytics could be better as I'd like to see more data about number of clicks vs. buys, percentage read, etc., but hopefully that will come in time.

Kristin Gleeson: I like that I can change price points so easily if I decide to run a special offer. If you do a $0.99 one, you have to be sure to untick the 75 percent profit and go for 35 percent or it won't go through. I also like that it makes the changes quickly.

Kindle Scout

Amazon describes Kindle Scout, launched in 2014, as "reader-powered publishing for never previously published ebooks." You post the first pages (about 5,000 words) of your book on the Kindle Scout website for a 30-day "scouting" period, alongside other new works. Readers are invited to nominate their favorites. If your book is then selected for publication on Kindle Press, Amazon has the exclusive, worldwide rights to publish your book in digital and audio formats in all languages for a five-year renewable term. Otherwise, you automatically get all your rights back at the end of a 45-day exclusivity period from submission.

If you're not selected for publication, you must request removal of your work from the Kindle Scout site. Otherwise, your campaign page will remain online. Amazon says:

Authors do need to contact Kindle Scout if they want their page completely removed. However, after a campaign ends, only readers who nominated a book will be able to easily view it (if the author doesn't ask us to take it down).

Eligible categories include Romance, Mystery, and Thriller, Science Fiction and Fantasy, and general Literature and Fiction books. Action and adventure, contemporary fiction, and historical fiction are accepted within the Literature and Fiction category.

If selected, you receive a $1,500 advance and a 50 percent royalty rate. You can also earn royalties with enrollment in the Kindle Owners' Lending Library, and Kindle Unlimited, as well as being eligible for targeted email campaigns and promotions. (Note: "eligible for," not guaranteed).

How to: Upload a fully edited, ready-to-publish book (50,000+ words) in Word format. You will also need the book title, cover, book description, your bio, and photo. You will be notified within two days if your submission is suitable for a Kindle Scout campaign.

Pros: Small advance, a promotional boost, and eligible for Amazon's marketing muscle behind the book.

Cons: Unlike most publishing contracts, the Kindle Press publishing agreement is not negotiable. Read with a steely eye. The grant of rights includes translation rights, and if these are exercised by Amazon, your royalty drops to 20 percent of net, which is low. ALLi recommends 50 percent of net or 25 percent of list price as a fair translation deal.

Stacey Cochran: Kindle Scout offers an innovative way for indie authors to raise their profiles. The crowdsourced process galvanizes reader support for all the authors ahead of publication and excites readers. I've been blown away by the personal and professional touch of the entire Kindle Scout team, and I have grown close to many of the other authors. It has supercharged my career like nothing else I've ever known.

You need to pace yourself. Plan out something you're going to do for each of the 30 days of your voting period. You have to be proactive about spreading the word and asking people to nominate your book. I planned a 30-day Facebook Tour, wherein I asked people in advance if they would host me on their Facebook walls on a given day to discuss my book *Eddie and Sunny* and Kindle Scout. The discussions would take place in the comments section of the original post the host would make, and we'd often have 100 or more comments by the time the 60-minute chat was done. The original post would link to the Kindle Scout page for my book, and so it made it easy for folks to find and nominate my novel.

Sariah Wilson: Be prepared to market yourself relentlessly to get the nomination votes for your manuscript to get noticed. I contacted everyone I could think of, ran a sweepstakes, and generally did whatever I could for a good month to get people to nominate my book. Scout also offers readers a small sample of your work, so make sure the sample hooks potential readers and leaves them wanting more, and makes them want to nominate you so they can read the rest.

Kindle Worlds

This is Amazon's foray into fanfiction territory, allowing any writer to create text-only novels, novellas, or short stories inspired by popular books, shows, films, music, or games (what Amazon calls "Worlds"). It has secured the licenses for select rights holders (World Licenses) permitting you to publish new work inspired by its Worlds. Prices set are between $0.99 and $3.99; the standard royalty rate is 35 percent for works of 10,000 words or more. The content guidelines set out the type of fiction currently accepted. On submission, your work becomes exclusive to Amazon and sold in a new section of the Kindle Store.

How to: Kindle Worlds features an easy-to-use submission platform. After you choose a licensed World and read the content guidelines for that World, click Submit. Then upload your story as a Word file (DOC/DOCX), RTF, or TXT, create a cover from over a thousand free images or using your own image—though not all Worlds allow authors to upload this. The minimum length is 5,000 words.

Pros: Another revenue stream for new and established authors.

Cons: Currently only available in the US. You must have a valid US bank account and a corresponding US address to participate. Writers must be over 18, which excludes the age demographic that are the biggest contributors to fanfiction. Writers must adhere strictly to creative limits, which may be imposed by the copyright owners.

Christine Nolfi: By writing in a World, you grant binding rights. Familiarize yourself with the contract before you begin. Your sales aren't visible in your normal KDP account. Approximately two months after the publication of your first KW story, royalty information will appear in your Author Central Account > Sales Info > Kindle Worlds Royalties.

Kindle Singles

Launched in 2011, a Kindle Single is an ebook of between 5,000 and 30,000 words published through Amazon, currently in the US, UK, Germany, and Japan only. It is a platform for original novella-length fiction or long-form journalism, or as the company put it on the launch of the new format, Singles are "Compelling Ideas Expressed at Their Natural Length."

Singles are selected from new talent as well as established writers, authors, and journalists. Amazon both publishes its own signings and distribute curated works by other publishers under the Kindle Singles brand. Prices are set on average between $0.99 and $2.99, with royalties of up to 70 percent of revenue paid on a monthly basis, and authors (or their trade-publishers) retain all rights. Kindle Singles editor David Blum says: "Kindle Singles welcomes submissions from all writers via our submissions queue at kindlesingles@amazon.com. We're looking for high-quality writing between 5,000 and 30,000 words that takes readers places you can't get to any other way, on compelling journeys of fact and fiction presented at their natural length. We accept writing in any category except erotica, and we will reply to all submissions within six weeks."

How to: Kindle Singles is happy to consider manuscript submissions, or pitches, as well as titles recently published through Kindle Direct Publishing. Email kindlesingles@amazon.com, including the proposed title and a brief summary of the work.

Pros: A great outlet for shorter books.

Cons: Not open to all territories.

Mishka Shubaly: "I would encourage any talented writer with a compelling story to submit to the program. Do your research: read a broad selection of Kindle Singles to get an idea of what the editors want and what readers are reading. Then craft an amazing story and send it in. The best way to get your writing accepted for publication as a Kindle Single is to tell an amazing story that's right for the format. Familiarize yourself with the format and the market by reading six or eight popular Kindle Singles—they don't have to be mine, but hey, why not? Then craft the ultimate version of your story and send it in. When I started publishing with Kindle Singles, I was managing a bar a couple of nights a week, had few professional prospects, and no name as an author. Six bestselling Kindle Singles later, I have an agent, a book deal, a house, and a career. I hoped to make $500. Suffice it to say that my expectations were exceeded!"

Kindle Owners' Lending Library (KOLL)

The KOLL is a collection of books that Amazon Prime members can read for free once a month. You need to enroll a book in KDP Select for it to be included in this program. Your books will still be available for anyone to buy in the Kindle Store as before. For each page read, you are entitled to a share of the KDP Select Global Fund (see below for how the fund operates).

KOLL is currently available to Amazon Prime customers in the US, UK, Germany, France, and Japan.

How to: You must meet the KDP Select requirements and enroll your book in KDP Select (see below).

Pros: It can add to your income. Some of our members are now earning more from borrows than sales.

Cons: Exclusivity. You're committed to KDP only during the 90 days of your book's enrollment in the program; it cannot be available free, or for purchase, in digital format anywhere else online, including your own website. Payment per page is variable, and depends on the size of the KDP Global Fund for that particular month.

Tim Lewis: "It is not entirely accurate to say that you are being paid per page, as the set amount is not fixed. Yes, the more pages read the better. But you are in effect buying more tickets in the KU lottery rather than being paid directly per page read."

Kindle Unlimited (KU)

KU is Amazon's subscription service, allowing readers to read as many books as they like and keep them as long as they want for a monthly subscription fee. Any reader (not just Amazon Prime members) can subscribe to KU. You need to enroll a book in KDP Select (see below) for it to be included in this program. Your books will still be available for anyone to buy in the Kindle Store as before.

For each page read, you'll be credited with a share of the KDP Select Global Fund (see below for how the fund operates).

How to: You must meet the KDP Select requirements and enroll your book in KDP Select (see below). The price of your book must not change for 30 days, even if you renew your KDP Select enrollment during that time.

Pros: Can give your book a considerable income boost, as more readers choose the KU subscription model. KU is currently available to indie authors in the US, UK, Italy, Spain, Brazil, France, Mexico,

Canada, and Germany. The audience for Kindle Unlimited books has grown substantially and continues to grow

Cons: Exclusivity. You're committed to KDP only during the 90 days of your book's enrollment in the program; it cannot be available free or for purchase in digital format anywhere else online, including your own website. Payments may fluctuate due to the variable size of the KDP Global Fund.

Fenella Miller: "KU doubled my royalties in the US, and I've always found them quick to respond to any queries."

Prime Reading

Prime Reading debuted quietly in 2016. Like Kindle Unlimited, it offers monthly subscribers the opportunity to download books from a catalogue, but it offers unlimited downloads rather than the ten-per-month limit of KU.

Prime Reading is an invitation-only program. It is curated, meaning that approximately 1,000 titles are drawn from a selection picked by Amazon, rather than the much larger pool of KU-eligible titles. Authors selected for inclusion in the catalogue are compensated with a one-time payment (typically in the low four-figure range) rather than the per-page payment system used by KU. Participation is voluntary.

At the time of its rollout, Prime Reading featured a mix of indie authors (approximately 20 percent of the catalogue), Amazon's traditional publishing imprints like Thomas & Mercer and 47North (approximately 25 percent), F+W Media imprints (approximately 25 percent), Kindle Singles (approximately 13 percent), a small number of Kindle Scout titles (approximately 3 percent), and various small-to-mid-size publishers.

AMAZON PRINT PLATFORMS

CreateSpace (CS)

CreateSpace is Amazon's free online POD platform for indie authors. This service lets you sell your paperback book directly on the CreateSpace eStore, through Amazon regional stores (Amazon.com, Amazon.co.uk, etc.), as well as through your own website, live events, and the like.

To make things easy, the site offers ready-to-print templates that you can download for free and use to format your book. When you're ready, the platform uses two PDFs—a cover and a text file—to produce a print-ready book file.

The basic service provides free online tools like cover design options, but there are additional services available, for an extra fee, such as professional copy-editing. There is a set minimum selling price for your book based on printing and distribution costs, but you can set a higher price. It uses services such as IngramSpark to distribute on a wider scale.

A free CS ISBN can be assigned when you set up your book (though if you want to sell through bookstores, this is not recommended; see below). If you don't already have a website, CS also gives the option of setting up your own author page to connect with readers and publicize your work. You can also easily track sales of your books.

How to: Create an account on CreateSpace. Upload a PDF of your book based on CS specifications, using the supplied templates to create print-ready files. Go to your bookshelf and click the Add New Title button.

Then, complete the fields in Step 1 (Your Book) and Step 2 (Rights & Pricing), and you'll be ready to publish.

Pros: POD means the book is printed on demand when customers order. Manufacturing and shipping is taken care of, removing a big administrative headache, as your book remains in stock, without you having to hold inventory. You can also link from CS to a Kindle version of your book.

Cons: Compared with printing a consignment, POD books are still expensive, leaving little profit for the author and making them more expensive than trade-published books if sold through bookstores. If you use a CS ISBN, it may not be accepted by bookstores. ALLi advice is to use your own ISBN.

(See more on using CreateSpace and IngramSpark together in the next chapter.)

KDP Paperbacks

KDP Paperbacks is a new program that entered public beta testing in 2017. Because the program is still under development, several key features are currently not available. The most serious omissions at this time are at-cost author copies and proof copies, and distribution to bricks-and-mortar stores and libraries. Amazon promises that these services will be added soon.

KDP Paperbacks does hold several advantages over CreateSpace, notably distribution to Amazon's Japanese site and integrated reporting of paperback and ebook sales in one place.

At present, KDP Paperback's missing features make CreateSpace the more desirable option. However, that's expected to shift as Amazon adds expanded distribution and proof copies back into the program.

AMAZON AUDIOBOOKS

Audio Creation Exchange (ACX)

B ack in 2009, as the market for digital media was growing, about 100,000 books were published, but fewer than 5,000 of these were produced in an audio version. Amazon Audible saw the opportunity in helping rights owners to close this gap in the market, and created its ACX platform to link authors and narrators and distribute the resulting audiobooks.

Using ACX, authors can narrate and produce their own books in audio, then distribute them via Audible.com in the US and Audible.co.uk in Great Britain and Northern Ireland only, at this time.

Alternatively, an author can use the marketplace functions on ACX to find and hire a professional audiobook producer and narrator to bring a title to life. There is also potential to sell the rights of the work to an audio publisher. This is a market set to grow, with famous authors such as Neil Gaiman now using ACX tools to liberate audio rights to his work and produce audio versions.

How to: Your audiobook must be ready for retail before uploading, and follow the Audible Submission Requirements.

Pros: ACX provides a great extra source of income from your book. Readers can move effortlessly between the ebook and audio formats of a book, picking up where they left off on the other.

Cons: Limited territories at this time. Audio production costs with ACX are relatively low but still represent a significant investment: do factor in hiring a professional audio producer.

Pam Dixon: My experience with ACX has been extraordinarily good. I am working on my 17th audiobook production with the same narrator. In addition, many of my productions were awarded ACX stipends, which minimized my out-of-pocket costs. My favorite thing about ACX is its customer support. It's outstanding. I've always opted for 50/50 royalty split—another means of limiting upfront costs. In my view, it is worth the effort. I like having the additional revenue.

Jane Dixon-Smith: ACX is a brilliant tool for finding and pairing narrators with authors and in turn producing excellent audiobooks. As you can agree your own terms with the narrator, whether it be a straight 50/50 split of the 40 percent royalty, meaning 20 percent each of what the book is sold at, or a fixed fee per finished hour, you can pick whatever suits you and the narrator. I found it pretty easy to find a suitable narrator for *The Rise of Zenobia*, first in the Overlord series, my fictional account of the third-century Palmyrene rebellion against Rome. Paul Hodgson was both professional and talented. Finding marketing opportunities once the audiobook was completed has been the toughest part.

BOOK PROMOTION ON AMAZON

B elow are some of the promotional tools our members have found most useful.

KDP Select

This program allows authors to run free promotions of their book on Amazon. The author gives exclusivity to Amazon for 90 days; in return Amazon pays higher royalties (70 percent versus 35 percent) in some territories; the book is available through the Kindle Owners' Lending Library, and Kindle Unlimited (see above). Since 1 July 2015, royalties are based on the number of pages read (as opposed to qualified borrows).

KDP Select also gives the option of offering your book free for up to five days, a strategy which can increase subsequent sales. It also makes your book eligible for Kindle Countdown Deals (see below), a limited-time promotional discounting for your book.

How to: You can enroll existing titles from the bookshelf in one of two ways: scroll to the column titled KDP Select and click on Enroll, or click the Edit Book Details link found in Other.

Pros: Opens platforms like KU and KOLL and promotional tools like a five-day window in which your book can be discounted. Backed by a good marketing strategy, these can give a powerful income boost to your book.

Cons: Exclusivity. You're committed to making the digital format of that book available exclusively through KDP Select during the 90 days of its enrollment in the program; it cannot be available free or for purchase in digital format anywhere else online, including your own website.

See KDP Select terms and conditions for more information.

For more details on how KDP calculates how many pages a reader has read, see Amazon's KDP FAQ.

KDP Select Global Fund

Amazon sets aside a monthly fund for the specific purpose of making the KDP Select program appealing to KDP publishers. "The size of the global fund is calculated to make participation in KDP Select a compelling option for authors and publishers," says Amazon.

The amount of the payment you receive from the fund varies, depending on the size in a given month and the number of authors being paid from it in that month.

Amazon calculates your share of the KDP Select Global Fund by counting pages of your book that KU or KOLL customers read for the first time (see below). Here's an example, assuming the fund is US$10m and 100,000,000 total pages are read in the month:

The author of a 100-page book borrowed and read completely 100 times would earn $1,000 ($10m multiplied by 10,000 pages for this author divided by 100,000,000 total pages).

The author of a 200-page book that was borrowed and read completely 100 times would earn $2,000 ($10m multiplied by 20,000 pages for this author divided by 100,000,000 total pages).

The author of a 200-page book that was borrowed 100 times but only read halfway through on average would earn $1,000 ($10m multiplied by 10,000 pages for this author divided by 100,000,000 total pages).

KDP reviews the size of the fund each month, and the fund is increasing significantly as more books are being borrowed and read through the KU program. In January 2016, it stands at US$12 million. KDP announces each month's KDP Select Global Fund amount on the KDP website and community pages.

For more FAQs about Amazon's KDP Select Global Fund, go to kdp.amazon.com.

Caroline Batton: KDP Select has worked well for me. The downloads make up 2/3 of my total "sales," though I get less per download (88p) than I do a sale (£1.11). Sadly, I'll never know if those downloads would be sales if I weren't in Select, but I doubt it. Be interesting to see what the new page-count system of paying means.

Kindle Countdown Deal (KCD)

This is another KDP Select benefit under which authors provide limited-time discount promotions. Readers see the regular price and the promotional price on the book's detail page, as well as a countdown clock showing how much time is left at the promotional price.

How to: Find the book you'd like to set up in your bookshelf and under the Book Actions menu, click Promote and Advertise, Kindle Countdown Deal, and create a Countdown Deal for that book.

Pros: A promotional tool that's popular with readers. A number of ALLi members use it to increase visibility for a new book.

Cons: Only available in the US and the UK. Some members report it made "no difference." In Amazon.co.uk, there is no symbol to tell a reader it's a Countdown Deal.

Amazon Marketing Services (AMS)

AMS offers various ad campaigns that are displayed to Amazon shoppers. There are different types of ads available: Sponsored Products, which appear above, below, or to the side of search results and product listings; Headline Search Ads, which appear above

Amazon search results; and Product Display Ads, which appear on product detail pages, customer reviews, and alongside search results.

Readers who click your ad are brought to your book's product detail page. You are charged only when your ad is clicked. Your actual cost-per-click (CPC) is determined in an auction with other eligible ads. You are charged $0.01 more than the second-highest bid in the auction for a click, up to your maximum CPC bid.

How to: You can create an AMS account directly on the KDP website. Choose the book you want to promote, specify how you want your ad to be targeted, a start and end date, and a maximum cost-per-click bid (minimum CPC bid is US$0.02 and minimum campaign budget is US$100). You can choose to have your ad delivered to customers who previously browsed the Kindle Store for a particular genre (targeting by interest), or to customers interested in specific products on Amazon (targeting by product).

When you target by interest, your ads will automatically be considered for placement on Kindle e-readers. When you target by product, your ads will not be eligible to appear on Kindle e-readers.

Pros: A good way to increase visibility and discoverability of your book.

Cons: Can be expensive, unless you have a well-worked-out strategy.

AMS is not currently available in all countries. The company is gradually rolling out the program to various regional stores over the next few years.

Amazon Giveaway

You purchase the prizes you want to award from Amazon and pay for sales tax and shipping to the winner(s). Since winners and location are not known when you set up a giveaway, you are charged an estimated amount to cover sales tax and shipping, and are refunded any excess when your giveaway ends. If prizes are unclaimed when your giveaway ends, those are returned and included in your refund.

How to: Select a prize from eligible items sold on Amazon.com and complete a two-step form to set up your giveaway and prizes. Amazon emails you a link, which you then use to promote your giveaway.

Pros: A great way to win new readers and fans. You can send a custom message to the losers of the giveaway, so this is another opportunity to make an offer—and to somebody who has demonstrated interest in your work.

Cons: People may sign up for the prize without any real interest in your work.

Timothy Bond: I've done several Amazon Giveaways. You pre-purchase the total number of books your giveaway might award, at retail, plus shipping. They will refund you for anything you don't give away. You get to provide the basic text for the contest, the text for the "Congratulations," and the text for "Sorry, you didn't win." You also set the terms yourself and what you want the outcome to be. You can encourage them to follow you on Twitter to enter the contest, for example. I used the "Sorry" text to provide a link to sign up for a free download of my ebook—and get on my mailing list in the process. I added 200+ people to my list each time I ran a giveaway.

APPLE IBOOKS

Apple iBooks is available for all iOS-capable products, so readers can easily take their library on the go and have it synced to other devices—laptop, phone, iPad—as they switch. The program features the intuitive user-friendliness that Apple has become known for.

A free download of the ebook design program, iBooks Author, allows writers to create Multi-Touch books (multimedia: animations, video content, and interactive 3D objects) in addition to regular ebooks. Additional features like readers' ability to highlight and share quotes via social media without leaving the e-reading app offer an interesting new way for authors to interact with their readership as well as possibly gain new interest.

There are system requirements. It is a proprietary format: you must own a Mac to create a book on iBooks. There are also restrictions around the mention of third-party book retailers, which makes iBooks more of a hassle to set up than Kindle. The process to get a publisher account takes several days. You must verify your bank account and tax ID number/EIN before you can upload. (This step can be skipped if you plan to only give books away for free).

While the author experience is not quite as user friendly as some other platforms like Kobo, the reader experience is very streamlined and books are available in 50+ countries, so the effort is very much worth the gains.

See below for a comparison between Amazon and Apple.

INGRAMSPARK

IngramSpark's service is aimed at "publishers looking for print and distribution services," and is unique in offering both ebook and print book in the same platform. You can pick and choose and use Ingram for ebook distribution only, or (more commonly) print book alone, or some combination of the two. IngramSpark allows you to opt out of distribution and go direct, on two platforms only at the moment: Amazon and Apple.

With an easy-to-navigate setup and estimated revenue calculator to help authors see what they'll actually be getting in return for their cover price, IngramSpark offers an author-friendly publishing experience, without having to go through multiple platforms. ALLi members receive substantial discounts on their services; check the discounts and deals page in the Member Zone.

Where IngramSpark comes into its own is in the POD services. More on this in the chapter about print books.

KOBO

K obo is an Open Platform, which allows readers to buy and read multiple digital formats on one e-reader, and it supports 60+ languages in 190 countries.

The upload is simple and highly user friendly, and authors can modify how they'd like to control their rights. The promotion service is in beta, and tracking analytics on sales and revenue is available, with easy-to-read graphics and reports, so authors can stay easily informed throughout promotions and marketing periods.

NOOK

NOOK is owned by Barnes & Noble, and many of our members, especially US members, have sold significant numbers of books there, but it is widely recognized that the NOOK platform is struggling and that Barnes & Noble's business is not what it used to be.

Nonetheless, it remains one of self-publishing's most significant platforms and ALLi still recommends direct upload and direct contact with NOOK, to see if you can get your books featured on the platform. When NOOK makes the effort to merchandise a title, it can still move books. Barnes & Noble still represent a sizable portion of the US book business, with a tremendously loyal group of customers and a huge mailing list.

PART VII

CHOOSING A LIBRARY SERVICE

LIBRARIES AND INDIE AUTHORS

One other service that deserves a special mention is low-tech and has been around a long time: libraries. Unlike bookstores, the people who work at libraries know books inside out. Many of them treat authors like rock stars. And they talk to readers all day long.

They are arguably the most important influencers in the book ecosystem. And they do an amazing job for the reading and writing community.

We have a section on how to get your book into libraries in our guide *Opening Up to Indie Authors*. Here our focus is the many services now stepping up to provide a link between your publishing platform and the ebook library infrastructure—mostly in the US, where there are thousands of libraries with the facility to loan ebooks.

Libraries are keen to offer self-published books, but with over 600,000 indie titles published every year in the US alone, librarians don't have the time or resources to filter the good from the bad.

Librarians also face tight budgetary constraints. Traditionally, mainstream publishers have sold print copies to libraries at a high markup (often five to ten times the price paid by consumers). After the book is checked out 20 or 30 times, it may need to be replaced.

Absurdly, this print model has been carried over into the digital age, with Digital Rights Management installed in the ebooks purchased by libraries, which both limits the number of individual checkouts and requires a "copy" to be repurchased after an overall number of loans or a preset period.

GETTING YOUR BOOKS INTO LIBRARIES

We looked at the three major services that connect independent authors to the ebook library system: ebooksareforever, SELF-e, and OverDrive.

All these services are operating in an emergent sector, and so there is no perfect system. Independent authors should follow our assessment of each and decide which is right for their needs and philosophy at the current time, while also taking into account future intentions based on pledges we received from the business operators.

ebooksareforever

"A platform to help libraries sustainably purchase ebooks from independent authors and publishers."
Launched: March 2014
Authors: Mark Dawson, Hugh Howey, CJ Lyons, Joanna Penn, HM Ward

The philosophy of ebooksareforever is based around sustainability. The team believes that libraries should be able to buy ebooks at affordable prices and—since they are not physical, degradable items—own and offer them to loan for eternity.

Co-founded by authors JA Konrath and August Wainwright, ebooksareforever sells DRM-free ebooks with no relicensing restrictions.

We deliver a curated collection of titles from independent authors and independent publishers and make it as simple as possible for both the author/publisher and the library to interact with the collection and to fairly compensate the author/publisher for every transaction.

— AUGUST WAINWRIGHT, CO-FOUNDER,
EBOOKSAREFOREVER

How it works: Every author and book is approved by a curation team. "We need this because we're working hand in hand with libraries," says Wainwright, "and we need to deliver what they're asking for.

We assess by reviews, number of titles the author has available, whether those titles are in a series, quality of cover art, interest in libraries, and genre saturation in our system. We couldn't be taken seriously if, say, 80 percent of our titles were romance. It equally wouldn't work if every book had to have at least 200 reviews on Amazon.

— AUGUST WAINWRIGHT

If your book is rejected, you can reapply 60 days later.

Each book is purchased by a library on perpetual license. They pay once, and they can use it forever. Only one copy can be checked out at a time.

Do authors get paid?: Yes. Titles are sold to libraries for $7.99 (full-length) and $3.99 to $4.99 for shorter works. Authors receive 70 percent of every sale.

Future plans: The ebooksareforever team say they hope to evolve the submission/rejection process once the business grows, but the current focus is on building a robust system that is trusted and popular with libraries.

They are also working on "patron apps" that will break the business out of the US and allow global libraries to purchase titles, with patrons loaning copies using universal apps. This system should also see broader opportunities for author payment.

There are also plans to allow libraries to purchase lower-priced "unlimited use" licenses, on approval of author/publishers. In this case, one copy could be checked out an unlimited number of times.

Pros:

- Free to submit
- Author payment
- Set up by authors for authors.

Cons:

- Rigorous curation favors series and higher-profile authors
- US-only.

SELF-e

"A unique discovery platform for participating public libraries across the US that enables patrons to read ebooks on any device, at any time. This free discovery service is available to all authors with electronic rights, no matter which self-publishing service they use."
Launched: Summer 2014
Authors: Hugh Howey, CJ Lyons

At the author level, SELF-e is built from the permafree marketing concept, which values long-term author exposure over short-term income.

Ebooks are vetted by *Library Journal*, the national publication for the library community. If accepted, they are displayed to librarians via BiblioBoard's loan and acquisition system, which, it's claimed, is used by around 2,700 libraries and reaches 30 million patrons.

SELF-e has attracted criticism over its business model, which charges libraries to acquire titles but offers no royalty to authors. There are also serious questions over the relationship between SELF-e, through its parent company Library Journal, and the controversial publishing service provider Author Solutions.

ALLi also raised concerns over SELF-e's connection to Library Journal's "2015 Self-published Ebook Awards," urging changes to some ambiguous terms and conditions, especially around "irrevocable" rights and other atypical language.

SELF-e will only work for authors who can compromise to the principle of discoverability over payment. It's suited to authors who view it as part of their marketing plan, where they have confidence in the quality of their work and want to expose it to the kind of attention that will eventually lead to sales.

— MITCHELL DAVIS, BIBLIOBOARD

SELF-e is effectively a partnership between BiblioBoard and Library Journal.

How it works: SELF-e operates on two tiers. The author submits their book, via the Library Journal system. If selected, it's made available to loan via "Library Journal SELF-e Select", which is offered to US libraries nationwide.

If the book isn't selected, then it's deferred to the "Statewide Indie

Anthology," and made available via the local library system on a state-by-state basis.

Do authors get paid?: No. SELF-e is focused on discovery. According to Library Journal's Patron Profiles report, "over 50 percent of all library users go on to purchase ebooks by an author they were introduced to in a library."

Future plans: As Library Journal's Ian Singer told ALLi earlier this month, "We just launched our first module (200+ self-published titles) a few weeks ago. We have the ability to track circulation of titles, and as the modules grow, we absolutely intend to share that information and that could very well lead to royalties. But I'm not promising anything."

Pros:

- Not restricted to US authors
- Quick and easy submission
- Greater potential for selection due to two-tier system.

Cons:

- No author payment
- Ethical concerns over connection to Author Solutions.

OverDrive

"Borrow and enjoy free ebooks, audiobooks, and more from your library or school's digital collection. All you need is an internet connection, a library card or student ID."

Launched: 2002 (introduction of "Digital Library Reserve" system)

Authors: Supports Smashwords and Matador titles

OverDrive is the world's largest library ebook platform. It offers a procurement and checkout system for 20,000 public libraries around the world, including 90 percent of US public libraries.

A significant moment for self-published authors came in May 2014, when indie distributor Smashwords announced a partnership with OverDrive, gaining access to the library system for over 200,000 indie titles.

Faced with the option of purchasing a single James Patterson novel for around $40, or ten thrillers from today's most popular indie authors at $4 each, libraries now have exciting new options to build patron-pleasing ebook collections.

— MARK COKER, OWNER AND FOUNDER, SMASHWORDS

How it works: Ebooks are supplied, via a publishing platform, to library databases, where librarians decide which titles to take.

The curation process varies depending on platform, but Matador uses NetGalley to connect with librarians, while Smashwords titles—in a similar process to ebooksareforever—are curated for quality and library requirements, and the titles that pass are then made available to librarians.

"Smashwords leverage our knowledge of what books are selling at retail," says Mark Coker. "Librarians can then take those lists with confidence that they're dealing with books that have already pleased readers."

Do authors get paid?: Yes. Smashwords authors and publishers can set custom library prices through the Smashwords dashboard. They then earn 45 percent for each title sold to a library.

Future plans: An issue for library acquisition/loan systems is the reliance on software—usually supplied by Adobe—which takes a cut for every transaction.

Smashwords has told ALLi that it hopes to find a way for libraries to work around this via a system that can license titles to libraries without taking payment for each loan. That would remove a long-term expense for budget-squeezed librarians and remove limits on access to lower-cost books.

Pros:

- Authors can set price and get paid for library sales
- Global (but US-skewed).

Cons:

- No support for titles priced at $1.99 or lower
- Curation based on previous visibility and retail success
- Favors assisted publishing platforms.

The Bottom Line

It's important for authors to recognize that these three services are not like for like. They offer different options depending on territory, career priorities, and marketing strategy.

Authors must have a clear sense of what they hope to achieve from their book's availability in a library system and choose accordingly.

SELF-e, for example, is not a sales solution with paid revenue. It's a curated discovery channel and if, as an author, you have an issue with offering free content to a broader readership—perhaps out of concerns over sales cannibalization—then SELF-e is not for you.

But, aside from concerns over relationships with businesses like Author Solutions, it is a potential path for independent authors to gain access to an area traditionally ring-fenced by the big publishers.

As with all aspects of self-publishing, it's crucial to seek professional help from service providers and demand the highest possible standards to ensure your books are indistinguishable from those produced by traditional publishers.

Whatever the methods of curation, libraries will be more prepared to take a risk on self-published titles over traditional, because the pricing tends to be lower, but only if the book looks professional and credible.

Although we are obviously sensitive to moral issues around author payment and business ethics, the current routes for access to libraries are more about visibility than bank balance. At the moment, there isn't a huge amount of money in the library market, but smart authors should select a solution they're comfortable with and use it as part of a longer game of profile-raising.

"Library patrons do purchase books," says Smashwords' Mark Coker. "That's because libraries are engines of discovery."

PART VIII

CHOOSING A RIGHTS SERVICE

KNOW YOUR RIGHTS

Once author-publishers have mastered the intricacies of production, their attention turns to the question of licensing their publishing rights.

- How might they sell their books in English in overseas stores?
- How might they sell translation rights?
- What about other subsidiary rights, like radio, film, and TV? As we write, the biggest publishing sensation is Andy Weir's *The Martian*. This book's pathway to publication is a rights success story. Podium sought out the author for his audio rights and won a ton of awards with the production of his audiobook, after which he got his print publishing deal, which led to the movie deal.

Rights business has traditionally only been conducted through such personal and business relationships, but technology has again come to the rescue of the author.

"The advent of online global platforms, right down to social media, the internet, and email means potential licensers and licensees can engage 24/7 whatever their territory," say Tom Chalmers of rights platform IPR License.

When IPR License quizzed a cross-section of published and aspiring authors, it found writers' understanding of the foreign rights market "was worryingly lacking."

- Almost half of authors (47 percent) admitted they did not know or were unsure if they owned the world rights to their book.
- Only 13 percent of respondents had licensed their work to an overseas publisher, representing a potentially huge opportunity missed.
- 28 percent of authors didn't know when they did or didn't have rights to license.
- Over a third (38 percent) failed to recognize that "a right of passage" (sic) was not a saleable right.
- Many published writers surveyed are not quite sure if they still own their own world rights or not.

IPR LICENSE AND PUBMATCH

S everal websites cater to matching publishers with authors but the most popular ones with indie authors are PubMatch and IPR License, and ALLi has a relationship with both. IPR License has a yearly fee of $79, while PubMatch has both free and paid services. Both offer discounts to ALLi members (see Discounts & Deals page in the Member Zone) and a dedicated ALLi page.

IPR License also offers ALLi members a one-to-one phone consultation with one of its team members reviewing the author's current situation and providing insight on future rights opportunities in their arena and areas to target.

Following this phone consultation, each member receives a Preliminary Report, which provides an in-depth critique of their author profile and book records to ensure all relevant information is up on the platform and is maximizing their visibility and making them as appealing as possible to rights buyers.

While these rights platforms are helping to break down some boundaries for rights holders, and simplifying and strengthening the rights process, making home and international markets ever more accessible, licensing rights is not easy and requires the same sort of dedication as selling your book directly to readers.

The more you sell already, the easier it is to sell rights.

IPR License

London-based IPR License was founded in 2012 by Tom Chalmers. As director of an independent publishing company, Chalmers was aware of the lack of a dedicated trading service for literary rights holders and rights buyers. He set up Legend Press in 2005 without any financial backing, and recognized the need to generate immediate revenue to bridge the gap until the company's future books could be produced and sold. It was then that he realized the opportunities in rights licensing.

After manually building a list of names and sending them copies, he licensed the second novel acquired into seven editions and four languages, providing the key revenue to get the business started. The possibilities in licensing remained in his thoughts as his publishing businesses grew and new ones started.

When he returned to this arena in 2011, he found himself thinking again about the huge amount of business not being completed in the multibillion-pound book and journal licensing sector. The predominance of book fairs and back-and-forth negotiations between rights agents and commissioning editors left a gap in the marketplace, as he saw it, for a platform that would provide for "365-day 24/7 trading of book and journal rights." He had two core aims, he says.

Firstly, to develop a platform on which a potential buyer could enter a specific list of requirements of work they were looking to license. A global search would then be completed and the potential buyer would receive a list of works meeting his requirements. Secondly, if the buyer and seller agreed a deal then, in this digital age, the transaction could be completed online.

— TOM CHALMERS

And so IPR License was born. "IPR License was not built to change the way rights business is completed but to support it," he insists. "And most importantly, to be able to complete more of it, for individual or small or large companies."

Rights holders assign records (information about their books) to their account and add new records—whether already published or not —as well as adding additional information to their records.

Those looking to purchase rights can use the search facility to locate work of specific interest to them that is available to license in their territory and then contact the rights holder directly through the messaging system.

IPR License has developed a fully transactional online rights solution, TradeRights. The TradeRights marketplace was developed in partnership with the Copyright Clearance Center and Frankfurt Book Fair.

IPR License also runs a "Know Your Rights" campaign for authors, with a dedicated web resource to tackle the issue of rights, and an online rights clinic for authors to post questions via Twitter, which are then answered by industry professionals.

PubMatch

PubMatch, based in the US, offers another platform that enables writers and publishing professionals to come together, a kind of networking site where authors can be matched with publishers, publishers with the perfect manuscript, and designers with the perfect author.

PubMatch's mission is to create a worldwide community for the publishing industry that encourages the creation of business relationships and the worldwide spreading of ideas. PubMatch will facilitate communication, data warehousing, and the simplification of rights marketing for publishers, agents, authors, and others, making it the go-to place for the international publishing community to find new titles and new talent.

PubMatch is a partnership between *Publishers Weekly* and the

Combined Book Exhibit family of companies. Publishers Weekly is the publishing trade magazine in the US market, offering reporting, commentary, reviews, and announcements. The Combined Book Exhibit family of companies has over a century of experience in the publishing industry, specifically in the arena of trade shows, marketing, and connecting publishers for the exchange of ideas.

Seth Dellon, Director of Business Development at PubMatch, LLC, says:

> *The Combined Book Exhibit (founded 1933) and sister company and organizer of the USA Pavilion, the American Collective Stand (founded 1983), have traveled the country and the world experiencing the international publishing industry firsthand. Watching, participating in, and reporting on the business deals done in these different venues inspired us to create a venue for such business and connections to be available 365 days a year.*
>
> — SETH DELLON

The digital age has made communication constant and simple, but not necessarily focused. A meeting in 2008 at the Beijing International Book Fair placed publishers from the US and publishers from China in a room to discuss potential partnerships. Alas, with little pre-planning, not much was achieved in terms of connecting. However, that awkward silence did serve as motivation because it was that silent room that inspired PubMatch—an online arena where publishers, agents, and authors from anywhere in the world could have focused discussions dedicated to foreign rights.

Since then PubMatch has grown into a worldwide community with thousands of members who connect by creating a custom professional profile, listing books they represent, and having searchable access to the global rights community. This enables a rights buyer from France to find a book from the US with available

French rights, or an agent with a science fiction title that has available Dutch rights can search for a publisher in Holland.

The PubMatch network enables members to plan ahead for fairs like BookExpo America by tagging users who are attending the fair, giving them resources to connect, and providing them with tools to make their onsite experience better.

Buying and selling rights is a critical element in the publishing industry, driving revenue and exposing authors to new markets, but rights buyers tend to be conservative and this aspect of publishing is only slowly warming to indie authors.

ALLI AND HRM

As well as working closely with the two largest rights-selling platforms, ALLi also holds a list of indie-friendly agencies. One such is **Hershman Rights Management**, which runs an innovative method for authors to instantly receive a representation offer, eliminating months of waiting time.

The instant approval process is for authors who are already published but want representation for their other subsidiary rights, such as their audio or foreign rights. It gives authors an instantaneous turnaround, which, till then, was nonexistent in the rights world.

ALLi is also investigating the feasibility of working alone on this, with the aid of a rights assistant.

PART IX

IN-DEPTH REVIEWS BY GIACOMO GIAMMATTEO

HOW TO READ THE RATINGS

We have done extensive research into providers offering services in the following categories: direct retail, ebook distribution, print distribution, full-service publishing packages, and subscription services.

Some of the providers offer services in several areas, but in most instances we categorized them by their primary service, along with mention of them in the other categories.

Additional services considered include: cover design, ebook conversion, editing, copy-editing, content editing, proofreading, layout/formatting, and marketing and promotion.

For those providers offering them, additional services are listed with their profile.

Sourcing Information

All information in this guide was gathered from the service providers' websites, FAQ sections, help guides, and general descriptions of services, together with recommendations from our members, ALLi's own information, and feedback from the wider author community. In many cases, we spoke to representatives from the providers over the phone, or communicated via email.

If the information wasn't readily available, every effort was made to search the website from top to bottom to find it.

At this point, requests for further information and clarification were also made to the service via helplines and webchats, and we also emailed consultants and/or staff in an effort to be accurate and comprehensive. Despite these efforts, some services failed to provide information, and to date have not replied to these phone calls and emails. In such instances, we have avoided speculation and drawing conclusions, and stated that the information is lacking.

Tables

Where possible, the guide gives an easy and graphical example of how sales are split, or costs are broken down.

Currency Exchange

The global nature of the self-publishing industry means we can use providers from all over the world. Prices shown are subject to change, and currency exchange rates fluctuate.

Updates

We continue to make efforts to find all necessary information and to fill gaps in future editions.

Our goal in producing this book is to provide valuable information to the indie author community and so the ratings in this section reflect what our Watchdog team felt was the value of the overall package offered to authors by a particular provider. A low rating does not necessarily mean that the quality of the book was low, for example.

In order to conserve space, and to provide the most beneficial information, we have only listed full details on the providers that we, as a group, felt were the most useful. Other less useful services, as we see it, are listed with links to their websites and a rating by the team.

There are hundreds of self-publishing services and more springing up every day. If we missed someone, it doesn't mean they aren't reputable; it might mean we either didn't have the data or couldn't obtain enough information to include them in this analysis, or they haven't yet come into our radar.

We would like to see more transparency from all service providers. Far too many of them have set up to take advantage of authors who have dreams of striking it rich with a bestseller. If the vendors want to play in this game, they should compete based on the quality of their services, not by tricking people into buying a package.

During the course of this research, we ran into far too many authors who had fallen victim to false claims and packages worded to make it sound as if they were offering a lot more than they were.

Try to look beyond what the provider is offering, and focus on the motivation. What do I mean by this? Take a company like AuthorHouse. Included in its services are listings for various *Kirkus* magazine reviews and ads that cost anywhere from $3,000 to $7,000. There is one $72,499 ad they offer to place in the *Reader's Digest*. In case you're wondering if you read that figure wrong, no, you didn't.

Compare AuthorHouse with companies like IngramSpark, iBooks, KDP, Kobo, NOOK, or Smashwords. These providers have a singular focus. They don't offer other services and have no distractions. Their business is books; they don't try to sell you additional things to make money.

That is not to say that there isn't ever a requirement for full-service package providers, but if you want to purchase such a service, make sure that you are dealing with a provider that sells books, not just services.

And ask questions not only of the vendors you are considering, but also of yourself. It's imperative that you know what help you want and what you're willing to do yourself.

You also have to know what your budget is, and how much you can afford to lose. That's right, I said lose. Go into this with the assumption that you won't make one dime. Won't sell one book. If you approach it with that attitude, you won't get in trouble. You might be disappointed, but you won't put yourself in a financial bind.

Most books will not sell enough in five years to earn the author $10,000 in royalties, and that is before expenses are deducted. So when you see some of these publishing packages that cost $5,000–10,000, think hard about how you'll pay for that.

Our mission here is not to discourage you, but to provide data so you can make a realistic decision on how to approach this like a business. I realize it's your dream; it's my dream too. But if you're not careful you can dream yourself right into the gutter.

The idea of these in-depth ratings is not only to give you analysis of some of the major players in the field, but also to show you how to analyze different kinds of services yourself.

SERVICE CATEGORIES

Direct Retailers

These are the primary channels that many authors, and almost all of those who are making a living from author-publishing, opt to deal with directly. Whether or not that is the best choice for you is for you to decide.

- Amazon's KDP and CreateSpace
- Apple's iBooks
- Barnes & Noble's NOOK
- Google Play
- Kobo Writing Life
- Ingram Lightning Source and IngramSpark.

Ebook Distributors

This section contains all of the major players whose main business is ebook distribution. I want to make one important note. When you read provider terms and conditions, you'll read terms like "zero commissions," or "100 percent royalties," or "85 percent royalties."

You are not doing a like-by-like comparison, unless you know what that 100 percent or 85 percent is based on.

In some cases, as you'll see below, 85 percent of net can be more than 100 percent of net. It all depends on how "net" is calculated and what deal was negotiated with the retailer in question.

The prime example of this is Barnes & Noble. Smashwords and Draft2Digital have the best deals of any distributor when it comes to B&N. You can see the full breakdown below, but with Smashwords and Draft2Digital, authors receive 60 percent of the list price (even at prices below $2.99); with most other distributors, authors receive 50 percent of the list price (which they call "100 percent" royalty).

Be vigilant—read the small print.

- BookBaby
- Draft2Digital
- EBookPartnership
- IngramSpark
- Smashwords
- XinXii.

Print Distributors

Many of the decisions regarding printing your books will depend on your goals. If you only intend to sell online, you'll have fewer decisions to make. If you intend to try to get into bricks-and-mortar stores, you have a lot more to consider. Quality also comes into play in all cases and, of course, cost.

- CreateSpace
- Hillcrest
- IngramSpark
- Lightning Source
- Matador
- Lulu
- Thomson-Shore.

At the end of the reviews, we do a comparison of the largest print providers: CreateSpace, Ingram, and Lulu.

Subscription Services

As if there wasn't enough confusion in the publishing industry, 2013 and 2014 introduced more. The ebook retail market was already a battlefield, and a few providers were showing signs of fatigue, notably Kobo and Barnes & Noble. Now a handful of providers have entered the fray by offering subscription services. And from the looks of it, they have designs on taking a good-sized chunk out of the ebook market.

The subscription service providers face a lot of challenges, not the least of which is convincing a reluctant publishing industry to offer their content in an "all you can eat" option to a ravenous group of readers. But that's not the only challenge. They also have to convince the readers to shell out hard-earned cash on a monthly basis for the privilege of reading books—readers who have the option of downloading enough free and $0.99 books to keep them occupied for several lifetimes.

What that means is the content must consist of titles that will not be the kind of titles offered up in the daily free and bargain emails.

If that wasn't enough, they have to do all of this while walking a tightrope, because the deals they struck with the publishing companies to compensate authors put them in a precarious position. If a reader devours two titles per month that are priced at $9.99—and assuming the big publishers have a deal similar to Smashwords—then the subscription providers lose money. Only one title per month and the reader will soon realize that they aren't getting their money's worth.

The trick—I think—is for them to fool the readers into thinking they are getting a bargain. How do they do that? By offering a mix of titles that consist of big names from traditional publishing, backlist items, and a healthy offering of indie titles, which tend to be priced lower.

It will be interesting to see how this plays out over the next couple of years. Of one thing I'm confident—subscription services are here to stay. I think they will settle down, some of the early adopters will realize it's not for them and cancel subscriptions, and others will slowly be drawn to it. In the end, a few players will probably be lost (Entitle and Oyster both announced closure in 2015) but the ones that remain will likely be stronger. No matter what you think of subscription services, they are here to stay, and you shouldn't ignore them. It's one more avenue of sales.

Assisted Publishing Package Providers

This is the area where most authors run into trouble. There are excellent providers out there, who create beautiful books and a viable route to market, and those who operate at the opposite end of the scale, providing poor service and a lot of upselling. The providers we have analyzed below are:

- Archway
- AuthorHouse
- Author Solutions
- Authoright
- BookLocker
- Bookmasters
- Breezeway Books
- Hillcrest Media
- Indie Reader
- Matador, UK
- Outskirts Press
- SilverWood
- Thomson-Shore.

THE REVIEWS

E ntries are listed in alphabetical order and compare service
provision as far as practicable. You will find Giacomo's rating
out of 10 near the start of each entry.

DISTRIBUTORS AND ASSISTED SERVICES

Apple iBooks

apple.com
Giacomo's rating: 8.5/10
Model: Retailer.
Setup fees: Free.
Services provided: Ebook sales.
Ebook conversion: EPUB/ISBN required.
Reach: All iBooks stores. Currently 52 countries.
Royalties: 70 percent to author regardless of pricing or territory.
Payment schedule: Monthly. Sales reports daily.

Notes: Apple is not the easiest retailer to go direct with. For this reason, and because authors need a Mac or access to a Mac to set up an account, some choose to access Apple services through a distributor, or in many cases to ignore them. I strongly believe they shouldn't be ignored. Apple is, by most accounts, the #2 retailer of ebooks worldwide after Amazon. In the US, some people place Apple at #3, behind B&N. In either case, Apple sells a lot of ebooks. Even more importantly, the market is expanding on a continual basis, with hundreds of millions of devices capable of running the iBooks software.

With the release of iOS8, iBooks comes preinstalled on all Apple devices. That might not seem like much at first pass, but when you consider that Apple sold ten million new iPhones on a three-day launch weekend, it puts things in perspective. That's ten million people who have iBooks on their phone; and remember, these new phones are bigger. The 6+, which is the biggest seller, is almost like a small tablet, making it comfortable to read a book on.

Aside from that, though, there is another reason why I believe Apple should not be ignored or treated as a second-tier channel. It's Apple's attitude toward indie authors. It is the only retailer that I know of that actively promotes indie authors. It is also the only retailer that pays everyone the same—no matter what. If you have one book listed with Apple, you get 70 percent of the sale price. If you are one of the big publishing houses and have thousands of books listed with Apple, you get 70 percent. It also pays the same no matter what country you sell in.

Pros and cons: Setting up an account with Apple is tough. It might take two weeks to get approved the first time. Apple is strict about what it accepts. But once you're set up, it's a breeze. One of the best features with Apple is that you can control prices for each country and set sale prices on the built-in calendar system. For example, if I plan a promotion next month and want my book to go on sale on the 15th and back to regular price on the 17th, this can all be set in advance—and by country. And if I want to sell my books in Argentina,

Brazil, and Italy for $0.99 while keeping them priced at $5.99 elsewhere, it's no problem. It only takes a few minutes to set that up.

Archway Publishing

archwaypublishing.com
Giacomo's rating: 1/10
Model: Full service.
Packages: $1,999–$13,999.
Services provided: I didn't list services provided or royalty rates, because this is a service I cannot recommend. Archway is a joint venture between Author Solutions (a company named in almost every predator alert in the industry) and Simon & Schuster. Its pricing is extremely high and its terms are so unfavorable to authors that I felt it was not worth giving it page time. If you want to explore it further, click the link to the website.

AuthorHouse

authorhouse.com
Giacomo's rating: 1/10
Model: Full service.
Packages: $349–$4,249.

AuthorHouse is owned by Author Solutions, the same company tied to Archway and named in many predator reports. AuthorHouse is another company out to make its fortune on self-published authors. No page time.

————

Authoright

authoright.com
Giacomo's rating: 5/10
Model: Full service. (In my opinion, Authoright functions more as a project manager on the author's behalf.)
Publicist fees: US Publicist, $3,095; Atlantic Publicist, $5,495.
Packages: Complete publishing packages (Concierge*) from $6,000–8,000.
Print: Included with package.
Distribution: Physical books: Amazon, Ingram, Barnes & Noble, and Waterstones.com; Ebook: KDP, iBook, Kobo, NOOK.
Sign-up cost: Included with package.
File conversion: Included with package.
Yearly fee: No.
Additional services:

- Book cover design: $595.
- Editing: Full copy-edit, content, proofreading = $33 per 1,000 words.

Extra services and costs:

- Literary agent submission service: $695.
- Content editing: Quote.
- Book to film: $1,395.
- Book advert: $795.
- Book trailer: $1,895.
- Social media campaign: $1,795.

*The Concierge includes copy-editing and proofreading (up to 90k words), but structural editing would be an extra cost, and website design, social media, and book trailer services are separate as well. Here's a complete rundown of what is included in the Concierge package:

- Full proofreading and copy-editing of the text (up to 90k words) to eliminate any errors.
- High-end book cover design.
- Formatting and layout of the book in both paperback and ebook formats.
- Comprehensive consultation regarding pricing, title choice, release timing, and overall marketing strategy.
- International distribution: The book will be available through all leading online retailers and to order through physical book retailers, and all major ebook marketplaces.
- An eight-week publicity campaign in the US and/or UK, with the goal of having you and your book reviewed and discussed in the media.
- High-touch service: Contact any time to have your questions answered by industry experts; advice and support throughout.

The only potential costs above the Concierge fee would be purchasing copies of the book for your own use (at a base print cost + shipping).

Notes: Authoright is more of a marketing services company with the flexibility of adding other self-publishing services to the mix. The services offered include book cover design, copy-editing, proofreading, and layout and formatting of your book. If you elect to have Authoright distribute your print books and ebooks, it will also handle setting up those processes. I believe its prices are high, but it's not surprising since it is basically a marketing company.

I spoke with an Authoright representative on the phone. They were professional, polite, knowledgeable, and did not try to sell pie-in-the-sky expectations. When I asked about getting into bookstores, their response was realistic, and they were spot on about what a self-published author might expect. They also offered cautious advice about the dangers of returns, and again were spot on. They didn't promise unrealistic results from their press release distribution efforts either. Instead, they said most clients get one or more pieces of coverage.

There is plenty of room in the publishing services segment of the industry for marketing services. It is one of the areas authors have no clue about. I would prefer, however, that providers like Authoright be more transparent in how they present themselves. In fact, I think they might be doing themselves a disservice by trying to be all things to authors; instead, perhaps they should simply offer marketing services. We know there's a need.

Pros: If you are looking for publicity and marketing services, this might be the place for you to go. I'd suggest thinking hard about the money spent versus what you realistically anticipate earning from your book.

Cons: Extra services and costs don't seem to be in the best interest of authors, in my opinion.

———

Author Solutions

author solutions.com
Giacomo's rating: 1/10
Model: Full service.

You should be wary of any company connected with Author Solutions. Here are a few:

- AuthorHive
- AuthorHouse
- AuthorHouse UK
- Author Learning Center

- Booktango
- iUniverse
- Trafford
- Xlibris
- Palibrio.

Note: Not worth mentioning except to say it is among the worst suppliers, in terms of value for money, reaching readers, and author care.

―――――

BookBaby

bookbaby.com
Giacomo's rating: 7/10 for ebook distribution
Model: Ebook distributor. (BookBaby offers all the services of a full-service company, but its strength seems to be ebook distribution.)
Print: Cost/100: $7.90 (POD); Cost/1,000+: $6.59 (offset).
Royalties: 100 percent.
Ebook: $299.
File conversion: Yes.
Yearly fee: No.
Distribution: Amazon, Apple, Baker and Taylor, B&N, Ciando, Copia, Ebsco, ePubDirect, e-Sentral, Gardners, Kobo, Page Pusher, Scribd (see chart).
Royalties: 100 percent of "net" (see chart).
Additional services:

- Book cover design: $149–$279.
- Book printing: Printing costs are high. Even with the $200 discount that comes with the premium service it is higher than CS or LS for 100 books. Above 100, it would be too high to be competitive.

- Editing: I have found almost all full-service companies that offer editing services to be higher than normal in price. BookBaby was no exception.
- Formatting.
- ISBN: $19.
- Website hosting: If you need this, it's nice to have an option with the provider, and the pricing wasn't outrageous.
- Book scanning services.
- Press releases.

Notes: BookBaby has one of the easiest sites to use, and its customer service is friendly and helpful. It also has a good list of distributors. In addition, it has a few unique offerings that many authors will like. I haven't tried the Bookshop offering yet, but it seems like a nice feature. I have tried some parts of the BookPromo, and I was pleased with it. I used the free review from Readers' Favorite and the Story Cartel offering. Between the two of them I received four reviews and, more importantly, four new fans.

The additional services will appeal to some people, and to others they won't. There's nothing wrong with that. BookBaby doesn't force you to choose anything you don't want.

As far as distribution goes, you'll have to look closely at BookBaby's website, as it is making a number of changes at time of writing. For a while it had unique distribution options (Ciando, Copia, Ebsco, ePubDirect, Gardners, and PagePusher) but PublishDrive is challenging that.

Pros: Easy to use. Good customer service. Great ebook distribution.

Cons: Upfront costs. Add-on services expensive.

———

BookLocker

booklocker.com
Giacomo's rating: 5.5/10
Model: Full service.
Packages: B&W books with color covers.

Program	At-Your-Service	Expedited	Do-It-Yourself
Print publication time	1 month	2 weeks	1 month
Setup fees	$675	$999	$0
Paperback	✓	✓	✓
Hardcover combo $399	Add-on	Add-on	Add-on
Formatting assistance	✓	✓	
Paperback cover design	✓	✓	Add-on
ISBN and barcode	✓	✓	
Basic EPUB conversion	✓	✓	Add-on
Contract	Nonexclusive	Nonexclusive	Nonexclusive
First year POD fee	✓	✓	$18
Print proof	✓	✓	$35

Fig. 1—Booklocker Programs

Print programs include distribution through Ingram. Listed on Amazon, B&N, and Books-A-Million.

- Original cover design: See samples from BookLocker's cover designer on its website. (Click on each cover to see the entire cover front, back, and spine).
- Most EPUB/MOBI conversions are basic, have two or fewer graphics, and include an automated table of contents. Books with more complex formatting like extra graphics, footnotes, endnotes, an index, tables, etc. may require an extra fee. You can request a quote at any time.
- The first year's annual POD file hosting fees ($18) for the At-Your-Service and Expedited programs are included in the setup fees listed above.

Print: Does own printing and distributes through Ingram. Hardcover or paperback.

Royalties: 35 percent of the list price for public sales of POD books sold through Booklocker.com. 15 percent of the list price for POD books sold through other distributors, retailers, etc.

Ebook royalties: 70 percent of the list price for ebooks priced $8.95 or higher. 50 percent of the list price for ebooks priced under $8.95.

Distribution: Amazon, Apple, B&N, Kobo.

Royalties: 65 percent of the net amount Booklocker.com is paid for each ebook priced $10 or higher. 55 percent of the net amount Booklocker.com is paid for each ebook priced under $10. What this equates to is for books sold through Amazon or Apple that are under $10, and at least $2.99, the author would receive 38.5 percent of list price. With B&N it would be 35.75 percent. Minimum list price for ebooks is $2.99.

Changes: For print books, it's a flat fee of $199 if they require changes after the printer has processed the files. To change price only on ebooks is a $5 fee.

Payment schedule: Monthly.

Notes: BookLocker is run by Angela Hoy, a long-time advocate of writers and owner of WritersWeekly.com. Angela is upfront about everything and responded professionally to every question I asked her. She would be the first person to tell you that BookLocker is not for everyone. And it isn't.

For some authors the services offered will be just right, but for those authors who hope to "break out" or even make a decent supplemental income from self-publishing, there isn't enough to go around. Print costs are a big problem if you have any hopes of selling books in a bookstore; in fact, a standard 300-page paperback will cost an author almost twice as much as it would with CS or LS.

As far as the package pricing, I have no problem with the $675 fee or what you get for it, but the ebook royalty structure is out of whack, and the distribution is very limited. If you want more exposure you'd have to sign up with another aggregator, such as Smashwords or BookBaby. If you're going to go that route, you might as well use them for all the channels and earn more money. If you go with

Smashwords, you'd earn 60 percent at Apple and B&N versus 38.5 and 36 percent at BookLocker. And with BookBaby's free option, you'd earn 60 percent at Amazon and Apple and 50 percent at B&N. That kind of difference is too much to sacrifice.

Money isn't everything when entering a business relationship, and there is a lot to be said for the straightforward approach that Angela Hoy takes. She earns even more respect for her honesty and openness about who should and shouldn't sign up with BookLocker.

Bookmasters

bookmasters.com
Giacomo's rating: 4/10
Model: Full service.
Packages: $199–$799–$999–$1,599. Ebook conversion included in the top three packages. Formatting included in all. Template cover included in first two packages and custom cover in top two.
Print: Does own printing and distributes through Ingram.
Royalties: Author gets 100 percent.
Sign-up cost: Setup fee of $495. Also a $40 per month reporting fee for sales and customer data. And $7 per month storage fee for fewer than 550 copies.
File conversion: $60 for PDF, and $0.95 per page for EPUB.
Distribution: Currently distributes to over 70 retailers including the Apple iBookstore, Amazon, Amazon UK, Barnes & Noble, Sony, Kobo, OverDrive, and others.
Royalties: 70 percent for Apple, and 50 percent for Amazon and B&N, and "most" others.
Changes: "We consider the PDF file we receive for conversion to be final and ready to be converted. Any editorial or author-preference changes can be made before conversion but will incur an additional formatting fee. Changes requested after an ebook has been converted

and distributed will also incur an additional formatting fee. We will then redistribute your new ebook files, but we cannot guarantee that the retailers will replace the old file with the new file."

Additional services:

- Book cover design: Custom ($199–900).
- Editing: Quote.
- Formatting: Quote.

Payment schedule: Monthly.

Notes: I spoke with a representative from Bookmasters. It has a professional website, with professional reps, many of whom have years of experience in the publishing field. While the packages aren't as expensive as some I've looked at, they have a few hidden costs that are deal killers as far as I would be concerned. Chief among them are the monthly costs for reporting of sales data. In addition, the charges for signing up for distribution are hefty, and the royalty payments—even though they claim to pay 100 percent—are below industry average.

––––––

Breezeway Books

breezewaybooks.com
Giacomo's rating: 3/10
Model: Full service.
Packages: $499–$2,999.
Services provided:

- POD printing and distribution.
- Ebook production and distribution.
- Cover design.

- Editorial.
- Formatting and conversion.
- Marketing and promotion services.
- ISBNs.
- Ghostwriting.
- Website design.

Royalties are low and costs are high. Its top-end editing service can run as high as $0.08 per word. That equates to $8,000 for a 100,000-word book. To give you an idea, less than 5 percent of authors will earn that much from their book.

———

CreateSpace

createspace.com
Giacomo's rating: 8.5/10
Model: POD printer (with added services/packages).
Initial/setup fees: Free.
Services provided: POD printing distribution.
Cost for one 300-page POD paperback (6x9): $4.46/£3.70.
Extra services:

- Cover design.
- ISBNs.
- Editing.
- Kindle conversion.
- Interior formatting.
- Marketing.

You can look at the CreateSpace website for costs on these services, as there are a number of options.
Sizes available: Paperback only. No hardback.

Royalties:

- CreateSpace: 80 percent to author for books sold on the CS store (minus cost of book).
- Amazon: 60 percent to author when sold through Amazon (minus cost of book).
- Expanded distribution: 40 percent to author when sold through these channels (minus cost of book).

Payment schedule: Monthly.

Reach: Amazon US and EU with the standard distribution. Expanded distribution provides access to Ingram, Barnes & Noble, libraries, and other stores.

Contract term and rights: Nonexclusive license to publish, distribute, and sell.

Notes: CreateSpace is owned by Amazon and it shows in the user-friendly website. If you have a print-ready file and a cover, you can set up your book in less than an hour. CS offers authors an inexpensive, easy way to get their books into print, and distribute them through the major online retailers in the US and Europe.

I'm not nearly as fond of its other offerings. I found some of them to be within reason, if not a little high priced, but others—especially editing—seemed very high. And I found it odd that CS offered paid-for reviews with Kirkus and Clarion, especially considering Amazon's stance on paying for reviews.

Another great benefit of CS is that authors can buy books at cost, and if you live in the US, shipping is not only reasonably priced, it's fast. In Europe or the rest of the world, alas, it's very slow. In many cases, I can ship books directly from CS at one-third of the cost I would have to pay. The other huge benefit is the customer service. You have an option for online chat, or you can hit the button that says "Call me" and your phone will ring in seconds. The reps are friendly and knowledgeable, and they do everything they can to solve your problems.

Print quality is good. I don't think it's as good as LS/Spark, but it's good. Perhaps the best thing about CS is its policy on changes. If you opted for the DIY process and you find later you need to make changes, it costs you nothing. Simply upload the new files and republish.

———

Draft2Digital

draft2digital.com
Giacomo's rating: 9/10
Model: Ebook distributor.
Print: No.
Sign-up cost: Free.
Changes: Free. (This is a huge benefit.)
Reach: Apple, B&N, Kobo, Page Foundry, Scribd.
Royalties: 85 percent of net.
Payment terms: Per month.

Notes: Draft2Digital offers ebook distribution to most of the primary players, as well as to CreateSpace for print books. Its website states it is pursuing deals with half a dozen other channels, including Google, Tolino, and OverDrive.

As far as royalties, it pays 85 percent of net, and net is the same as terms offered to authors who go direct. Draft2Digital also has a sweet deal with B&N, where the author receives 60 percent of list price even if the books are priced below $2.99. The only other aggregator I know that has this deal is Smashwords.

See our in-depth coverage at the end of the chapter.

———

eBookPartnership (EBP)

eBookPartnership.com
Giacomo's rating: 6.5/10
Model: ebook distributor.
Sign-up cost: For 1–4 titles submitted it charges a setup fee of $50/£37.50 per title and an annual fee (from the beginning of the second year) of $40/£29 per title.
If you have 3 or more titles you pay the publisher rate, which is $40/£29 per title per year from the outset. Requires ebook file.
Changes:

- Ebook content changes: From $45 (editorial changes to ebook files post or mid-conversion.)
- Updating retailer listings: $20 (uploading new files, covers, or metadata, or relisting with retailers.)
- EPUB file fixes and validation troubleshooting: From $45.

Services offered:

- Standard ebook conversion: Price for ebook conversion to MOBI and EPUB formats is $199/£149 for a book that is mainly text and no longer than 75,000 words.
- Ebook cover design: Premium cover design—$225/£149. Incorporating stock/library images as required, with Photoshop processing as needed, and with added title and author text.

Other services:

- Websites for Writers.
- ISBN allocation: Free if you use its conversion and distribution service or $15 if not.
- Fixed-layout ebook distribution.

- Print book scanning: From $199 (price based on a 300-page novel.)

Royalties: 100 percent of net (see below for specifics.)
Payment schedule: Monthly (prefer PayPal).
Reach and royalties:
Ebooks:

- Amazon—70 percent (same as direct).
- Apple—70 percent (same as direct).
- Barnes & Noble (includes NOOK UK)—50 percent.
- e-Sentral—75 percent.
- Gardners (includes Baker and Taylor)—50 percent.
- Google Play—52 percent.
- Ingram (distribution through Ingram gets you into Copia, Diesel, ebooks.com, Infibeam, and many other channels)— 62.5 percent.
- Kobo—70 percent (same as direct).
- Magster—60 percent.
- OverDrive (24,000 retailers and libraries)—50 percent.
- Waterstones (UK)—50 percent.

Subscription services:

- Bookmate—50 percent.
- Scribd—50 percent.

Notes: I'm not a big fan of the "pay for distribution" option, and I'm even less a fan of the yearly fee, but with that said, and assuming you have three or more titles, the $40 per year isn't a deal breaker. Even if your books are priced at $2.99, and assuming you're only getting 50 percent royalties, you would only have to sell 28 books per title to break even. Keep in mind, though, that means 28 books outside of the channels you opt to go direct with or that you could have been allowed access to somewhere else for free. So, if you submit your books directly to Amazon and B&N, that means you'd need to sell those 28 per title on the remaining channels.

The way I look at it, the access to Ingram, OverDrive, Google, Gardners, and Waterstones could easily cover the cost of your yearly fee. If you don't go direct with the four major players, then signing up with EBP would be far less of a decision. Remember, though, to make sure you have your files the way you want them, as changes will cost you dearly. I like EBP, and the people behind it are as customer friendly as you can get. But the ebook distribution market is changing quickly, and EBP seems to be lagging behind with upfront fees and charging for changes and for file conversion.

———

Google Play

play.google.com/books
Giacomo's rating: 6/10
Model: Retailer.
Initial/setup fees: Free.
Services provided: Ebook sales.
Ebook conversion: EPUB/ISBN required.
Reach: Worldwide.
Royalties: 52 percent to author if direct. 45 percent if through a third party.
Payment schedule: Monthly. Sales reports daily.

Notes: I found Google to be the most difficult to set up with directly. It was not intuitive and there were hoops that it made you jump through that seemed unnecessary. Managing your books is not easy either. And getting sales reports is so tedious it's almost not worth it. I found a few annoying things about Google. It is very aggressive about discounting your books. This can cause big problems with Amazon (which will price match) especially at the lower price points. For example, let's assume you set a price on Google of $2.99. If it discounts it, and Amazon matches, your royalty at Amazon drops from 70 percent to 35 percent. Not something you want to happen. I had to set one of my novellas at $3.99 on Google in order to prevent this. Google also seems slow to respond to price changes. This can have a big effect on promotions, so be aware of that. Another thing I didn't like about Google was the commission—52 percent is too low.

——

Hillcrest Media Group

hillcrestmedia.com
Giacomo's rating: 5.5/10
Model: Full service, ebook only, print only.
Packages:

	Basic	Advanced	Premium	Professional
Price	$1,697	$2,497	$3,997	$5,997
Custom book cover	✓	✓	✓	✓
Custom interior formatting	✓	✓	✓	✓
ISBN, LCCN, and barcode	✓	✓	✓	✓
100% royalties	✓	✓	✓	✓
Available on Amazon, B&N, and other retailers	✓	✓	✓	✓
Books in Print	✓	✓	✓	✓
Physical proof	✓	✓	✓	✓
Free copies	5	10	15	20
Search Inside!	✓	✓	✓	✓
Website and hosting	$399	Bronze	Silver	Gold
Google Books submission	✓	✓	✓	✓
Copyright registration	✓	✓	✓	✓
Author sales reporting	✓	✓	✓	✓
Submission to search engines	$99	✓	✓	✓
Back cover sales copy	$199	✓	✓	✓
Yearly book fee	$99	✓	✓	✓
Returns program	$199	✓	✓	✓
Expanded distribution		$1,299	✓	✓
Order fulfillment	$499	$499	✓	✓
eBook creation & distribution	$799	$799	$799	✓
Basic editing	pricing below	pricing below	pricing below	75,000 words

Fig. 2—Hillcrest Publishing Services

Print: (POD and offset)*.

Cost for printing 1–100 books: $5.40 per book.

Distribution: Ingram/Baker & Taylor royalties: 100 percent.

Yearly fee: $99.

Ebook: $299 for a basic ebook (to set this in context, Draft2Digital will give you this same service for free.)

Sign-up cost: $799 (included with top package).

File conversion: Included.

Yearly fees: Amazon and iBookstore Distribution Only: $49. Complete Distribution (Global, Amazon, and iBookstore): $79. Library Distribution: $29. Personal Sales Page: $25.

Distribution: Amazon, Apple, B&N, Kobo, and 30 more.

Royalties: 70 percent from Amazon and Apple, 40–55 percent from others.

Changes: Content changes submitted at end of each quarter. $50 per hour charge. Changes to metadata (price etc.) incur a charge of $30.

Additional services: Design, book fulfillment, printing, ebook publishing, editing, ISBN, websites.

Payment schedule: Monthly for print, quarterly for ebook. Payments made by check.

Notes: Hillcrest now offers three options to self-publishers: Mill City Press, its full package; Publish Green, an ebook-only service; and bookprinting.com, its print-only option.

Book cover, interior layout, and ISBN included. The most expensive package includes basic editing (up to 75,000 words) and ebook layout and conversion. If you buy the most expensive package and get the ebook layout and basic editing, it will set you back $8,142 for a 100k word book.

Of all the services I looked at, the editing seems to be the most expensive. Basic copy-editing is $0.02 per word, which means for a 100,000-word manuscript you'd pay $2,000. The top end is the Publishing Prep, and it costs $0.045 per word, or $4,500 for the same manuscript. In addition, the royalties on ebooks were substandard. It lists as paying out 100 percent royalties, but that seems to be only with the big three—Amazon, Apple, and B&N. For the others, it cites royalties of 40–55 percent.

The site is impressive. It has what appear to be great packages, until you break down the costs and start comparing. I think it has the ability to put together some great options for self-published authors; unfortunately, I don't think it is at that point yet.

Pros: Complete packages, full coordination, handholding through whole process.

Cons: Expensive. Some services very expensive. Yearly fees are excessive.

———

IngramSpark

ingramspark.com
Giacomo's rating: 8.5/10
Model: POD printer.
Initial/setup fees: $49 per cover/text file (print). Includes ebook if set up at same time.
Services provided:

- Inclusion in the Ingram catalogue.
- Print distribution.
- Barcode generation.
- Ebook distribution.
- Ability to set wholesale discount (30 percent, 40 percent or 55 percent).
- Books returnable.
- Title setup.
- Loading, storing, and managing book, ebook files, and metadata per title.
- Book and ebook—$49 (submitted at the same time).
- Ebook—$25 (if submitted separately).

- Titles are eligible for automatic free setup with an initial order of 50+ copies. When a print order is placed for 50 copies within 60 days of title setup, the customer will receive a $49 refund.

Extra services and costs:

- Ingram catalogue: $12.
- Barcodes: Included.
- Revisions (per cover or text): $25.
- Ebook distribution: Included.
- ISBNs: IngramSpark is now offering ISBNs for $85.

Sizes available: Hardback and paperback. Wide variety of sizes.
Royalties: Print—author receives net after the wholesaler discount and unit cost are deducted from list price. Ebook—author receives 40 percent of list price.
Cost for one 300-page POD paperback: $4.86/£3.33; 100 @ $4.59; 1,000 @ $3.24.
Payment schedule: Monthly. No charge or minimum limit.
Reach: All Ingram channels, Amazon, B&N, Gardners, Bertrams, Blackwells, Baker & Taylor, Book Depository. On the ebook side, you reach 190 of Ingram's CoreSource retailers.
Contract term and rights: Nonexclusive license to publish, distribute, and sell

Notes: Spark offers almost all the benefits of Lightning Source at a slightly reduced price. The cost per book, the quality, and the distribution are identical to Lightning Source. You also get access to the same ebook distribution channels, but that comes at a price. It only pays 40 percent of list price for ebooks. And perhaps the killer is that you cannot opt out of channels, except Apple and Amazon.

Spark has expanded its discount options and now offers authors the choice of 30–40 percent and 55 percent—and it does allow for returns. The print prices allow you to be competitive, at least in the

POD market, and with Ingram's distribution you have the possibility, no matter how slim, of getting your books into independent bookstores.

I like what Ingram has done with Spark—to an extent—but it's set up for people who are familiar with the publishing business and it's not as user friendly as it should be. On the plus side, it offers authors returns, and a 55 percent discount, which very few of the POD companies allow. I would recommend its POD service, but I'd stay away from the ebook distribution until it's improved; there are better options.

See a more detailed analysis at the end of the chapter.

Kindle Direct Publishing (KDP)

kdp.amazon.com
Giacomo's rating: 8/10
Model: Retailer.
Initial/setup fees: Free.
Services provided: Ebook sales.
Ebook conversion: Free.
Reach: All Amazon Kindle stores, including USA, UK, Canada, Brazil, Japan, India, Italy, Germany, France and Spain, Mexico, Australia.
Royalties: 70 percent to author if price is between $2.99 and $9.99; 35 percent to author if priced below $2.99 or above $9.99. Also note that authors will not earn 70 percent in all countries unless they are enrolled in Amazon's exclusive Select program. Currently the territories of India, Japan, Brazil, and Mexico only pay 35 percent if the author is not in Select.
Payment schedule: Monthly, by check or via bank transfer depending on country of residence. Payment limit can be as low as $10.

Notes: Uploading a book to KDP is easy. Amazon does things right when it comes to making things simple to use. If you have your data ready, it takes no more than half an hour to upload the details and have your book ready for publication. Amazon only allows you to select two categories for your book, so think carefully about how you want to be categorized.

Amazon also requires authors to price their ebooks so that the price listed on Amazon is the lowest or equal to the lowest they offer it anywhere, and 20 percent less than any print edition. It enforces this strictly, and will price match aggressively.

If you are on the 70 percent option, you will be paid on the sale price, not the list price. If you are on the 35 percent plan, you will be paid on the list price if Amazon matches another retailer. To my knowledge, Amazon is the only retailer that requires this of authors.

Listing with Amazon is a no-brainer. No author can survive without it. With that said, I do not recommend signing up for KDP Select—the exclusive option.

This, of course, is a hotly debated issue and many authors swear by it. I don't, for one reason. Imagine you go to a book signing and 100 people show up, clamoring for your book. Instead of signing a book for all 100, you randomly pick 60 of them and tell the others they'll have to wait. Maybe forever.

That's exactly what you're doing if you go Select. Amazon has a commanding lead in the ebook marketplace—about 60 percent—but that means that for every 100 people who want to buy your book, 40 won't be able to. To put it in different terms—for every 10,000 who want to buy your book, 4,000 won't be able to.

And if you plan on selling internationally, which is where the growth hasn't peaked yet, the differences could be bigger.

———

Kobo Writing Life (KWL)

kobo.com/us/en/p/writinglife
Giacomo's rating: 7/10
Model: Retailer.
Initial/setup fees: Free.
Services provided:

- Ebook sales.
- Free conversion to EPUB from multiple formats.

Royalties: 70 percent to author if priced between $1.99 and $12.99. 45 percent if outside that range.
Payment schedule: Monthly via direct debit.
Reach: Kobo stores worldwide, including Canada, UK, US.
Contract term and rights: Author retains all rights.

Notes: The Kobo site was very user friendly. It took no time to set up an account and upload books. Once you have it set, managing the books is a breeze also. Changing prices in different territories or to place a book on promotion takes minutes, and sales reports are visible daily on the dashboard. Kobo pays strong royalties, and has a good reach. It is especially strong internationally, with many authors experiencing better sales with Kobo than any other retailer in Australia, Canada, France, and other territories.

Kobo continues to innovate, as evidenced by its strong push to ally the service with independent bookstores, a program that is gaining some traction. I like Kobo, and I think it will continue to improve and pick up steam on the international front. I have concerns about how much headway it'll be able to make in the US market, but time will tell.

———

Lightning Source

lightningsource.com
Giacomo's rating: 9/10
Model: POD printer.
Initial/setup fees: $75 per cover/text file (print).
Services provided:

- Print distribution.
- Barcode generation.
- Ebook distribution.
- Ability to set wholesale discount (from 20–55 percent).
- Ability to allow returns.

Extra services and costs:

- Ingram catalogue: $12.
- Revisions (per cover or text): $40.

Binding available: Hardback and paperback.
Royalties: Author receives net after the wholesaler discount and unit cost are deducted from list price.
Cost for one 300-page POD paperback: $4.86; 100 @ $4.59; 1,000 @ $3.24.
Payment schedule: Monthly. No charge or minimum limit.
Reach: All Ingram channels, Amazon, B&N, Gardners, Bertrams, Blackwells, Baker & Taylor, Book Depository. Ebooks are handled by IngramSpark.
Contract term and rights: Nonexclusive license to publish, distribute, and sell.

Notes: Lightning Source is owned by Ingram, the largest distributor of books in the world.

Lightning Source doesn't offer many bells and whistles, but what it does offer is a personal customer service representative for each account, either in the US or the UK. Of all the service companies, this is unique. Each representative has a personal email and a direct-dial phone number.

Reports are easy to access online, and if you need books shipped it's a simple process. There is a $1.50 handling fee per order placed by author/publisher, but authors are not charged for shipping of wholesale orders. Lightning Source does not provide ISBNs, and doesn't offer add-on services. It offers the highest-quality printing and the best worldwide distribution.

Files are uploaded in PDF for interior and cover. Cover templates are generated on the LSI website. For ebook distribution, file formats are Adobe PDF or EPUB.

Lightning Source offers the best in POD technology combined with Ingram's worldwide distribution to 38,000 retailers. In my opinion, Lightning Source offers the best quality of any POD provider or printer. It focuses on doing one thing and does it well. The cost per book is on par with CreateSpace, and I haven't found anyone who does it for less.

With Lightning Source an author can also opt to have their books returnable, which means there is a possibility that the bricks-and-mortar stores might stock them. It's still a long shot, but it is a shot.

Pros: Highest-quality print books. Best distribution with worldwide reach. Ability to control discounts. Ability to offer returns. Option to be included in Ingram's catalogue. Personal representative. Barcode generation. Easy shipping of books.

Cons: Not as simple to use as some services. CS is definitely easier. LS is not set up for the author with one or even a few books. Since IngramSpark opened, most, if not all, indie authors have been directed there. LS is telling people that to open an LS account you must have 10–20 titles; otherwise, they should sign up with IngramSpark.

———

Llumina Press

See Breezeway Books.

————

Lulu

lulu.com
Giacomo's rating: 2/10
Model: Print distributor/full service.
Packages: Both DIY and full-service packages available: $99–$3,299.
Services provided:

- POD printing.
- Ebook distribution.
- Print distribution.
- Cover design.
- ISBNs.
- Free EPUB conversion.
- Publicity, marketing, and promotional materials.
- Ghostwriting.
- Formatting.
- Photobooks.

Unit cost for one 300-page POD Book (6x9): $7.25.
Changes: A batch of 25 changes to a project as part of a publishing services package costs $105. It costs $210 to republish a revised project and resend to distribution.
Reach: Apple, Amazon, B&N.

Notes: For the serious author who is interested in distributing their books, the cost of printing a book with Lulu is far too high. In three examples I used for judging prices, Lulu's cost was 50–70 percent more expensive than Lightning Source or CreateSpace. An indie author using any POD service is already hampered by high print costs. There isn't room in the margins for padding if you want to price your book at a level that tempts readers to buy.

My bigger issue with Lulu is its add-on services. Everything I looked at pointed to high prices. I don't think I've seen editing services priced as high as Lulu's. If an author opted for its full developmental editing package, the cost for a 100,000-word book would be $8,100. Copy-editing alone would be $2,300, and line editing comes in at a whopping $3,700.

But that pales in comparison to the Trifecta Review or the Kirus Premium review services. The Trifecta gives you three (make note of that number—three!) reviews—one each from Kirkus, Clarion, and Blueink—for the princely sum of $3,899. For those of you who don't have a calculator handy, that's $1,300 each. Since Kirkus offers indies a review for the measly sum of $425, that means Lulu is charging more than $1,700 apiece for Clarion and Blueink.

And they're not done with you yet. For a mere $4,599 you can purchase a Press Release Video Edition, or for $8,399 an Online Newsmaker Publicity Campaign. If you are flush with cash, you can spring for the $11,999 Video Newsmaker Publicity Campaign.

If you're only going to get a book printed by Lulu—and you don't mind paying a very high premium—you might do okay. But don't expect to be able to sell it anywhere and make money; there isn't enough left over for you.

———

Matador

troubador.co.uk
Giacomo's rating: 8/10
Model: Full service. I list Matador as a full-service provider, and it is, but it approaches it differently than most others. Matador doesn't try

to sell authors packages; instead, it offers each step of the process as a separate service and allows authors to choose what they need. Details are below.

Print: Setup costs $1,135/£680 (includes setup, ISBN, barcode and QR code, typesetting and proof revisions, custom cover design.)

Print costs: $6.50/£3.92 per unit. Price drops significantly at higher volumes: 100 @ $5.34 per unit; 500 @ $3.94 per unit; 1,000 @ $3.40 per unit.

Storage: Up to 300 books, storage is free. 300+ books @ $32 per month.

Ebook: (As add-on to print publication). Conversion to EPUB and Kindle formats: $250/£150. Distribution to retailers worldwide: $66/£40.

Services provided:

- Onscreen copy-edit: $650/£390.
- Proofread: $567/£340.
- Marketing: Book Trade Marketing and Distribution, $417/£250; Book Trade Marketing & Distribution PLUS Media/Public Relations Marketing $1,002/£600; Starter Ebook Marketing $417/£250; Extended Ebook Marketing $626/£375.

Sizes available: Paperback and hardback.

Royalties: 85 percent of net sales.

Payment schedule: £400 deposit, with the balance on prepress and print costs when ready.

Reach (ebooks): Amazon, Apple, Barnes & Noble, Waterstones, Kobo, Blinkbox, Google, OverDrive, Gardners, and WHSmith.

Packages and costs: Matador will prepare a quote in advance covering all services and costs. Author chooses what they want.

Notes: Matador's primary strength lies in the realm of traditional publishing. It offers the same high-quality service for print production as you'd find from any traditionally published source. It can, and will, do POD services, but its true strength shines with print runs of at least 300 books. As you can see by the cost per unit at the higher print runs, it makes a significant difference in the price/profit for the author.

If you're serious about trying to place your book in the UK bricks-and-mortar stores, you should look closely at Matador. Unlike most services catering to the self-publishing market, Matador has a dedicated sales team that "hand sell" your book. It treats each author as a true partner, knowing that its reputation is at stake alongside yours and it is selective about which books it publishes.

Matador has a nice distribution reach for ebooks, which includes the standard Big Four, but also Waterstones, Blinkbox, Google, Gardners, WHSmith, and OverDrive.

I'm sure you can find a company offering less expensive packages, or individual services, but that's not always what a decision should be based on. Matador keeps a keen eye on the bottom line, but doesn't sacrifice quality. If you are concerned about the appearance of your book, about the quality of the interior, and if you want to be successful in the UK market, I would give Matador a serious look. Compare a few services, weigh the price you'd have to pay versus quality, and then make your decision.

———

NOOK Press

nookpress.com
Giacomo's rating: 7.5/10
Model: Retailer.
Initial/setup fees: Free.
Services provided:

- Ebook sales.
- Free ebook conversion to EPUB.

Royalties: 65 percent to author if priced between $2.99 and $9.99. 40 percent if outside that range.

Payment schedule: Monthly. Daily sales reports.

Reach: NOOK stores, including BN.com, Nook.co.uk.

Contract term and rights: Nonexclusive license to publish, distribute, and sell.

Notes: The NOOK press site is easy to upload to directly, at least in the US. B&N lets an author select five categories, which is nice compared with the two Amazon allows, as it helps with visibility. Sales reporting is easy and accessible, and Excel spreadsheets are prepared monthly for download.

NOOK is often dismissed by indies and the publishing industry, and yet there are authors outselling Amazon on the NOOK platform. With one of the promotional ads I ran, NOOK outsold Amazon by almost two to one. I reached the #2 spot on all of NOOK that night and only reached #62 on Kindle.

A lot of rumors have circulated about B&N going bankrupt, as Borders did, or at the very least getting out of the NOOK business. I think that regardless of what happens with B&N, the NOOK business will survive. Books might be read on someone else's hardware, but the content will still be sold. It might not be by B&N, but whoever it is will continue to be a major player in the market.

———

Outskirts Press

outskirtspress.com
Giacomo's rating: 2/10
Model: Full service.
Packages: $199–$5,979.
Services provided:

- POD printing and distribution.
- Ebook distribution.
- Cover designs and templates.
- Editorial work.
- Marketing services.
- Marketing materials.
- ISBNs.

Notes: I didn't go into the details of Outskirts' packages. Everything about this site made me want to run away—quickly. I did look into the packages and into some of its other services. This will give you an idea of what you're dealing with:

"IPad/iPhone Premium Edition with Private Label iBooks Distribution. [Their wording not mine.]

Cost = $699."

What you get for that—an ISBN and a listing on Apple in your name.

The bottom line is if you had your own ISBN (most places charge $19 if you don't have one), you could do all of this for nothing!

Here's another Outskirts service.

"Promotional Materials (save 25 percent on over 2,000 promotional items like bookmarks, postcards, and more). Price: $1,099."

From what I could tell, these are items you could purchase for less than $150–200.

It will also arrange for Amazon Search Inside the Book for a little more than $100, or guarantee you a radio interview for $499. Just to let you know, Search Inside is free, and anyone who spends a little time working on it can arrange a radio interview if you have something interesting to talk about.

Everything on this website screamed at me to leave and not come back. I listened to the voices. If you want to check it out, the link is above.

———

SilverWood Books

silverwoodbooks.co.uk
Giacomo's rating: 7.5/10
Model: Full service (Author Services Provider).
Packages: $1,100/£680–$2,500/£1,800.
SilverWood is very much a custom provider of services. Authors can opt into additional services and choose from a list of add-ons, or they opt not to.
Services provided: Professional editing, proofreading, page layout, book cover design, POD, author website design, and book publicity.
Print: POD or offset.
Print distribution: Gardners, Bertrams, Coutts Information Services, Macauley, Central Books, Ingram.
Bindings available: Paperback and hardback (most sizes).
Royalties: SilverWood retains 15 percent of list price for books sold using its trade accounts, with the balance passed to the author.
Ebook distribution: Amazon's Kindle, Gardners Books, Ingram Book Group, Apple's iBookstore, Diesel ebooks, WHSmith, Kobo, and Barnes & Noble NOOK.
Contract term and rights: Author keeps all their own rights. Contract is nonexclusive and has a 30-day termination clause.

Notes: SilverWood doesn't take on every author who comes to it. That alone should tell you how different it is. From the first meeting to the final product you will know you are in the hands of professionals who care not only about what they do, but also about you, and your project.

The quality of its books is equal to that of the big publishers, and SilverWood has been successful in getting its authors' books into many of the independent stores. It has a close working relationship with Foyles Cabot Circus, the Bristol branch of the UK's largest independent bookseller, and selected SilverWood titles are guaranteed placement in the store throughout the year.

SilverWood is not for everyone. Helen Hart, the publishing director, will be the first one to tell you that. It isn't the least expensive, but it certainly isn't the most expensive either. SilverWood's goal is to help you produce the best possible book, while maintaining realistic expectations. Helen won't try to sell you services you don't need, and she might not even take you on as a client if your expectations are out of line. If you're looking for high-quality work and want to produce a book you can be proud of, you might give SilverWood a close look.

———

Smashwords

smashwords.com
Giacomo's rating: 9/10
Model: Ebook distributor.
Initial/setup fees: Free.
Ebook conversion: Free.
Other free services provided:

- Ebook distribution.
- Preorder distribution to iBooks, NOOK, and Kobo.
- Conversion to multiple formats.
- Retailer.
- Free ISBNs.
- Free unlimited anytime updates to books and metadata.
- Centralized metadata management and consolidated sales reports and tax reporting.
- Merchandising tools (coupons, interviews, enhanced series metadata).

In addition to the other tools, Smashwords offers three free books, and video tutorials. These books and videos are all about promoting best practices. *The Secrets to Ebook Publishing Success* teaches a writer to think and act like a professional publisher. Smashwords has a new presentation on preorder strategy, and a very informative presentation on Apple merchandising.

Royalties: Depends on which channel the book is sold through. Author receives 85 percent or more of the net sale proceeds in most cases. (For detailed breakdown see chart.)

Payment schedule: Quarterly.

Reach: Smashwords store, iBooks, Barnes & Noble, Diesel, Kobo, Baker & Taylor, Amazon (limited), Page Foundry, OverDrive, Scribd, Txtr. (See chart for complete list.)

Contract term and rights: Nonexclusive license to publish, distribute, and sell.

Notes: If you haven't figured it out by now, I'll come right out and say it—the publishing world is in an obvious state of flux. The worst part is that so many companies are rushing to take advantage of self-published authors with shoddy services and exorbitant prices. When doing this job, it can sometimes seem as if the entire industry is rife with charlatans, and so it's nice to find providers whose goals are in total sync with authors. Smashwords falls squarely into this category.

Its philosophy is simple and its motivation is clear. In order for it to make money, authors have to make money. It doesn't charge for anything except selling your book. It sells no additional services. It has no sales team. What it does—what it is driven by—is the same thing that drives you, as an author. Its goal is to deliver the best product and negotiate the most favorable deal for authors with distributors and retailers.

Mark Coker, president of Smashwords, has lived up to that, as evidenced by the agreements he has managed to wrangle for authors against many of the other distributors. Smashwords' deal with B&N is second to none. It's so good that the 85 percent royalty you earn with Smashwords yields more than the 100 percent from BookBaby, or eBookPartnership, or any of the others. In fact, if you sell a lot of books under the $2.99 price point at B&N, you will likely earn more with Smashwords than you would going direct with B&N. And the deal negotiated with Scribd is better than anyone anticipated.

Smashwords doesn't rest on its laurels either. In addition to Scribd, deals have been signed with Txtr, a major player in the European market, and OverDrive, the largest distributor to libraries around the world.

We have heard and read complaints about Smashwords, mostly in regard to sales reporting, website interface, slow response times on price changes, and slow customer service. I tested these as best I could.

- Customer service: Each email I sent was responded to within 48 hours.
- Price changes: Apple's change took effect the same day.
- Sales reporting: Smashwords now offers daily sales reporting from B&N, Apple, and Kobo.
- Website interface: I had no problem with the site. I uploaded six books in a couple of hours, and had zero problems. I used EPUB. I have never tried a Word file.

I think you have to ask yourself what is most important. For me, I want a distributor with the best reach, and who negotiates the best deals. I want to maximize earnings. I want to know I can trust that distributor to be around next month and next year, and I want to know I can trust it to have my best interests as part of its philosophy.

Pros: It provides an online bookstore for authors to sell their own books, coupons, and a host of sales tools like author interviews, the Series Manager, and one of the best tools available—the ability for indies to offer preorders on Apple, Kobo, and B&N. Ability to make unlimited changes for free.

Cons: I have heard complaints of slow customer service and sales reporting, as well as issues with the free conversion tool.

———

Thomson-Shore

thomsonshore.com
Giacomo's rating: 7/10
Model: Full service.
Packages: Thomson-Shore offers packages, but is open to print-only options as well.

Thomson-Shore	Basic	Professional	Book Launch	Book Shepherd
Total cost of services	$2,895	$3,895	$4,855	$7,295
100% profits to author	✓	✓	✓	✓
No obligation to purchase books	✓	✓	✓	✓
Retain full control of all rights	Contract can be terminated by author at ANY time			
Full pricing control by author	✓	✓	✓	✓

Fig. 3a—Thomson-Shore Services

Thomson-Shore	Basic	Professional	Book Launch	Book Shepherd
Email and phone support from production manager	✓	✓	✓	✓
Book Shepherd to help you develop idea or manuscript to trade standards	N/A	N/A	N/A	✓
Book project plan	N/A	N/A	N/A	✓

Fig. 3b—Thomson-Shore Mentoring

Editorial	Basic	Professional	Book Launch	Book Shepherd
Free editorial evaluation	✓	✓	✓	✓
Copy-editing	Optional	Optional	Optional	✓
Content or developmental editing	Optional	Optional	Optional	Optional
Book development guide	N/A	N/A	N/A	✓

Fig. 3c—Thomson-Shore Editorial

Design	Basic	Professional	Book Launch	Book Shepherd
Custom interior design	✓	✓	✓	✓
Custom book cover design	✓	✓	✓	✓

Fig. 3d—Thomson-Shore Design

Registrations	Basic	Professional	Book Launch	Book Shepherd
Copyright filing and Library of Congress	✓	✓	✓	✓
ISBN registration with one of our imprints	William Charles Publishing	Eligible for elite imprints	Eligible for elite imprints	Includes elite imprint or custom print
Ghost publish and create own custom imprint and ISBN	Optional	Optional	Optional	Eligible for elite imprints

Fig. 3e—Thomson-Shore Registrations

Book Production	Basic	Professional	Book Launch	Book Shepherd
Physical book printing	POD or offset	POD or offset	POD or offset	POD or offset
Ebook formatting and distribution	Amazon, B&N, iBooks, and all major retailers			
Books for author at printing cost	✓	✓	✓	✓

Fig. 3f—Thomson-Shore Production

Sales and Distribution	Basic	Professional	Book Launch	Book Shepherd
Trade distribution and fulfillment services	Ingram and Seattle Book Co.	Ingram and Seattle Book Co.	Ingram and Seattle Book Co.	Ingram and Seattle Book Co.
Free warehousing of printed books	✓	✓	✓	✓
Marketing				
Online retailer optimization	✓	✓	✓	✓
Edit your cover copy and author bio	✓	✓	✓	✓
Publishing University		✓	✓	✓
Develop marketing strategy with marketing director		One hour consulting	Three hours consulting	Weekly consulting
SEO optimization with keyword analysis	SEO optimization with keyword analysis	✓	✓	✓
Title, subtitle, cover copy, bio, and catalog description development		✓	✓	✓
Book review submissions			✓	✓
Membership in IBPA or AuthorU			✓	✓
Business cards and bookmarks			250 of each	500 of each
Book-signing poster			✓	✓
Sales onesheet			✓	✓
Press release				✓
Total cost of services	$2,895	$3,895	$4,855	$7,295

Fig. 3g—Thomson-Shore Distribution

Print: $5.40 per book.

Distribution: Ingram and in-house services for worldwide distribution. Clays, the UK print and distribution giant, is now a partner. Offers industry standard 55 percent discount and returns.

Print: If set up separately, $35 setup fee and $2.35 per page for layout/typesetting. (Included with package.)

Ebook: If done at same time as print, $250. (Included with packages.)

Reach: Amazon, Apple, B&N, Kobo, Smashwords.

Changes: No charges for metadata. Content changes are $45 per hour.

Additional services provided:

- Editorial review: Free.
- Line/copy-editing: $0.01 to $0.015 per word.
- Content editing: Quoted per book.

- Developmental editing: Quoted per book.
- Custom cover design: $695.

Bindings/sizes available: Any print option.
Royalties: Ebooks: 12 percent distribution fee on net royalties.
Payment schedule: Quarterly.

Notes: For the past 40 years, Thomson-Shore has provided the highest-quality book printing and binding and the very best in customer service to the publishing industry. It offers the best printing technology, and has recently partnered with Clays, the UK's biggest print and distribution company, to offer true global print solutions.

If you want handholding, or if you're after a no-nonsense, high-quality operation to print your books and help you get started, you might give serious consideration to Thomson-Shore. As we've already discussed, the publishing business is changing rapidly. Many companies are expanding services to satisfy the huge demand from new authors rushing to get their books to market. As with any situation like this, there are people eager to take advantage of others.

And then you have companies like Thomson-Shore, who are reputable and have been in the business a long time. In fact, Thomson-Shore recently bought Seattle Book Company and PublishNext, two other long-time reputable companies in the business. Combined they are a strong new resource for authors and small publishers who want to produce and deliver a quality product.

With that said, I wasn't impressed with the package prices, especially at the high end. The Basic Package wasn't too bad. If you look closely at the individual prices you'll see it isn't trying to gouge the author, but simply quoting prices for a top-notch product/service. The price for line editing was among the lowest of any provider I looked at, competing with individuals offering the same service. The print prices are in line with the most competitive in the business, and the fact that it doesn't charge for storage of books is testament, again, to the fact that Thomson-Shore is not trying to take advantage of the authors. The problem I see is that Thomson, like many companies, bundles services that not all people will want, which means an author ends up paying for things they either don't need, or don't want.

Look at the Basic Package. For $2,895 you get a few "must-have" services, such as custom book cover design, and custom interior design for the print book and ebook. Those services alone might cost you $1,700 from a top-notch vendor; but assuming that, it still leaves almost $1,200 to pay for the "other" services. I'm not saying it's out of line, but not everyone would want them. (Publishing consultation, phone support, editorial evaluation, ISBN, free warehousing of books, editing of cover copy and bio.) When you move up the ladder to the higher-priced packages, I think the benefits are less obvious.

My advice—if you consider Thomson-Shore, look closely at what you are paying for versus what you really need.

XinXii

xinxii.com
Giacomo's rating: 7/10
Model: Ebook distributor.
Ebook conversion: "Free high-quality conversion to EPUB and MOBI. You want your ebook to be distributed by us? We convert your ebook to the EPUB format (for iBookstore) and MOBI format (for Amazon) for free."
Ebook: Free.
Traditional fees/costs: Do not exist at XinXii. No sign-up fee, admission fee, delivery fee, service charges, conversion charges, payment processing fees, retailer discounts, credit card charge-backs, publishing fees, webhosting fees, webspace (unlimited) fees, transaction fees.
Distribution reach: Amazon, Angus & Robertson, Barnes & Noble, Buch.de, Buecher.de, Casa del Libro, Der Club Bertelsmann, Donauland, Family Christian, Fnac, Hugendubel, iBooks, Indigo,

Kobo, Libris BLZ, Livraria Cultura, Mondadori, Telefonica, Otto Media, PagePlace, Rakuten, Thalia, Vodafone live, Weltbild, Whitcoulls, WHSmith. (Plus XinXii website.)

Royalties: 50 percent of net sales for all channels except the following: O2, Sony Mobile PlayNow, T-Mobile, T-Zones & Vodafone live! (40 percent for these).

The "net sales" is equal to the ebook's net sales price (sales price excl. VAT).

Payment schedule: PayPal or bank transfer, paid monthly. Weekly sales reports.

Contract term and rights: No contract duration, no exclusivity. There is no contract duration: the "Delete" button will allow you to easily remove your title from XinXii whenever you want to. And there are no exclusivity agreements when you publish a title on XinXii: publish it wherever you want.

Notes: I found XinXii to be a refreshing company to deal with. The website was easy to use, the instructions clear, and the process went smoothly. I set up an account and uploaded six books in less than one hour. XinXii's philosophy reminded me of the way Smashwords handles things, which is good. It doesn't charge an upfront fee. It doesn't charge for converting your document. It doesn't charge for the web page it gives you, or anything else. It's all based on royalties, so just like with Smashwords, if the author doesn't sell books, XinXii doesn't make money. I like that. Also (like Smashwords) it gives authors tools to help them sell. Here are a few of them:

- Author badges.
- XinXii author page.
- Book trailer.
- Coupon codes.
- Offline book marketing.
- Pinterest.
- Press releases.
- Social bookmarks.

- Social networks.
- Social news.
- Tips by experts.
- Twitter.
- WiseStamp.

As far as distribution, many authors might not be familiar with the names on this list, but it is an impressive group of channels. I've included a few details below.

Angus & Robertson is the largest bookselling chain in Australia.

buch.de internet stores AG is the second-largest internet media dealer in the German-speaking region. The online shop offers you millions of books, ebooks, films, games, etc.

buecher.de is one of the leading German book and media retailers online with more than seven million products. Among the German titles there are more than 120,000 ebooks in other languages as well as entertainment media such as games, music, and movies.

Casa del Libro is the leading Spanish bookseller chain, not only with 37 stores but also online with seven million unique users.

Der Club Bertelsmann is one of the largest book and media clubs in the world with more than three million products and 300 branches in Germany.

Donauland is Austria's largest book and media club with 400,000 members.

Family Christian is the largest Christian bookselling chain in the USA.

Fnac is not only a leading provider of products in the sphere of technology, leisure, and culture, but also the largest bookstore in France with more than 50 million printed books per year. The website fnac.com has 750,000 visitors a day and is one of the leading ecommerce websites in France. XinXii distributes to fnac.com and fnac.pt.

Livraria Cultura is the largest bookselling chain in Brazil.

Mondadori is the largest publishing company in Italy.

Thalia is the market leader in retail bookselling in German-speaking countries. Thalia sells its own-branded Oyo e-reader along with a catalogue of around 300,000 ebooks.

Weltbild is one of the largest internet, book, and media retail companies anywhere in Europe. Weltbild has established the company as one of the top brands in the retail sector. Weltbild is the second-largest online book retailer.

Whitcoulls is the leading bookstore chain in New Zealand. WHSmith is the leading bookselling and newspaper chain in Great Britain. It has more than 500 bookstores as well as supplies bookstores at stations/airports and an online bookshop.

EBOOK DISTRIBUTORS

Which One to Use?

This table compares the pros and cons of several popular ebook distributors. The industry is in a state of flux, so what is true today might not be true next year, or even next month. New players enter the market, new channels open up, and a new technology can change everything in a heartbeat.

We chose a few of the higher-rated companies to compare, but the data is included for you to make your own decisions. We did our best to verify all data, but if you see something wrong please let us know.

Channels	BookBaby	Draft2Digital	eBookPartnership	Smashwords
Amazon*	70%	-	70%	60%
Apple	70%	60%	70%	60%
Baker & Taylor	60%	-	-	60%
B&T Axis	-	-	-	45%
B&N	50%	60%	50%	60%
Bookmate	-	-	50%	-
Ciando	60%	-	-	-
Copia	70%	-	-	-
Ebsco	70%	-	-	-
ePubDirect	50-60%	-	-	-
e-Sentral	75%	-	-	-
Gardners	50%	-	50%	-
Google Play	-	-	52%	-
Ingram	-	-	62.5%	-
Kobo*	70%	60%	70%	60%
Library Direct	-	-	-	70%
Magster	-	-	60%	-
OverDrive	-	-	50%	50%
Page Foundry	-	60%	60%	60%
Page Pusher	60%	-	-	-
Scribd	70%	60%	60%	60%
Storytel	-	-	-	-
Txtr	-	-	60%	60%
Waterstones	-	-	50%	-

Fig. 4a—Ebook distributors

Amazon pays 70 percent on books priced $2.99–$9.99. All others are 35 percent. If you are not in the KDP Select program, the territories of Brazil, India, Japan, and Mexico are a maximum of 35 percent.

Ciando is one of the leading ebook retailers in Germany, now offering distribution through five websites, 60 regional libraries, and direct relationship with over 1,300 German bookstores.

*Kobo—70 percent of list price in US, CA, AUS, UK, and 45 percent in other territories.

Copia is a social media e-reading platform with an excellent following.

e-Sentral is Malaysia's #1 online bookstore.

Scribd is a subscription service with different requirements for what constitutes a "sale." Scribd has more than 500,000 books, each available in its subscription service plans.

OverDrive is not known by many authors, but is one of the big players worldwide, and will be a major force in the next few years. It also has an app for almost every mobile and desktop platform, including PCs, Macs, iPads, iPhones, etc. If you're wondering just how big it can be, last year more than 100 million ebooks were downloaded from OverDrive. You read that right—100 million!

Additional Costs

Costs	BookBaby	Draft2Digital	eBookPartnership	Smashwords
Sign-up fee	299	.	$50/40	.
Yearly fee	?	.	$40	.
Conversion	.	free	EPUB or $	Free
Changes	?	free	$*	Free

Fig. 4b—Ebook distributors, additional costs

Annual Fees

BookBaby (BB) Premium costs $299 per book. There are no charges per year after that.

eBookPartnership (EBP) costs $40 per title with five books, plus $40 per year per title after that. With both BB and EBP you can buy credits, so even if you don't have five books now, you can purchase the credits and obtain the discount.

Changes

EBP's policy on changes is on its website, but you do have to pay to make content changes or upload new files/covers, etc.

ISBNs

I strongly recommend that authors get their own ISBNs. Bowker sells them as does Nielsen, but they are ridiculously expensive for just one. If you buy ten at a time, the cost is $275, or $27.50 each. If you plan on being prolific, you can purchase 100 for $575, or $5.75 each. If you go with both print and digital editions, you'll need two ISBNs per book, so buying them in a block of ten gives you enough for five books. One of the downsides of using an ISBN from a distributor like

Smashwords (SW), BB or CreateSpace (CS) is that those companies are then listed as the publisher of record.

The Economics

For the sake of sanity, and because there are too many possible scenarios to consider, I restricted my calculations to two scenarios.

- Scenario 1: Using the distributors for Apple, B&N, and Kobo, and going direct with Amazon.
- Scenario 2: Going direct with Amazon, Apple, B&N, and Kobo, and using the distributors for all other channels.

SCENARIO 1

Because of the different royalty rates, the only way I saw to do this fairly was to make a table for each of the channels. The number of books sold is displayed on the top row, and the dollars earned on the rows next to each distributor.

B&N

Books Sold	1,000-99c	1,000-2.99	5,000-99c	5,000-2.99
BookBaby*	500	1,500	2,500	7,500
Draft2Digital	600	1,800	3,000	9,000
eBookPartnership	500	1,500	2,500	7,500
Smashwords	600	1,800	3,000	9,000
Direct	400	1,950	2,000	9,750

Apple

Books Sold	1,000-99c	1,000-2.99	5,000-99c	5,000-2.99
BookBaby*	700	2,100	3,500	10,500
Draft2Digital	600	1,800	3,000	9,000
eBookPartnership	700	2,100	3,500	10,500
Smashwords	600	1,800	3,000	9,000
Direct	700	2,100	3,500	10,500

Kobo

Books Sold	1,000–99c	1,000–2.99	5,000–99c	5,000–2.99
BookBaby*	700	2,100	3,500	10,500
Draft2Digital	600	1,800	3,000	9,000
eBookPartnership	700	2,100	3,500	10,500
Smashwords	600	1,800	3,000	9,000
Direct	450	2,100	2,250	10,500

*BookBaby's numbers represent the premium option—$299 per title.

Average Earnings

I averaged earnings based on market share. I used 20 percent total market share for B&N, 15 percent for Apple, and 5 percent for Kobo. I realize this might not reflect the worldwide market, but based on different channels represented, this was the best way to do it. If your numbers are considerably different, simply plug your data into the charts and see where you stand. Remember, Amazon is not included, so under the first column it represents 1,000 books sold on the three channels mentioned. Using market share statistics, out of those 1,000 books, 500 would be on B&N, 375 on Apple, and 125 on Kobo. Here's what the chart looks like.

Books Sold	1,000–99c	1,000–2.99	5,000–99c	5,000–2.99
BookBaby	600	1,800	3,000	9,000
Draft2Digital	600	1,800	3,000	9,000
eBookPartnership	600	1,800	3,000	9,000
Smashwords	600	1,800	3,000	9,000
Direct	550	2,025	2,750	10,125

As you can see, if the numbers I used for market share are correct, you would earn the same amount of money across all four distributors. The difference is that BB Premium and EBP cost money. So, am I saying don't go with the premium options? No. I'm simply presenting the data, as I understand it. Each author has to decide what to do based on where they sell and how much.

Note: There would be a big difference if you used a distributor for

Amazon, as BB and EBP both pay 70 percent and SW pays 60 percent. I didn't include Amazon because it seems as if almost everyone goes direct with it.

SCENARIO 2

This didn't turn out at all like I expected, because I had no idea when I started this that authors would earn the same using SW as they did using the premium options for the primary channels. As it stands, scenario 2 is simply a matter of deciding whether the other channels offered by the premium distributors are worth paying for. Let's take a look.

BookBaby

To justify using BB's premium service it's simply a matter of identifying the channels either not available for free elsewhere, or where BB has a royalty advantage, and then comparing those channels with BB's free offering.

The table below shows approximately how many books you need to sell at several price points to break even. And remember, this is per book, and only on the unique channels. If you have three books, you need to sell three times that many.

Channels include: Ciando, Copia, Ebsco, ePubDirect, Gardners, Page Pusher.

BB Cost	Books-99¢	Books-2.99	Books-4.99
299	600	166	100

When you look at these numbers, you might think—damn, I can easily sell that many books. And maybe you can. But please remember that this is with the above channels only. This is not counting books sold through Amazon, or Apple, or NOOK, or Kobo, or anywhere else you sell books. This might be a lot more difficult than you think.

You also need to add to this the difference in percentage/royalty you would receive from retail channels BB has in common with others. For example, you would earn 10 percent more on Scribd, and 15 percent more on e-Sentral.

I understand that BB's premium service comes with other benefits. Each person will have to determine whether those services add enough value to make the difference. You can look at what is included at bookbaby.com/ebook-services.

eBookPartnership (EBP)

Justifying whether to pay for EBP's service follows the same analysis as what we did for BB. The channels unique to EBP are: Bookmate, Ebsco, Gardners, Google Play, Ingram, Magster, Storytel, and Waterstones. You can go direct with Google Play, although the process is frustrating, but improving.

I included channels that overlap with BB because I doubt that anyone will pay for both distribution options, so the retailers I included were the ones not available as a free option. That leaves us with justifying the $50 cost ($40 with purchase of five credits) based on these channels. The calculations couldn't be simpler. Can you sell enough books on Bookmate, Ebsco, Gardners, Google Play, Ingram, Magster, Storytel, and Waterstones to pay for the service? The table below shows how many you need to sell, using 50 percent as the average royalty rate.

EBP Cost	Books–99¢	Books–2.99	Books–4.99
50	100	33	20
40	80	27	16

This chart might make you think—damn, I can easily sell 20 books at $4.99.

If you have a good following in the UK, Waterstones alone could easily pay for the cost of premium distribution, and Bookmate, Ebsco, and Magster are up-and-comers in the market. Ingram is a long-established player and brings a host of additional channels.

The decision boils down to knowing where you sell. If you don't know where you sell, and how much you sell, and at what price point, I suggest you go with free options until you get a handle on your numbers. I certainly recommend keeping a spreadsheet of sales by date, retail channel, price, and geography. These are all important factors to consider when determining who to use for distribution and what price to set for your books.

Before you decide on EBP, though, remember that it charges for making changes. That cost could be huge. Don't forget that when you do your calculations.

MY STRATEGY

I go direct with Amazon, Apple, Barnes & Noble, Google Play, and Kobo. I use SW and I opt in for every channel except the five I go direct with. I have recently put a few books into SW's catalogue for Apple, B&N, and Kobo, still going direct with Kindle and Google. I wanted to try this out because of the terms at the lower rates. It can make a huge difference on promotions.

The Promotions Consideration

If there is one factor that makes a huge difference to an indie author, it's the ability to run promotions and sales whenever you want, and often on a moment's notice. If you can't respond quickly it can cost you dearly. When I run ads on some of the bigger promotion sites, such as BookBub, e-readernewstoday, Kindle Books and Tips, or, if I ever get accepted, Pixel of Ink, I need to be able to adjust price up or down quickly. In the past you could only do this if you went direct, as no distributor could offer response times that fast. Now, however, SW and Draft2Digital both have response times that typically take place within hours. I have already tested this with SW on B&N, and on Apple, and it worked fine. Kobo was slower to respond. I don't have any books on Draft2Digital yet, but I know it is also very good.

This can make a huge difference, because if you have a successful promotion, you want to take advantage of the recommendation algorithms that kick in at the peak of your run. When your book has reached its highest ranking (as best as you can determine) you want to raise the price to take advantage of the push from the retailer. (Some authors opt for a different strategy of continuing the sale at a low price.)

Another big reason for wanting to do this with SW or Draft2Digital is if you have books you are promoting below $2.99. Both of these distributors offer 60 percent of list price at B&N regardless of the price point. It could make a big difference on a big promotion, or on any book like a short story or novella that is priced below $2.99.

Payment Terms

SW pays quarterly. Draft2Digital pays monthly. BB and EBP pay monthly (assuming minimums are met).

SUMMARY

BookBaby

BB has come a long way in the past year. I have always liked BB's clean, easy-to-use site, and the channels it offered.

Pros: Good channels, including all of the major ones, plus Ciando, Copia, Ebsco, Ebook Direct, e-Sentral, Gardners, Page Pusher, and Scribd. BookPromo™ package offered to authors.

Cons: Charges upfront for service.

Other: For authors looking for a complete publishing package, BB has a range of services you might like. It offers cover design, print books, website hosting, editing services, book scanning services, and press releases. I have no idea how it rates in any of these areas as I haven't used BB.

Draft2Digital

This company has made huge strides in the past two years, and is continuing to aggressively pursue new channels and strike great deals for authors. Kris Austin, the CEO, is about as author friendly as you can get.

Every program he puts in place is geared with the author in mind. As far as channels, it currently has B&N, Apple, Kobo, PageFoundry, and Scribd. It is close to finalizing deals with Google and Tolino, and is talking with OverDrive. It is also in active negotiations with several other retailers, including Ingram and Omnilit.

Pros: Great channels, excellent author-focused attitude, great customer service, free service, and free conversion of files. Also offers preorders for Apple, Kobo, and B&N. (Plus exciting new services coming.)

eBookPartnership

It has a lot to offer, not the least of which is an excellent distribution network on the international front.

Pros: Great channels of distribution, including all of the big ones, plus Bookmate, Ebsco, e-Sentral, Gardners, Google Play, Ingram, Magster, OverDrive, Storytel, and Waterstones.

Cons: Costs $50 per title, and $40 per title per year after that.

Other: EBP also offers additional services for authors who need them, including a variety of ebook conversions, book scanning, cover design, and website hosting.

Smashwords

This is the original and largest indie ebook distributor, but that hasn't stopped Mark Coker from innovating or from continuing to improve.

Pros: Free service, free changes, preorders to Apple, B&N, and Kobo. SW authors also benefit from an online store and coupons for custom author promotions.

SW also introduced a website redesign that made the site more mobile friendly, introduced enhanced metadata for series books with its Series Manager tool, and introduced Smashwords Interviews, an author self-interviewing tool that helps readers learn the story behind the author.

SW has strong distribution channels, including: all the big channels, plus Baker & Taylor Axis, Library Direct, OverDrive, Scribd, and Txtr. Easy system for uploading, and conversion is free. SW already had one of the best distribution channels, but it continues to improve.

One of the biggest pluses, for me, is the ability to opt in/out of channels and to make changes to a book's content and/or price with no charge. To me, this is critical. The only two distributors who offer this are SW and Draft2Digital.

The Bottom Line

Financially, the decision on which route to go will vary depending on your price point and your projected sales, but decisions are seldom strictly financial ones. Other factors come into play. Here are a few to consider:

- **Ease of use.** SW and Draft2Digital have easy-to-use sites, as does BB. I haven't uploaded to EBP, but I've heard from a few people who say the site compares favorably.
- **Customer service.** I love that BB has phone support, but that's only for the premium option. It has email support for all others. SW and EBP also have email support. From the authors I've spoken to, and from my dealings with Kris Austin, I can say that Draft2Digital has excellent customer service; it's one of its strong suits.

Each person's circumstances will be different. Before you decide, think of how each factor might affect you.

If you have to make changes after uploading, you'll incur steep charges at BB or EBP, while SW and Draft2Digital are free. Look hard at the charts. It doesn't take long to rack up expenses that would eliminate all potential profits.

Another factor is the conversion cost. I have mine in EPUB so I don't face the issues, but if you're trying to upload Word documents it will cost you at BB unless you go premium.

Be honest about how many books you think you'll sell, and at what price. Then look at the charts and determine what makes sense. Don't make a decision based on how many you'd like to sell. Be realistic. Remember, this is how many you'll sell outside of Amazon, and any other channel you go direct with. Most authors won't hit the breakeven point.

My Take

It's an absolute no-brainer to go with Smashwords. It has great channels, great support for authors, and it's free. You can't argue with that. Draft2Digital has that same attitude, as does PublishDrive. One of the things I like best about SW and Draft2Digital is their approach to the business. They are not trying to sell authors anything. Neither Draft2Digital nor SW makes any money unless the author makes money, and yet they have costs associated with hosting the site, etc. The only way they make money is to help authors sell books, and they don't charge for doing that.

For the premium options you'll have to run the numbers. I haven't gone with them, but some people might consider EBP if only for Waterstones and Ingram. Don't let Ingram fool you. Ingram is the largest book distributor in the world and has a substantial ebook network. You can see a list here. And Waterstones is a major player in the UK market.

Note: I looked into two other distributors but didn't include the details.

I didn't include IngramSpark because you cannot opt out of its distributor list, with the exception of Apple and Amazon. It also only pays 40 percent across the board. Ingram has done wonders for its print distribution, and I spoke to some of the folks at Spark about its ebook pricing. It is looking at making a lot of changes to its model, but it takes time. I hope it gets to it soon, as I think it can be a major player in the game and bring great new channels to the table.

There are many other distributors we looked at. Some of them might offer the perfect combination for you. We listed what we felt were the best options, but we welcome your feedback, which will be incorporated into future editions of the guide.

SOME PRINT BOOK DISTRIBUTORS COMPARED

T he chart below is to help you determine which provider is best for your print needs. They have been chosen either because they represent the best options in ALLi's opinion (IngramSpark and CreateSpace), or because they are companies that many authors use.

Some providers are primarily UK based, and while all of the providers might offer service in the UK, I did not have specific UK print prices in all cases.

Setup fee

In some cases print distribution is offered as part of a publishing package, included along with other services.

	CS	Hillcrest	LS	Lulu	Matador	Spark	Thomson
$ per book	$4.46	$5.40	$4.86	$7.25	$6.50	$4.86	$5.40
Discount*	20/ 40/60	55	20/30/ 40/55			30/ 40/55	55
Returns	no	✓	✓	no	✓	✓	✓
Hardback	no	✓	✓	✓	✓	✓	✓
Setup fee	no	pkg	75	pkg	pkg	49	pkg
Yearly fee	no	99	12	no	no	12	no

Cost per book

All prices were based on the same criteria: a 6x9 trade paperback with 300 pages, B&W interior, cream paper, perfect bound, and gloss finish on cover. POD prices were quoted in all instances. As you can see, the cost is fairly close from all but one of the companies. Lulu was double in almost every example I ran. And at higher volumes the ratio was worse. Lulu also has a close association with Author Solutions, a non-recommended service.

CS comes in as the lowest-priced provider for low quantities, but if you calculate higher print runs, they all become competitive. At 100 copies LS and Spark are within pennies of CS's price, and at 500 or 1,000 copies all of the other companies, except Lulu, are considerably less (approximately $3.25 per book).

Discount/returns

Most of the companies offer the industry standard 55 percent discount, which almost all bookstores require to consider stocking your books. You can get by with less for online stores.

Quality

We hope to have examples of print books produced by all companies featured in this guide in our next update. In the meantime, comparing CS, LS, and IS, our conclusion is that CS makes a good book, but LS and IS make a better one.

Hillcrest, Matador, SilverWood, and Thomson are providers known to produce very high-quality books.

With CS, 20 percent is for the CS online store. The author earns 80 percent of the sale price minus the cost of the book.

The 40 percent rate is for online stores like Amazon. The author earns 40 percent of the sale price minus the cost of the book.

The 60 percent rate is for expanded distribution, which, theoretically, will allow you to get into libraries and independent bookstores. I say theoretically because CS does not allow for returns, and almost all stores require a book to be returnable.

Hillcrest, Matador, and Thomson are all set up on the 55 percent discount and all allow returns.

IngramSpark—When IS started out, it only allowed a 55 percent return, but it has since opened up the option for authors to allow 40 percent discounts as well. It also allows returns.

Lightning Source—LS is the most flexible on discounts. An author can set the discount as low as 20 percent. At 30 percent you still have a good chance of getting into online stores. You can also go with the standard 55 percent or other choices in between. Returns are allowed.

Note: It's important for authors to understand that the chances of getting accepted into a large number of independent stores is slim. I don't like to be the one to say "never," but the odds aren't good. My advice is that unless you have an excellent reason to think you can be the exception to the rule, go with a 40 percent discount and do not choose the "returns" option. That will allow you to sell online and even in a few select independent stores.

Hardback, setup fee, and yearly fee

The hardback or not decision is easy. Only CS doesn't have an option for hardback. As far as the setup fee, where it reads "package," the price is included in the package options. Even with those companies, however, I believe all of them have separate plans for authors who want print only. Contact them and ask.

Questions to Ask

Choosing a print partner is not as much about money as it might seem at first. It's a decision that can only be answered after you determine exactly what you want to do with your printed book.

- Are you going to be primarily an ebook author with a few printed books for promotional purposes?

- Are you going to restrict print sales to online, through the print book retailer and your own website?
- Are you going to limit yourself to a few local or handpicked bookstores?
- Are you going to go all out and try to get a distributor and do a print campaign, with the associated trade-style publicity in newspapers and other media that is necessary to sell books in this way? If yes, why?
- Have you realistically budgeted time and money costs?

Ninety-nine percent of indie authors will find it a super-stretch challenge to sell widely through bookstores, even as they set out to conquer the world. Be realistic and you'll save yourself money.

And if things go well, and your books begin selling like hotcakes, you can then ramp up.

In the next section, we compare the two biggest print options for indie authors, and the two recommended by ALLi: CreateSpace and IngramSpark.

CREATESPACE AND INGRAMSPARK

Lightning Source (LS) and IngramSpark (IS)

L ightning Source and Spark are both owned by Ingram, both using the same print technology and offering the same services as far as printing and distribution goes. The differences are in the setup costs and in the discounts allowed, and that Spark also offers ebook publishing.

LS assigns a representative to each account, so you can talk to a real person. Ingram is now, however, encouraging all new author-publishers to use IS instead of LS. It intends to have a customer service rep on the platform but that is not yet in place.

CreateSpace (CS)

CS is a great platform for indie authors, giving access to Amazon's retail power at good rates.

PRINT BOOK DISTRIBUTION OPTIONS

I've seen a lot of comparisons between CreateSpace (CS) and Ingram (either Lightning Source or Spark). In almost every instance I walk away thinking that it wasn't a fair comparison. There is a lot of misinformation.

I hope I can build on the information already given and provide a little objectivity, to help people decide which company they should choose for their print needs.

Features	CreateSpace	IngramSpark
Changes	No charge?	$25
Cost per copy B&W	$4.55	$4.86
Cost per copy color	$21.85	$8.40
Cost of setup	$0	$49*
Yearly fee	$0	$12
Customer service	Excellent, instant chat online	Good
Discount	30/40/60%**	40/55%*
Distribution	Amazon/Extended	Worldwide
Ease of setup	Very easy	Easy
Hardcover	No	Yes
ISBN	Yes	Yes
Quality	Good	Excellent
Returns	No	Yes
Shipping	Excellent US/Okay int'l	Very good US/excellent int'l

Specifications used for book calculations—B&W and color: paperback, 6x9, cream, perfect bound, gloss finish, 300 pages.

Discounts are figured using both options with IngramSpark. CS has only one option for expanded distribution. CS discount for Amazon is 40 percent, and for expanded distribution is 60 percent. Spark discount is your choice—30 percent, 40 percent, or 55 percent. [Note:** This can make a huge difference.]

*Spark will refund the setup fee if you purchase 50 books within the first two months.

Shipping

Calculations are for one book, to three locations, and standard shipping was figured in each case. In addition, I listed expedited and time estimated for delivery. All currency is local: US dollars, UK pounds, AU dollars.

	US (#days) US$	UK (#days) £	AU (#days) AU$
CS-Standard	3.59 (5–7)	5.00 (8–10)	15.51 (11)
CS-Expedited	11.18 (3)	9.01 (2–3)	30.58 (3–4)
Spark-Standard	5.30 (7–10)	3.50 (3–5)	10.83 (3–5)
Spark-Expedited	12.88 (4–6)	6.85 (1–2)	15.97 (1–3)

As you can see from the chart, while CS is great for US shipping, it falls apart in the international arena. Its US shipping is even better than what is cited online, as I have found that deliveries usually arrive before the estimates. International is another story. On the other hand, IngramSpark shipping is way behind CS for domestic, costing you more for slower delivery.

I did numerous giveaways on Goodreads, and I usually opened them to international readers. Three times I had to ship to AU. The first time I used CS and had to spend almost $30 to make sure it arrived within two weeks! CS has improved since then, but not by much. Afterward I used Ingram and paid one-third of the price and it still arrived in fewer than seven days.

Ingram has worldwide distribution with printing facilities in many countries, so you can ship almost anywhere at reasonable prices, and expect delivery in a reasonable time frame. The cost to ship to Queensland, AU was less than $15 and that included the price of the book. If you intend to distribute internationally, this is a huge advantage.

Note: Shipping policies and terms are always changing. What is true today might not be the same tomorrow, so before you use these numbers in your budgets, check them in real time.

Discounts

This is one of the big factors in making a decision, and it is the one that confuses most indie authors. I'll try to break it down to simple terms.

- CreateSpace takes 40 percent when you sell on Amazon.
- CreateSpace takes 60 percent for expanded distribution (other online stores, libraries, and bookstores).
- With Spark you can choose whether to allow 30 percent, 40 percent, or 55 percent for distribution.

This is all very important.

Most of the authors I speak with know very little about discounts and how they work. They simply sign up with CS and go about business. But remember, you're not just an author; you are now in business for yourself, and you should pay attention to the details, especially discounts.

WEIGHING THE OTHER FACTORS

Comparing always turns out to be far more complex than expected and this was no different. Comparing print distributors involves a lot of options; it's not simply looking at price and quality. This is where the "ease of use" comes in.

Ease of Use

Whether you categorize this as ease of use or difficulty of setup, doesn't matter. It's like asking if the glass is half full or half empty. No matter which term you use, CS comes out on top by a wide margin. Using CS is easy. You can upload your file, and—if you are prepared— you can finish in less than an hour. It even offers an expert option to save time if you know what you're doing.

Spark is not as easy. The Ingram site was designed for publishing professionals and the process reflects that. It's not difficult once you get to know the system, but the learning curve is steeper.

I have heard a lot of complaints about the difficulty of working with Ingram. I'll be the first to admit it isn't as easy as CS, but I also have to be honest and say it really isn't that difficult. If you are prepared (like you should be with CS or Ingram) and you have the files and information you need in front of you, it takes very little time or effort to do it right. In fact, it takes me about the same amount of time to upload a book to Ingram as it does with CS, although I've been through this before.

Customer Service

CreateSpace really shines here. It has an online chat system that is second to none. If you need to speak to a representative, enter your phone number and hit the "Call me now" button and your phone will ring within seconds. (No kidding—seconds!)

Spark is working hard on improvement, and I have to give it credit for that. In recent months, I have seen one of its top management team join discussion groups to answer questions and provide advice. That shows its head is in the right place. A huge step in the right direction.

Changes

When I mention changes what I really mean is the costs associated with making changes, and, once again, CreateSpace wins this hands down. If you make an error—and many indie authors do—you simply upload a new file. No charge.

With Spark, if you make an error, you upload a new file, but you will have to pay $25. This is not an insignificant factor or one to be overlooked. Everyone makes mistakes, especially indie authors, and if you have to upload a new file to fix them, it will cost you with Spark.

ALLi members are regularly given a discount that allows free revisions.

Cost Per Copy

As you can see, the cost per copy is very close on B&W—within $0.40 —but the cost for color shows a tremendous difference—about $13 for a 300-page book. This one isn't even a contest. If you need a color book, especially if it has more than a few dozen pages, you should definitely use Spark.

ISBN

CS offers several options for ISBNs. The free and $10 options are only good if you want to distribute solely through CS; they can't be used anywhere else. The $99 option can be used elsewhere, but not if you opt into expanded distribution. Here's why.

As we already discussed, CS uses Ingram for distribution. So if you purchase the CS ISBN and opt for expanded distribution, when you go to publish with Ingram and use the same ISBN, it will show as already being in its system, as CS has it assigned.

There are two ways around this.

- Buy the CS ISBN for $99 but do not opt into the expanded distribution.
- Buy an ISBN from IngramSpark (less money) and use that for both Ingram and CS.

Of course, the other option is to use your own ISBN, which is my preferred choice. Bowker sells them in the US, and Nielsen sells them in the UK.

Hardcover Books

CreateSpace does not offer hardcover. Spark does.

Returns

If you don't plan on aggressively pursuing bricks-and-mortar stores, don't choose the Spark 55 percent discount, and don't make the books returnable.

Time to Publish

This is another area where I've seen a lot of authors and bloggers talk about how quickly CS gets its book to market, but Ingram is so much slower. It's yet another case of not comparing apples with apples.

Yes, CS can, and will, get your book published on Amazon quicker than Ingram can get it published anywhere. But there is that little point of CS being owned by Amazon. I think that helps. On the other hand, CS won't get you into B&N, or BAM, or anywhere else faster than Ingram. In fact, CS uses Ingram for distribution.

Quality

This one is close to my heart. People value things differently, but to me, quality is the most important aspect. In this area, Ingram shines.

- The print is a rich, crisp black.
- The cream paper doesn't look as if had been left out in the sun.
- The white paper is bright and clean.
- The covers are true to the colors you submit, and the covers fit perfectly.

With CS I have experienced a number of problems with covers, but the biggest complaints have been with the ink. It almost always appears faded, and I haven't been happy with the cream paper.

SUMMARY

CreateSpace has the edge on:

- Price per unit, B&W
- Ease of use

- Customer service
- Changes
- ISBNs (if you don't use your own ISBN)
- Setup costs and yearly fees
- Domestic shipping.

IngramSpark has the edge on:

- Price per unit, color
- Discounts
- Distribution
- Hardcover
- Quality
- Returns
- International shipping.

The Bottom Line

I have seen a lot of providers rush in to take advantage of authors during this surge in self-publishing. Most of them are easy to spot if you dig deep enough, but some aren't. The difficult part, being an author, is in being able to spend the time to validate a provider and see if what it's selling is, in fact, a good deal.

Sometimes even a good provider offers services that aren't the best.

CS is a top choice for fulfilling an author's print needs, but I suggest a word of caution about some of its other offerings. From what I've seen, you can do far better shopping elsewhere for things like cover services and/or marketing help.

Look at intent. Any time that you are evaluating a vendor or a service provider, look at what its intent is. In the case of CS, it offers a lot for free or at a very reasonable price, but is it so it can "upsell" you other services?

On the other hand, Ingram has no hidden agendas. It offers print services. It doesn't charge a commission; it doesn't offer cover design, or marketing, or layout, or ISBNs, or anything else. Ingram makes money when you sell a lot of books. That is its motivation—to sign up customers who will sell a lot of books. In other words, it wants the same thing I do.

You might think it's great that CS offers to sell you an ISBN for $99 that you can put your own imprint on. But step back a minute and think. If you spend another $196 you can have ten of them. And let's not forget that CS is not doing this out of the goodness of its heart; it makes $98 per ISBN at that price. Yes, you didn't read that wrong. It buys them for a maximum of $1 apiece. (Actually less.)

So What Do I Do?

Long ago I stopped looking at any provider or service as good or bad. I look at them with one thing in mind—how can they help me achieve my goals?

So instead of saying: CS doesn't have the best quality. Ingram's customer service isn't as good or Ingram's distribution and discounts are better, I use the best from each provider. This is ALLi's recommendation for best practice when printing a book.

I use CS for Amazon only. That means I do **not** sign up for expanded distribution there.

I use CS for US shipping to readers who order from my website, or for giveaways, or to send review books to bloggers, etc. CS really shines in this department. It's inexpensive and it's quick.

I use Ingram for all other distribution. That means every book that goes to B&N, or BAM, or Charter Books, or to libraries, or if they get ordered by bookstores... those books come from Ingram. If I send books to independent bookstores in an effort to get in with them, I use Ingram also. I do this for two reasons: I feel the quality is better; but mainly I don't want the bookstore to see the book as available only through Amazon. Many booksellers will not stock Amazon.

I also use Ingram if I have to ship to AU, or UK, or anywhere in the world except the US. And I use Ingram for an initial order to myself to keep for autographed books. The people who ask for autographed books are most likely your best customers. Give them your best material.

CreateSpace offers:

- Fast and good distribution to Amazon
- Fast and affordable shipping to US customers
- Shipping "review copies" to bloggers and/or for giveaways like on Goodreads.

IngramSpark offers:

- Distribution to all stores except Amazon
- Fast and affordable shipping to international customers
- Shipping high-quality copies as samples to bookstores, for autographed copies, etc.

Our Recommendation

Each person has to look at their own situation and determine what strategy suits them best. For some, it might be CreateSpace only. For others, IngramSpark only.

For most authors, though, ALLi recommends the combination of CreateSpace with IngramSpark as the best solution. For detailed information on how to use CreateSpace and IngramSpark together, see Karen Myer's post on the self-publishing advice blog.

AMAZON VS. APPLE

BY GIACOMO GIAMMATTEO

The answer to the question of who is the best ebook retailer is more complicated than it might appear. Right now, Amazon sells the most books. We all know that. And we all love that.

When asked which ebook retailer is number two to Amazon, Jeremy Greenfield from Digital Book World used to say: "I wish I could give you a clear answer, but after nearly a month of investigation into whether Apple or Barnes & Noble is now the second-largest ebook retailer in the US, this is the best I have: it depends." I think Apple has secured the number two spot.

I hear a lot of complaints about Apple, most of them having to do with how difficult it is to deal with, or how strict it is about accepting material, or how you need a Mac to submit a book. All of that is true, to an extent. But none of that has much to do with the long term.

Even if it took you two weeks to upload a book (and it certainly shouldn't), what's two weeks when your book will be there for years, theoretically forever? And yes, Apple can be strict about what material it accepts, but that's better for indie authors in the long run. As to needing a Mac... I wish it wasn't so, but there are workarounds, from using Mac in Cloud, to using one of the aggregators, like Smashwords or Draft2Digital or PublishDrive or

StreetLib, that distribute your book to lots of retail outlets, including iBooks.

COMPARING APPLE AND AMAZON

Feature	Amazon	Apple
Categories	2	3
Commissions 0.99-2.98	35	70
Commissions 2.99-9.99	70	70
Commissions 10.00+	35	70
Commissions int'l (Brazil, Mexico, Japan, India if not in Select)	35	70
Coupons	✗	✓
Delivery charges	$0.15 per megabyte	up to 2GB free
Exclusivity	required for some benefits	✗
File type	MOBI	EPUB
Free books w/ Select	5 days per quarter	anytime
Free books w/o Select	✗	anytime
Payment terms	60 days	32 days
Price matching enforced	✓	✗
Pricing internationally	some control	complete control
Reach globally	12 territories	51 countries

Categories

Amazon lets authors select two categories for books, although it does restrict some of the categories and won't let you choose them. Apple allows you to select three categories with no restrictions.

Commissions

Notice I said commissions. Technically, these are not royalties but that's a discussion for another time. The payment process is complicated here, on Amazon's side. The chart lists it but here are the details and some additional information.

Amazon

If your book is priced between $0.99 and $2.98, you are paid a 35 percent commission. If it is priced between $2.99 and $9.99, you are paid 70 percent.

If it is priced at $10 or more, you are paid 35 percent.

If you are not in Select (Amazon's exclusive program) you will be paid 35 percent in the following countries: Brazil, India, Japan, and Mexico.

If that wasn't complicated enough, Amazon also charges a delivery fee if your book falls into the 70 percent commission range.

Apple

You receive 70 percent no matter what price or where it's sold.

Before Apple entered the scene, Amazon paid indie authors 35 percent across the board. It wasn't until it became obvious that Apple was coming out with an iPad that Amazon said, "Holy shit, I better pay these guys more." Those are my (Jim's) words, by the way, not Amazon's, but you get the gist.

So it raised the royalties to 70 percent, which was no coincidence, given that it was the percentage Apple was paying musicians and app developers.

Coupons

Apple provides coupons to give out to customers, bloggers, and reviewers. It's a nice touch and easy to use. Amazon does not.

Delivery Charges

This is one of those things that, when first looked at, seems like nothing, but the more you look, the more you see.

My charges for normal mystery books average $0.10–0.12 per book. On a book priced at $2.99, that reduces your earnings from $2.10 to about $2.00. That represents an effective cut of about 4 percent. So in reality, you're getting 66 percent instead of 70 percent.

The actual charges amount to $0.15 per megabyte. This could get serious if you have a 10MB file and are selling your book for $4.99. Instead of receiving $3.50, you'd get $2.00. That's taking your commission from 70 percent to 40 percent. A huge cut in commissions.

This is so important that I want to spend a moment on it. If you're a typical novelist and your book is primarily text, it won't affect you much. Maybe the 3–4 percent I cited above. However, if you produce cookbooks, illustrated books, nonfiction books heavy with charts, tables, graphs, and images—then these delivery charges mean a lot.

Take a look at this example.

Megabytes	Cost of book	Apple pay	Amazon pay	Apple %	Amazon %
1MB	$4.99	$3.50	$3.35	70%	67%
5MB	$4.99	$3.50	$2.75	70%	55%
10MB	$4.99	$3.50	$2.00	70%	40%

Before you go thinking "A 10MB file is a lot...", consider that many of the cookbooks run from 20–50MB or more. The *Complete Cooking For Two Cookbook* weighs in at a whopping 90MB! Of course, at that size it has to be priced much higher, so it falls into the 35 percent commission range, which means Amazon doesn't charge a delivery fee—but Amazon now keeps 65 percent of sales.

This book lists at a Kindle price of $29.95, which means Amazon rakes in $19.47 per book! If an indie author produced this book, they would only receive $10.48 per book.

One thing to note before we move on: if you had that same cookbook on Apple and priced it at $29.95, your commission would be $20.96.

Note: Amazon only charges you if you are in the 70 percent commission plan.

Exclusivity

Amazon demands exclusivity if you want to participate in the Lending Library, Kindle Unlimited, or Kindle Select, which allows you to give books away free for five days per quarter. Select also pays equal commissions in Brazil, India, Japan, and Mexico.

Apple has no exclusivity.

File Types

Amazon uses MOBI files, and Apple uses EPUB.

Free Books

As noted above, with Amazon you must be in the Select program in order to give away books for free, and even then it's limited to five days per quarter.

With Apple, you can give books free at any time.

Payment Terms

Amazon pays 60 days after the end of each month, while Apple pays 32 days after the end of each month.

Price Matching

Amazon insists on having the lowest price, no matter where your book is sold. It will typically price match if it finds the book at a lower price elsewhere, but can take other actions, such as removing your book from KDP.

Apple has no such requirements.

This is a big concern for me. I don't want anyone dictating the price I set for my books. Suppose I want to offer Apple readers a special deal on the anniversary of the launch of the iPad, or do the same for NOOK readers when a new e-reader comes out. The problem is that Amazon won't allow it.

Pricing Internationally

With Amazon, there is some control over how you price your books on the international front, but with Apple there is complete control. This can be a big factor if your strategy is to use price to break into a new market. With Apple you have 51 countries where you can adjust price individually, and even put the price in the local currency.

Territory Pricing

If you don't immediately grasp the significance of territory pricing, let me provide some detail. One of the biggest problems with selling internationally is the high cost of books in other countries related to the cost of books in the US. We might be able to sell a solid mystery or fantasy for $5.99, but take that price to Mexico, Brazil, or India, and your book will likely sit on the virtual shelf forever.

We have had the ability to manage prices individually as long as we went direct to the retailer. As an example, on Apple's iBooks I price differently for many of the 51 countries it offers. So I sell for $5.99 in the US, $3.99 in the UK, and $0.99 in many countries like India, Japan, Mexico, etc. (You can also set prices according to local currency, which makes it nicer, too.)

Here's a quick chart to show you how you could set prices.

Currency	Price
US dollar	$5.99
UK pound sterling	£1.99
Brazilian real	R$.99
Mexican peso	$4.99
Euro	€2.99
Chinese yuan	¥12.99

The currency shown above might not mean much to you if you're not familiar with the rates, but the table below shows what it would look like if you simply let an app automatically adjust price to other currency (based on a $5.99 US price).

Currency	Price
US Dollar	$5.99
UK pound sterling	£3.93
Brazilian real	R$15.57
Mexican peso	$92.00
Euro	€4.85
Chinese yuan	¥36.95

As you can see, this pricing strategy is offering discounts to other countries and offering them in the countries' own currency. And don't forget that Amazon often charges a surcharge of up to $2.00 per book or more in some countries, making our books unaffordable.

Global Reach

With Amazon you can sell your book in 12 different territories. Apple offers 51 countries.

Sales Reporting

Amazon is updated every few hours. Apple is updated daily.

Scheduling Promotions

Amazon allows you to schedule Countdown promotions if you're in Select. Apple allows you to schedule promotions any time for various countries.

Uploading

Amazon is very easy. You can upload your file in minutes. Apple is much more time-consuming, and you need access to a Mac. This is a big drawback for Apple, and a feature I wish it would change.

MY PREDICTIONS

I believe that Apple will continue to increase market share for iBooks worldwide in the coming years. I think people have underestimated the impact of two simple things regarding iBook sales:

- Apple pre-installing iBooks on all devices running the newer iOS.
- The new, bigger phones.

Many younger people have now switched from reading on a Kindle app to reading almost exclusively on their phones. The vast majority of Kindle readers don't actually own a Kindle; they read Kindle books on other devices. And Apple has hundreds of millions of devices in use. A lot of the new iPhone purchases are by people new to Apple, and they are coming into the Apple ecosystem with iBooks preinstalled, so if they want to read books, it's not a stretch to think they're more likely to opt for iBooks.

Combine that with the fact that a lot of authors are finally recognizing that Apple is worth considering as a retail channel, and you have the makings of a shift in the market. A larger selection of books/authors draws more readers, and more readers draw even more authors. All in all, watch the Apple space and make sure you're there.

THREE BOOK AGGREGATORS

W e cover a lot of aggregators in the Reviews section, and we document the pros and cons of each service. We've chosen three for more detailed analysis, to point up the things to watch out for when making your own assessments.

- BookBaby
- Smashwords
- Draft2Digital

As well as these, aggregators of note include PublishDrive, StreetLib and Smashwords, though SW's interface is now looking very dated.

BOOKBABY

During the past few months, BookBaby has added several new channels and beefed up its services. I spent about an hour on the phone with Steven Spatz, BookBaby's president, and I also took time to check out the new features of the site and communicated with some existing customers via email. I've included results below.

The lists and chart below outline BookBaby's services. We're only covering ebook distribution, but I wanted you to know what other options it has:

- Ebook publishing and conversion
- Ebook distribution
- Bookshop
- Ebook cover design
- BookPromo
- Custom-printed books
- Website hosting for authors
- Editing services
- Book scanning services
- Ebook press releases.

And just so everyone knows—I use BookBaby as one of my distributors.

Factors for Consideration

- Cost
- Ease of upload
- Conversion quality
- Conversion costs
- Sales reporting
- Payments
- Channels
- Royalties
- Change costs
- Speed of changes
- Preorders
- Customer service
- ISBNs.

Cost: BookBaby switched to a premium service only model in 2014. The cost is $299, but with no yearly fees afterward.

Ease of upload: The BookBaby site is very easy to use. It took me less than ten minutes to upload a book.

Conversion quality and cost: BookBaby's new premium service includes conversion and provides a few other benefits as well.

Sales reporting: Sales reporting is straightforward and easy to use.

Payments: Payments are made monthly through direct deposit, PayPal, or check.

Channels: BookBaby has great reach and will get your books into the following channels:

- Amazon
- B&N
- Apple
- Kobo
- Copia
- Ebsco
- ePubDirect
- Gardners
- Baker & Taylor
- e-Sentral
- Scribd
- Storytel
- Ciando ebooks.

Royalties: See the chart for details.

Content changes: "For spelling and/or minor grammar fixes for your previously submitted ebook, please contact us with the changes you would like to make. You may make multiple changes in a single set of corrections. Includes reconversion and redelivery to all ebook retailers."

- $50: 1–10 changes

- $75: 11–25 changes
- $100: 26–50 changes
- $150 per hour: 51+ changes
- Pricing and metadata changes: Free.

Speed of changes: BookBaby seems to be behind in the speed of processing changes. I'm saying this not from personal experience, but from talking to half a dozen people who related their experience to me. If you have a different example, please let me know.

Preorders: BookBaby does not offer preorders at this time.

Customer service: Customer service by email or phone.

ISBNs: BookBaby will sell you an ISBN for $19.

Extras: BookBaby has put together several unique offerings for authors and provides them free. A few are worth taking a closer look.

Bookshop: This is a chance to sell your book direct to customers. You can check out the details at bookbaby.com/bookshop/.

BookPromo™: This is a free bundle of promotional services to help BookBaby authors spread the word about their new books. The BookPromo™ bundle includes guaranteed book reviews, promotion opportunities, discounts on PR and book trailers, and much more.

What's included:

- Ebook discovery placements with Goodreads and Noise Trade
- Guaranteed book reviews with Readers' Favorite and Story Cartel
- Promotion through PR Newswire, Author Marketing Club, and WriterCube
- Discounts for PR and book trailers
- Exclusive guide: Ultimate Social Media Marketing for Authors.

I've tried several of these services and have been pleased with the results. During my discussion with Steven Spatz he talked at length about the BookBaby philosophy and how they are working toward helping authors achieve their goals. To that end, BookBaby is working on quite a few new options that will help. Keep an eye open for new developments.

An Analysis of BookBaby

Change can be good or bad, but the one constant is it always seems to confuse people. With that said, let's take a look at BookBaby's new distribution options.

Channel	Royalty	Available Elsewhere
Amazon	70%	(direct)
Apple	70%	60%
B&T	60%	50%
B&N	50%	60%
Ciando	60%	✗
Copia	70%	✗
Ebsco	70%	✗
EpubDirect	50–60%	✗
e-Sentral	75%	60%
Flipkart	60%	60%
Gardners	50%	✗
Kobo*	70%	60%
OverDrive	50%	50%
Oyster	70%	60%
Page Pusher	70%	60%
Scribd	70%	60%

The Bottom Line

I think BookBaby offers a lot to authors. It has a few unique channels and a couple of interesting and useful extra services that are free. My biggest problem with the service is that it still charges for content changes.

I'll admit this is a pet peeve of mine, and some of you might not mind it. But once you have ten books or more for sale, and you decide you want to make a change to your back matter, or you want to add links to a new book in each of your past books, or if you simply want to change prices, you'll face quite a few charges.

When that happens, you will mind.

SMASHWORDS

Mark Coker, CEO of Smashwords, was a pioneer in the ebook distribution business, and he continues to innovate and provide great new services for indie authors. In the past year, Smashwords has broken new ground with the addition of channels like Scribd (a subscription service), OverDrive (libraries), and Txtr, a great addition to the international retail market.

Smashwords also introduced daily sales reporting for Apple, B&N, and Kobo, and greatly improved the response time for publishing new books or making changes to existing ones.

Factors for Consideration

- Cost
- Ease of upload
- Conversion quality
- Conversion costs
- Sales reporting
- Payments
- Channels
- Royalties
- Change costs
- Speed of changes
- Preorders
- Customer service
- ISBNs.

Cost: Using Smashwords is free. No upfront costs, which shows that the company supports the authors. Its motivation is to help authors sell books. Just like with Draft2Digital, the only way Smashwords makes money is for you to sell books. As far as I'm concerned, this is the way it should be.

Ease of upload: I have never used the Meatgrinder for file conversion. But I did upload a finished EPUB and the process was simple. It took me less than ten minutes and I experienced no glitches or rejections of the files. (Smashwords recently announced that the wording on the copyright page doesn't need to show Smashwords as the publisher any more, which should make it even easier to upload files.)

Conversion quality and cost: I don't use conversion tools or software, and as I stated, I didn't try the Meatgrinder, but for anyone who does use it, it is free of charge, and Smashwords provides a style guide to help you through the conversion.

Sales reporting: Sales reporting is daily for Apple, B&N, and Kobo.

Payments: Payments are quarterly.

Channels: As far as distribution reach, Smashwords leads the pack.

- Amazon (limited)
- Apple iBooks
- Barnes & Noble
- Baker & Taylor
- Baker & Taylor Axis
- Kobo
- Library Direct
- Page Foundry
- OverDrive
- Scribd
- Smashwords online store
- Txtr.

Royalties: Royalties are 85 percent of net as a rule. Keep in mind that "net" can mean different things for different aggregators.

Royalties for the other channels are mostly 60 percent, with a few at 50 percent.

See the chart on ebook distributors for specifics.

Change costs: This is one of my pet peeves. I admit, it drives me crazy that most of the aggregators charge ridiculous amounts for authors to make changes to their files, and some charge even to change prices. Smashwords offers changes for free.

Speed of changes: Smashwords continues to push for improvement in this area. It uploads changes hourly to distributors. Apple and Kobo normally show changes within hours. B&N can take up to a day or so, depending on the time of day changes are submitted. Scribd is the fastest, with changes usually taking place within the hour.

Preorders: Smashwords offers preorders to Apple, B&N, and Kobo, and offers them both with and without assets. What that means is that even if your book isn't quite ready, you can list it for preorder while you finish it. This is a huge benefit, and not to be taken lightly.

Customer service: Customer service has taken hits in the past, but it has improved steadily and I consider it good. I have had occasion to use the customer service for several issues and always received a prompt and courteous response.

ISBNs: Smashwords offers free ISBNs, although I still recommend authors get their own ISBNs.

The Bottom Line

When you go to evaluate a distribution partner, I think you have to ask yourself what is most important.

For me, I want a distributor with the best reach, and who negotiates the best deals. I want to maximize earnings. I want to know I can trust that distributor to be around next month and next year, and I want to know I can trust it to have my best interests as part of its philosophy.

Smashwords fits the bill in all of those areas.

DRAFT2DIGITAL

Draft2Digital was conceived and founded by Aaron Pogue, a self-published author with years of formatting and document design experience. He recognized a need for good digital conversion combined with strong distribution, so he recruited a few friends with IT, finance, and business acumen and Draft2Digital was formed.

From the beginning, the philosophy was simple—this would be a company run by authors, for authors.

You might have noticed that I'm big on "intent." I believe that when it comes to selecting a self-publishing partner one of the most important things to look for is how the provider's interest aligns with your goals.

Cost: This one is easy. Using Draft2Digital is free. No upfront costs, which is how I like it. This tells me the provider supports the authors. Its motivation is to help authors sell books. Why? Because the only way Draft2Digital makes money is for you to sell books. As far as I'm concerned, this is the way it should be.

Ease of upload: I have to admit, Draft2Digital shone in this area. The process was simple and intuitive. I tested it out and it took me less than ten minutes to sign up for the service and upload a Word file.

Conversion quality and cost: I don't use conversion tools or software. I pay a third party to convert my books into digital and print format, so this was a first for me. I uploaded a Word file of my latest book to see how it worked. The process was fairly straightforward. I ran into a few hiccups with chapter headings and font styles, but after a short learning curve, it converted the file smoothly. I tested it on EPUB and MOBI and PDF. The EPUB and MOBI files were pretty damn good. The PDF looked good, but I haven't tested it yet with CreateSpace to see how it looks as an actual book.

I'll have to say that the conversions I do with Scrivener (for my beta readers) came out better than Draft2Digital's conversion, but—and this is a big but—Draft2Digital is offering this free, and I'm not one to complain about free things. For the price, the conversion gets an A.

Sales reporting: Sales reporting is daily, with the exception of Scribd. I am seeing this more often with many of the progressive aggregators. Smashwords recently went to daily sales reporting on the primary channels also. As the ebook market continues to grow globally and be integrated, I think we'll see daily reporting with almost all channels.

Payments: Payments are monthly and authors can opt for PayPal ($10 minimum), check ($25 minimum), or direct deposit for both domestic and international.

Channels: Draft2Digital doesn't have the reach of some of the bigger aggregators, but it is aggressively pursuing new channels. Currently it has B&N, Apple, Kobo, Page Foundry, and Scribd. It is close to finalizing deals with Google, and is talking with OverDrive, and is in active negotiations with several other retailers, including Ingram, Omnilit, and Tolino.

In addition to the ebook channels, Draft2Digital offers distribution through CreateSpace for print books. Right now it is only set up to do 8.5x5.5 but it is working on other sizes.

Royalties: Royalties are 85 percent of net. I always like to get specific on "net" as it can be quite different between aggregators. For Apple it is almost always standard. Apple pays everyone 70 percent, which means Draft2Digital pays 85 percent of that, or 60 percent of list price. B&N seems to be the one with big differences. Some of the aggregators, even the ones who claim to pay 100 percent of net, only pay 50 percent for B&N. Draft2Digital pays 60 percent, and that's even at the lower prices. So if you sell your book for $1.99 or $0.99, with Draft2Digital you earn 60 percent. If you go direct you only earn 40 percent.

Change costs: Draft2Digital offers changes for free.

I'll tell you why this is huge. Many indie authors, being inexperienced, make mistakes. Maybe they didn't hire a good copy-editor or proofreader. For whatever reason, they publish a book and discover later that it has mistakes. Now they are faced with fixing those mistakes and uploading it again. If they have to pay for the changes, that's double punishment.

Indie authors also experiment with prices. If you have to pay to change prices... well, that's ridiculous. Draft2Digital makes sure you can change what you need to without a penalty.

Speed of changes: Draft2Digital shines in this department also. It uploads changes hourly to distributors. Apple and Kobo normally show changes within hours. B&N can take up to a day or so, depending on the time of day changes are submitted. Scribd is the fastest, with changes usually taking place within the hour.

Preorders: Draft2Digital offers preorders to Apple, B&N, and Kobo, and offers them both with and without assets. What that means is that even if your book isn't quite ready, you can list it for preorder while you finish it. This is a huge benefit, and not to be taken lightly.

Customer service: Customer service is supposedly good. I can only say supposedly because I have never used it, not being a customer. But the people I've spoken to say they've had good experiences.

ISBNs: Draft2Digital offers free ISBNs, although I still recommend authors get their own ISBNs.

Extra services: Draft2Digital offers universal links, an audiobooks option and more. It is constantly innovating and upgrading.

The Bottom Line

Draft2Digital is author focused and friendly. It develops its programs and policies with the author in mind. This is the kind of place you want to do business with. It doesn't have a lot of extra services where it is looking to you for purchases. It is only concerned about helping authors sell books. If you sell books—it makes money.

Draft2Digital Commended by ALLi's Author Service Award

Orna Ross presented the award to Draft2Digital at the First Word Day, dedicated to international sales, at the NINC Conference 2015.

PART X

SERVICE RATINGS

ABOUT ALLI'S SERVICE RATINGS

The primary purpose of the ALLi Service Ratings is to separate reputable self-publishing services from the rogue operators who overpromise, overcharge, underdeliver, or in any way exploit authors.

ALLi is also willing to work with any service that wants to improve its offerings and bring them in line with our recommendations for current best practice for author services.

Contact the Watchdog Desk at any time if you would like to inform us about a service or discuss a rating.

Service providers are listed in alphabetical order for easy lookup, and are assigned one of four possible ratings:

PARTNER MEMBER
Services that have been carefully vetted and which align with ALLi's Code of Standards.

RECOMMENDED
Services that behave ethically and professionally, with pricing and value in line with industry norms.

CAUTION

Services that do not align with one or more aspects of the ALLi Code of Standards. These services should be avoided.

Watchdog Advisory

Services that have given rise to consistent complaints, and which may have been subject to legal action.

The ratings below are the opinions of the ALLi Watchdog Desk, based on careful appraisals of pricing and value, quality of service, contract rights, transparency, accountability, and customer satisfaction.

ALLi's ratings are updated frequently. Please see our online ratings (bit.ly/ALLI_Ratings) for the most current information. If you would like to suggest a service for evaluation or share your experiences with a service provider, please contact us online at (bit.ly/ALLI_Watchdog).

SELF-PUBLISHING SERVICE RATINGS

L istings are in alphabetical order. To avoid driving traffic to substandard services, we do not generally give a website address for those rated as Caution or Watchdog Advisory.

Abbott Press WATCHDOG ADVISORY
Author Solutions imprint

Adirondack Editing PARTNER MEMBER
adirondackediting.com

AIA Editing and Publishing PARTNER MEMBER
aiapublishing.com

Alison's Editing Service PARTNER MEMBER
alisonjack-editor.co.uk

Alliant Press WATCHDOG ADVISORY
Partnership between Alliant University and vanity press Author Solutions

Amazon (CreateSpace) PARTNER MEMBER
createspace.com
Read our comparison with **IngramSpark** in Part Nine, and how to
leverage the unique strengths of both services. Consult:
selfpublishingadvice.org/watchdog-ingram-spark-vs-createspace-
for-self-publishing-print-books, selfpublishingadvice.org/how-to-
use-createspace-and-ingram-spark-together

Amazon (KDP) PARTNER MEMBER
kdp.amazon.com
Read our comparison of publishing platforms in Part Nine, **Amazon
vs. Apple**. For more information, consult:
selfpublishingadvice.org/alli-watchdog-amazon-vs-apple

America Star Books WATCHDOG ADVISORY
Formerly PublishAmerica, a vanity press with a staggering number of
complaints. For more information, consult:
consumeraffairs.com/misc/publish-america.html

Amie McCracken PARTNER MEMBER
amiemccracken.com

Amolibros PARTNER MEMBER
amolibros-selfpublishing.co.uk

Angela McPherson PARTNER MEMBER

Anthemion Software PARTNER MEMBER
anthemion.co.uk

Apple (iBooks) RECOMMENDED
apple.com
Read our comparison of publishing platforms in Amazon vs. Apple.
For more information, consult: selfpublishingadvice.org/alli-
watchdog-amazon-vs-apple

Archway Publishing WATCHDOG ADVISORY
Simon & Schuster imprint outsourced to Author Solutions. For more information, consult: selfpublishingadvice.org/alli-watchdog-latest-on-author-solutions

Areo Books PARTNER MEMBER
areobooks.com

AtlasBooks CAUTION
A division of Bookmasters

Austin Macauley WATCHDOG ADVISORY

Author Accelerator PARTNER MEMBER
authoraccelerator.com

Author Connections PARTNER MEMBER
authorconnections.com

Author Design Studio PARTNER MEMBER
authordesignstudio.com

AuthorHouse WATCHDOG ADVISORY
Author Solutions imprint. For more information, consult: selfpublishingadvice.org/alli-watchdog-latest-on-author-solutions

AuthorHouse UK WATCHDOG ADVISORY
Author Solutions imprint. For more information, consult: selfpublishingadvice.org/alli-watchdog-latest-on-author-solutions

Author Learning Center CAUTION
Owned by Author Solutions; be extremely wary of any paid services. For more information, consult: selfpublishingadvice.org/alli-watchdog-latest-on-author-solutions

Author Marketing Club PARTNER MEMBER
authormarketingclub.com

Author Marketing Experts PARTNER MEMBER
amarketingexpert.com

Authoright CAUTION

Author Solutions WATCHDOG ADVISORY
Author Solutions has been the subject of multiple class-action
lawsuits in the US. For more information, consult:
selfpublishingadvice.org/alli-watchdog-latest-on-author-solutions

Author's Republic PARTNER MEMBER
authorsrepublic.com

Averill Buchanan PARTNER MEMBER
averillbuchanan.com

Bakerview Consulting RECOMMENDED
bakerviewconsulting.com

Balboa Press WATCHDOG ADVISORY
Hay House imprint outsourced to Author Solutions. For more
information, consult: selfpublishingadvice.org/alli-watchdog-latest-
on-author-solutions

Balboa Press UK WATCHDOG ADVISORY
Hay House imprint outsourced to Author Solutions. For more
information, consult: selfpublishingadvice.org/alli-watchdog-latest-
on-author-solutions

BAM! Publish (Books-A-Million) CAUTION

Barbara Bauer Literary Agency WATCHDOG ADVISORY

Bargain Booksy RECOMMENDED
bargainbooksy.com
See our evaluation of ebook discovery services for more information:
selfpublishingadvice.org/ebook-discovery-book-promo-services-
review

BB EBooks PARTNER MEMBER
bbebooksthailand.com

Berge Design PARTNER MEMBER
bergedesign.com

Better Scribe PARTNER MEMBER
betterscribe.com

Blank Slate Communications PARTNER MEMBER
blankslatecommunications.com

Blissetts PARTNER MEMBER
blissetts.com

Bluebird Consulting PARTNER MEMBER
bluebird-consulting.com

BlueInk Review PARTNER MEMBER
blueinkreview.com

BookBaby PARTNER MEMBER
bookbaby.com
Watchdog review available. See: selfpublishingadvice.org/allis-self-
publishing-watchdog-bookbaby

BookBub RECOMMENDED
bookbub.com
See our evaluation of ebook discovery services for more information:

selfpublishingadvice.org/ebook-discovery-book-promo-services-review

Book Country CAUTION
Book Country is owned by Author Solutions; while the community itself is innocuous, be extremely wary of any paid services

Book Cover Cafe PARTNER MEMBER
bookcovercafe.com

Book Create Service PARTNER MEMBER
bookcreateservice.com

BookGarage PARTNER MEMBER
bookgarage.com

Bookmasters CAUTION
Also operates as AtlasBooks

Bookprinting.com CAUTION
An alias of Hillcrest Media Group

BookPublishing.com (Jenkins Group) CAUTION

BooksGoSocial PARTNER MEMBER
booksgosocial.com

BooksOnline.directory WATCHDOG ADVISORY
Also operates ArtistsGallery.directory and
CreativeDesignersWriters.com

Booktango WATCHDOG ADVISORY
Author Solutions imprint. For more information, consult:
selfpublishingadvice.org/alli-watchdog-latest-on-author-solutions

Bookupy CAUTION

Breezeway Books CAUTION

Caliburn Press CAUTION

Chanticleer Book Reviews PARTNER MEMBER
chantireviews.com

Claus Lund Rosenkilde PARTNER MEMBER
rbforlag.dk
A new service that meets ALLi's Code of Standards. New Partner
Members remain under review during their first year of operation.

Clays PARTNER MEMBER
clays.co.uk

Clink Street Publishing CAUTION
The "publishing" arm of Authoright

Clio Editing Service PARTNER MEMBER
clioediting.com

Coinlea Services PARTNER MEMBER
coinlea.co.uk

Completely Novel PARTNER MEMBER
completelynovel.com

CreateSpace PARTNER MEMBER
createspace.com
Read our comparison of **IngramSpark vs. CreateSpace** in Part Nine,
and learn how you can leverage the unique strengths of both services.
For more information, consult: selfpublishingadvice.org/watchdog-
ingram-spark-vs-createspace-for-self-publishing-print-books,

selfpublishingadvice.org/how-to-use-createspace-and-ingram-spark-together

CreateThinkDo PARTNER MEMBER
createthinkdo.com

CreativeDesignersWriters.com WATCHDOG ADVISORY
Also operates ArtistsGallery.directory and BooksOnline.directory

Crystalline Noble WATCHDOG ADVISORY
Also operates BooksOnline.directory, ArtistsGallery.directory, and CreativeDesignersWriters.com

Daisy Editorial PARTNER MEMBER
daisyeditorial.co.uk

Damonza.com PARTNER MEMBER
damonza.com

Daniel Goldsmith Associates PARTNER MEMBER
danielgoldsmith.co.uk

DCP CAUTION
Operates msbuyer.com, a manuscript purchasing operation; actual company name and location are unknown, but operates under the alias "DCP"

Dead Birds PARTNER MEMBER
deadbirds.net

Design for Writers PARTNER MEMBER
designforwriters.com

Dog Ear Publishing CAUTION

Draft2Digital Partner Member
draft2digital.com
In-depth review available. For more information, consult:
selfpublishingadvice.org/draft2digital

eBook Dynasty Partner Member
ebookdynasty.net

Ebook Launch Partner Member
ebooklaunch.com

eBookPartnership Partner Member
ebookpartnership.com

eBooksAreForever Recommended
ebooksareforever.com
Review available. For more information, consult:
selfpublishingadvice.org/ebook-library-services-for-authors

Ebooks Cover Design Partner Member
ebookscoversdesign.com

Editorial.ie Partner Member
editorial.ie

Ellie Donovan PR Partner Member
ellydonovan.co.uk

Ellie Stevenson Partner Member
elliestevenson.wordpress.com

FastPencil Caution

FindPublishingHelp.com Caution

Fingerpress Ltd PARTNER MEMBER
fingerpress.com

Formatting Experts PARTNER MEMBER
formattingexperts.com

FreeBooksy RECOMMENDED
freebooksy.com
See our evaluation of ebook discovery services for more information:
selfpublishingadvice.org/ebook-discovery-book-promo-services-review

Fussy Librarian RECOMMENDED
thefussylibrarian.com
See our evaluation of ebook discovery services for more information:
selfpublishingadvice.org/ebook-discovery-book-promo-services-review

GABAL Global Editions WATCHDOG ADVISORY
GABAL imprint outsourced to Author Solutions. See:
selfpublishingadvice.org/alli-watchdog-latest-on-author-solutions

Get Published! LLC WATCHDOG ADVISORY
Author Solutions parent company. See:
selfpublishingadvice.org/alli-watchdog-latest-on-author-solutions

Girl Friday Productions PARTNER MEMBER
girlfridayproductions.com

Green Ivy Publishing CAUTION

Guaranteed Author (Leigh St. John) CAUTION

Gunboss Books PARTNER MEMBER
gunboss.com

Heddon Publishing PARTNER MEMBER
heddonpublishing.com

Helen Baggott PARTNER MEMBER
helenbaggott.co.uk

Hillcrest Media Group / Hillcrest Publishing Group CAUTION

Hobthross Ltd PARTNER MEMBER
hobthross.com/index.html

Hot Pink Publishing (Carla Wynn Hall) CAUTION

I_AM Self-Publishing PARTNER MEMBER
iamselfpublishing.com

iBooks (Apple) RECOMMENDED
apple.com
Read our comparison of publishing platforms in Amazon vs. Apple:
selfpublishingadvice.org/alli-watchdog-amazon-vs-apple

Independent Ink PARTNER MEMBER
independentink.com.au

Indie Authors World PARTNER MEMBER
indieauthorsworld.com

IndieBookLauncher PARTNER MEMBER
indiebooklauncher.com

Indie Writer Support WATCHDOG ADVISORY
Also operates ParaDon Books, ReadersBooks.info

Infinity Publishing CAUTION

IngramSpark PARTNER MEMBER
ingramspark.com
Read our comparison of IngramSpark vs. CreateSpace, and learn how
you can leverage the strengths of each:
selfpublishingadvice.org/watchdog-ingram-spark-vs-createspace-
for-self-publishing-print-books,
selfpublishingadvice.org/how-to-use-createspace-and-ingram-spark-
together

Inkitt CAUTION

Inkshares CAUTION

Inkslinger Editing PARTNER MEMBER
inkslingerediting.com

Inkwater CAUTION

IPR License PARTNER MEMBER
iprlicense.com

iUniverse WATCHDOG ADVISORY
Author Solutions imprint. For more information, consult:
selfpublishingadvice.org/alli-watchdog-latest-on-author-solutions

JD Smith Design PARTNER MEMBER
jdsmith-design.com

Jenkins Group CAUTION

Jessica Bell PARTNER MEMBER
jessicabellauthor.com/book-cover-design-services.html

Katharine D'Souza PARTNER MEMBER
katharinedsouza.co.uk

Kindle Direct Publishing (KDP, Amazon) Partner Member
kdp.amazon.com
Read our comparison of publishing platforms in Amazon vs. Apple:
selfpublishingadvice.org/alli-watchdog-amazon-vs-apple

Kirkus / Kirkus Indie Recommended
kirkusreviews.com/indie-reviews
Although Kirkus behaves ethically, we have concerns about some
aspects of its service; see: selfpublishingadvice.org/publishing-is-a-
kirkus-review-worth-the-price

Kobo Partner Member
kobo.com/writinglife

KT Editing (Katherine Trail) Partner Member
ktediting.com

Language + Literary Translations Partner Member
literarytranslations.us

Lateral Action (Marc McGuinness) Partner Member
lateralaction.com

Lawston Design Partner Member
lawstondesign.com

Library Cat Editing Services Partner Member
catrionatroth.blogspot.com/p/editing-services.html

LifeRich Publishing Watchdog Advisory
Reader's Digest imprint outsourced to Author Solutions. See:
selfpublishingadvice.org/alli-watchdog-latest-on-author-solutions

ListenUp Indie Partner Member
listenupindie.pub

Llumina Press CAUTION

Lucy Ridout Editorial Services PARTNER MEMBER
lucyridout.co.uk

Lulu CAUTION
Review available. See: selfpublishingadvice.org/publishing-allis-new-watchdog-checks-out-lulu

Mark Dawson (Self-Publishing Formula) PARTNER MEMBER
selfpublishingformula.com

Matador Publishing PARTNER MEMBER
troubador.co.uk/matador.asp

megustaescribir WATCHDOG ADVISORY
Owned by Penguin Random House, outsourced to Author Solutions. For more information, consult: selfpublishingadvice.org/alli-watchdog-latest-on-author-solutions

Mill City Press CAUTION

Month9Books (Georgia McBride Media Group) WATCHDOG ADVISORY
Allegations of failure to pay authors, accounting chaos, unprofessional behavior, and at least one lawsuit. For more information, consult: yainterrobang.com/month9books, accrispin.blogspot.com/2016/07/cutting-lists-isnt-new-q-with.html, accrispin.blogspot.com/2016/07/month9books-scales-back-its-list-amid.html

MorainesEdgeBooks.com PARTNER MEMBER
morainesedgebooks.com

More Visual (TheBookCoverDesigners.com) PARTNER MEMBER

thebookcoverdesigners.com

MSBuyer.com CAUTION
Manuscript buyer operating under the initials DCP; actual company name and location are unknown

My Book Cave PARTNER MEMBER
mybookcave.com

NetGalley PARTNER MEMBER
s2.netgalley.com

Nikki Busch Editing PARTNER MEMBER
nikkibuschediting.com/index.html

NOOK Press CAUTION
Review available. See: selfpublishingadvice.org/watchdog-nooks-author-services

Novel Thinking PARTNER MEMBER
novelthinking.co.uk

Oak Tree Publishing CAUTION

Octavo Publishing PARTNER MEMBER
octavopublishing.com

One Stop Fiction PARTNER MEMBER
onestopfiction.com

OodleBooks PARTNER MEMBER
oodlebooks.com

Opprimo Marketing CAUTION

Opuscule PARTNER MEMBER

Outskirts Press CAUTION

OverDrive RECOMMENDED
company.overdrive.com
Review available. See: selfpublishingadvice.org/ebook-library-
services-for-authors

PageMaster PARTNER MEMBER
pagemaster.ca

Palibrio WATCHDOG ADVISORY
Author Solutions imprint. For more information, consult:
selfpublishingadvice.org/alli-watchdog-latest-on-author-solutions

Palmetto Publishing Group RECOMMENDED
palmettopublishinggroup.com

ParaDon Books WATCHDOG ADVISORY
Also operates Indie Writer Support, ReadersBooks.info. David
Gaughran's experience highlights some of the concerns with this
company and its principal, Korede Abayomi. For more information,
consult: davidgaughran.wordpress.com/2016/01/13/the-one-where-
an-author-steals-text-from-my-book-to-sell-pirated-software

Partridge Africa WATCHDOG ADVISORY
Author Solutions imprint. For more information, consult:
selfpublishingadvice.org/alli-watchdog-latest-on-author-solutions

Partridge India WATCHDOG ADVISORY
Author Solutions imprint. For more information, consult:
selfpublishingadvice.org/alli-watchdog-latest-on-author-solutions

Partridge Singapore WATCHDOG ADVISORY

Author Solutions imprint. For more information, consult:
selfpublishingadvice.org/alli-watchdog-latest-on-author-solutions

Pauline Montagna Manuscript Services PARTNER MEMBER
paulinemontagna.com.au

Payhip PARTNER MEMBER
payhip.com

Pegasus Elliot Mackenzie Publishers WATCHDOG ADVISORY

PeopleSpeak (Sharon Goldinger) PARTNER MEMBER
detailsplease.com/peoplespeak

Perfect the Word PARTNER MEMBER
perfecttheword.co.uk

Peters Fraser and Dunlop PARTNER MEMBER
petersfraserdunlop.com

PickFu PARTNER MEMBER
pickfu.com

Pix Bee Design PARTNER MEMBER
pixbeedesign.com

PJ Boox PARTNER MEMBER
pjboox.com

ProofProfessor (Matt Rance) WATCHDOG ADVISORY

PublishDrive PARTNER MEMBER
publishdrive.com

Published.com CAUTION

Publish Green CAUTION

Raider Publishing WATCHDOG ADVISORY
Numerous complaints. For more information, consult:
accrispin.blogspot.com/2015/04/warning-raider-publishing-
international.html

Rancho Park Publishing PARTNER MEMBER
ranchopark.com

ReadersBooks.info WATCHDOG ADVISORY
Also operates ParaDon Books, Indie Writer Support

Readers in the Know PARTNER MEMBER
readersintheknow.com/home

Read Out Loud PARTNER MEMBER
readoutloud.in

Reedsy PARTNER MEMBER
reedsy.com

Rethink Press PARTNER MEMBER
rethinkpress.com

Reviewers for Books CAUTION

Robin Ludwig Design (gobookcoverdesign.com) PARTNER MEMBER
gobookcoverdesign.com

Rob Siders (52 Novels) PARTNER MEMBER
52novels.com

Rocket Science Productions / RSP Marketing Services CAUTION
"Phase One" of this vanity press scheme involves a $595 payment for

copyright registration and an ISBN; see **Part Four** to learn more about potentially worthless services marketed to indie authors

Rosenkilde & Bahnhof (Claus Lund Rosenkilde) Partner Member
rbforlag.dk
New service, under review

S & H Publishing Partner Member
sandhbooks.com

Sally Vince Editorial Services Partner Member
editorsal.com

Sarah Kolb-Williams Partner Member
kolbwilliams.com

Scarlett Rugers Book Design Agency Partner Member
scarlettrugers.com

Scotforth Books Partner Member
scotforthbooks.com
Scotforth Books is an imprint of Carnegie Publishing

Scribd Recommended
scribd.com
Scribd has a rocky history with regard to its subscription services, but these customer complaints do not extend to interactions with authors

Seenapse Partner Member
seenapse.it

SELF-e Caution
Review available. See: selfpublishingadvice.org/ebook-library-services-for-authors

Self-Publishing Formula (Mark Dawson) PARTNER MEMBER
selfpublishingformula.com

Serious Reading CAUTION

Shakspeare Editorial PARTNER MEMBER
shakspeareeditorial.org

SilverWood Books PARTNER MEMBER
silverwoodbooks.co.uk

Smashwords PARTNER MEMBER
smashwords.com

Standoutbooks PARTNER MEMBER
standoutbooks.com

Strategic Book Publishing and Rights Agency (SBPRA, Robert Fletcher) WATCHDOG ADVISORY
SBPRA has been the subject of multiple alerts at Writer Beware, and has been the subject of legal action compelling it to repay $125,000 to authors. For more information, consult:
accrispin.blogspot.com/2014/05/robert-fletcher-of-sbpra-to-pay-author.html, sfwa.org/wp-content/uploads/2014/05/2014-04-15-Judge-Streitfeld-signed-Order-Grant-Pl-M-Enforce-Settle-Agree-.pdf

Sweek.com PARTNER MEMBER
sweek.com

Swift Publishing CAUTION

Swoon Romance (Georgia McBride Media Group) CAUTION
See Month9Books for additional information

Tantrum Books (Georgia McBride Media Group) CAUTION
See Month9Books for additional information

Tate Publishing WATCHDOG ADVISORY
"Thumbs Down" assessment from SFWA. Tate is the subject of at least one lawsuit. Numerous complaints filed with consumer protection agencies. For more information, consult:
sfwa.org/other-resources/for-authors/writer-beware/thumbs-down-publishers,
accrispin.blogspot.com/2016/06/tate-publishing-enterprises-slapped.html

Terry Gilbert-Fellows (Blackheath Dawn) PARTNER MEMBER
blackheathdawn.co.uk

The Book Designer (Joel Friedlander) PARTNER MEMBER
thebookdesigner.com

The Creative Penn (Joanna Penn) PARTNER MEMBER
thecreativepenn.com

The Literary Consultancy PARTNER MEMBER
literaryconsultancy.co.uk

The Pen Factor PARTNER MEMBER
penfactor.com

The Soulful Pen (Carla Wynn Hall) CAUTION

Thomson-Shore RECOMMENDED
thomsonshore.com

Tom Evans, Bookwright PARTNER MEMBER
tomevans.co

Trafford Publishing WATCHDOG ADVISORY
Author Solutions imprint

Upgrade Your Story PARTNER MEMBER
upgradeyourstory.com

Voyage Media PARTNER MEMBER
voyagemedia.com

Wendy Toole Editorial PARTNER MEMBER
wendytooleeditorial.com

WestBow Press WATCHDOG ADVISORY
Thomas Nelson & Zondervan imprint outsourced to Author
Solutions. For more information, consult:
selfpublishingadvice.org/alli-watchdog-latest-on-author-solutions

Whitefox Publishing Services PARTNER MEMBER
wearewhitefox.com

Woman Safe Health PARTNER MEMBER
womansafehealth.com

Wordclay WATCHDOG ADVISORY
Author Solutions imprint

WriteIndia, aka Times of India WATCHDOG ADVISORY
Allegations of contract manipulation. For more information, consult:
accrispin.blogspot.com/2016/07/yet-another-post-on-why-you-
absolutely.html

Writing.ie PARTNER MEMBER
writing.ie

Written Word Media PARTNER MEMBER

writtenwordmedia.com

XinXii Recommended
xinxii.com

Xlibris Watchdog Advisory
Author Solutions imprint. For more information, consult:
selfpublishingadvice.org/alli-watchdog-latest-on-author-solutions

Xlibris AU Watchdog Advisory
Author Solutions imprint. For more information, consult:
selfpublishingadvice.org/alli-watchdog-latest-on-author-solutions

Xlibris NZ Watchdog Advisory
Author Solutions imprint. For more information, consult:
selfpublishingadvice.org/alli-watchdog-latest-on-author-solutions

Xlibris UK Watchdog Advisory
Author Solutions imprint. For more information, consult:
selfpublishingadvice.org/alli-watchdog-latest-on-author-solutions

Xulan Press Caution

York Publishing Services Partner Member
yps-publishing.co.uk

WE ARE HERE TO HELP

ALLi is willing to work with any service that wants to improve its offerings and bring them in line with current best practice for author services.

Please contact the Watchdog Desk at any time if you would like to inform us about a service or discuss a rating.

bit.ly/ALLI_Watchdog

PART XI

APPENDICES

ALLI CODE OF STANDARDS: PARTNERS

P artner Members of ALLi agree to uphold our code of standards.

Integrity

We recognize that Partner Membership of ALLi means our primary aim is to enable authors to effectively publish and sell books. We follow through on all promised services and fully honor all advertisements and publication agreement terms. We never spam, oversell, or harass authors to buy our services or sell a dream to the uninitiated.

Value

We add value to each publication commensurate with the fee charged, relieving authors of key publishing tasks, enhancing readability, design, or discoverability.

Clarity

We make it clear what we can and cannot do for the self-publishing writer and how our service compares with others.

Pricing

Our price quotations are accurate, transparent, and complete. Pricing is in line with market norms.

Partnership

We involve authors in planning and decision-making for key aspects of the publication process, from titles and cover design to sales and marketing strategies.

Service

We are accountable for our work. We keep authors informed each step of the way and provide good customer service and follow-up.

Communication

We provide helpful and timely information to authors at all stages of publication, and beyond, and facilitate authors to get any ancillary information that we cannot provide.

Community

We have a long-term commitment to author-publishing and support the empowerment of self-publishing authors.

FURTHER ADVICE

LLi's Self-Publishing Advice Centre, which includes our self-publishing advice blog, categorizes advice across the seven stages of publishing a book: writing, editorial, design, production, distribution, marketing, and rights. It also has a section on living the indie author life, including advice on time and money and creative inspiration.

SelfPublishingAdvice.org

GLOSSARY

A

abook
Abbreviation of audiobook. *Compare:* pbook and ebook.

acknowledgments
Recognition or honor given to people who have influenced a book or who have made a difference in the life of the author.

ACOS (average cost of sale)
Accumulated total of all costs used to create a product or service, including overheads, fixed and variable costs.

acquisitions board
A group of people who work for a publisher to make decisions about what books to accept for publication.

ACX (Audiobook Creation Exchange)
An Amazon-owned marketplace that matches authors with professional narrators and producers for the creation of audiobooks (abooks).

advance
An upfront payment made by a publisher, as an advance on expected

royalties, in exchange for the rights to publish and sell your book(s) and associated rights.

advance information sheet (AIS)

A short document providing basic book details and information about a book's availability and ordering methods. *Also:* sell sheet.

advance print run

Printing of a book completed before the book's official release date, usually for publicity purposes.

advance review copy (ARC)

A draft of a book sent to beta readers or reviewers prior to publication. *Also:* advance review/reader copy. *Compare:* proof.

aggregator

A service provider that publishes and distributes books to a variety of distributors and retailers. *Compare:* distributor.

algorithm

A process or set of rules used in a calculation; book retailers like Amazon use algorithms to calculate a book's sales ranking.

Amazon Author Central

A free resource that allows you to publish an Author Profile and feature books on Amazon.

Amazon Marketing Services (AMS)

An Amazon program that allows sellers to bid on advertisements displayed alongside search results, product listings, and customer review pages.

Amazon Prime

A subscription service for Amazon customers that offers discounted shipping, access to free entertainment, and other benefits.

Amazon Standard Identification Number (ASIN)

A unique, ten-character identifier for an Amazon product.

appendix

Part of a book that follows a chapter or that comes after all the chapters, with supplemental matter, such as tables or source material.

AskALLi

Alliance of Independent Authors campaign that pledges to answer any self-publishing question that any individual or organization may have.

assisted (self-)publisher
A company that provides book production, distribution, marketing, and other services to self-publishers.

Audible
An Amazon-owned company; the largest audiobook producer and retailer in the US.

audiobook
A recording of a book or magazine being read aloud.

author bio
A brief biography that may include a summary of books written, interests, and achievements.

author brand
A representation of your identity and image that helps your readers connect with you and your books.

author cooperative/collective
A group of authors who work together to leverage the skills of the group in order to advance members' publishing efforts.

author platform
The ability to sell books because of who you are or can reach.

authorpreneur
An author who successfully runs a publishing business.

author–publisher
A professional self-publisher writing for profit.

Authors4Bookstores
Alliance of Independent Authors campaign connecting writers and booksellers, for mutual benefit.

Author Solutions, Inc. (ASI)
A notorious vanity press operating under a variety of imprints.

B

Babelcube
Company that connects authors with translators and internationally distributes translated books.

back matter
The sections of a book following the last chapter. *Also* end matter.
Compare: front matter.

bar code
An image that encodes information into a series of vertical lines; a
book's ISBN encoded in this format.

Bertrams
The second-largest book wholesaler in the UK.

bestseller rank
See: sales rank.

beta reader
A person who provides early feedback or a critique of a book prior to
publication.

big data
An enormous supply of data, and often the analysis of such data.

Big Five
The five largest, New York-based traditional publishers: Hachette,
HarperCollins, Macmillan, Penguin Random House, and Simon &
Schuster. Formerly the "Big Six," until the merger of Penguin and
Random House in 2013.

BISAC
An acronym for Book Industry Standards and Communications.

BISAC codes
The BISAC subject headings list; a standard used to categorize books
based on topical content.

bitcoin
The most popular cryptocurrency, generally deemed the first of its
kind. The open source software comes with an elusive and mysterious
history. Satoshi Nakamoto is the name used by the unknown
person(s) who designed the bitcoin, but no one is really sure who
made it.

bleed
To extend an element that is printed right up to the page edge, such as
an image or background tint, beyond the trim size to allow for
variations in trimming.

blockchain

As part of the implementation of Bitcoin, the first blockchain database was devised to record the cryptocurrency transactions. Blockchain technology operates as a public, verified digital ledger that records transactions as a chain (string) of data, stored on a decentralized network. Information, once entered, can't be altered. Blockchain also has several non-cryptocurrency applications, including smart contracts and the recording of other digital assets.

blog

A regularly updated section on your website; a useful way to help you establish your subject matter expertise and connect with your readers.

blog hop

A list of web links that appears on multiple blogs, allowing readers to hop from one blog to the next in the series. *Also:* link-up.

blog tour

A series of pre-arranged blog posts, usually scheduled during the months just before and after a book launch.

Book2Look

A widget offering samples from your book alongside social links.

BookBaby

An ebook publisher and aggregator.

book block

PDF files that comprise all book content except the cover. *See also:* interior.

book blurb

A short description of a book, often used on the back cover.

BookBub

An ebook discovery service featuring a free daily email that notifies readers of discounted ebooks.

book categories

See: BISAC.

book chainstores

Book outlets that share a brand and central management, usually with standardized business methods and practices, and spread nationwide or worldwide.

book doctoring
See: content editing.

Book Espresso machine
A machine that can print and bind any book as print-on-demand within five minutes.

book fair
An exhibition and convention for publishers, authors, and booksellers.

book review
See: review.

Booksellers Association of Great Britain and Ireland (BA)
The trade association for booksellers.

Books In Print
A catalog, usually digital, primarily for use by bookstores and libraries, listing millions of books with ISBNs; published by Bowker.

book trailer
A video advertisement for a book, much the same as a film trailer.

Bowker
A for-profit corporation that is the sole provider of and registrar for ISBNs in the US.

bricks-and-mortar (brick) bookstore
A physical store; said of a retailer, in contrast to online operations.

C

call to action (CTA)
The part of a marketing message that attempts to persuade a person to perform a desired action.

case bound
A type of binding and the industry term for a book in hardback/hardcover format.

click-through
The process of clicking on a hyperlink or online advertisement to the target destination.

click-through open rate (CTOR)

Metrics used to measure the effectiveness of your email marketing campaigns.

click-through rate (CTR)

The average number of click-throughs per hundred ad impressions, expressed as a percentage.

CMYK

A color model for print books, using cyan (C), magenta (M), yellow (Y), and black (K). *See also:* RGB, greyscale.

codex

A physical book which may be constructed of vellum, papyrus, or similar materials, as well as paper, and handwritten or printed.

collaborative consumption

An economic model based on the sharing, swapping, and renting of services. The "sharing economy" or "collaborative economy" can be seen in platforms like Airbnb or Kickstarter and is growing in fintech (financial technology), through solutions like peer-to-peer lending.

commission (1)

A percentage of book sales paid to the author. Often used interchangeably with royalties.

commission (2)

To order or authorize the production of publications, services or materials.

content editing

Editing with a focus on broad issues such as pacing, character development, veracity, relevance, and structure. *Also:* structural editing, development(al) editing, book doctoring, or manuscript appraisal.

content editor

The person who conducts a content edit.

content marketing

The creation and sharing of useful material like videos, blogs, and social media posts to generate leads for your book.

conversion

The process of putting a manuscript into a digital format suitable for use by a publisher, such as converting a Word document into an EPUB file.

co-op advertising

Advertising whose cost is shared between or among different companies. Such advertising is especially advantageous to smaller companies with limited budgets.

copyediting

Editing with a focus on the detail, such as syntax, grammar, verb tense, word usage, punctuation, and consistency. *Also:* line editing.

copyeditor

The person who conducts a copyedit of your copy (manuscript material).

copyright

The exclusive legal right to publish, perform, or record a literary work, to profit from it, and to authorize others to do the same. *Compare:* license.

cost per click (CPC)

Internet advertising model used to direct traffic to websites, in which an advertiser pays a website owner when their advertisement is clicked. Also used to refer to the cost charged for each click through from the ad to the product. *Also:* pay per click.

cost per impression (CPI)

Also known as pay per impression. Internet advertising model, in which advertisers pay for the number of times an ad is shown on a website, regardless of whether or not it is clicked. *Also:* pay per impression.

co-venture

Undertaking whose costs and responsibilities are shared by more than one company or publisher.

cover design

Aesthetic layout on the covers of a book, usually intended to be attractive or alluring to the eye.

cover spread

The entire cover of a physical book, from the front, including the spine, to the back.

CreateSpace
An Amazon-owned publisher and distributor of self-published print books.

credit line
Line of text that assigns credit to the owner of the copyright of the material it refers to.

critique
See: content editing.

crowd-
A prefix used to denote a collaborative effort by a group.

crowdfunding
Funding a project by raising small donations from many contributors.

crowdsourcing
Gathering information, feedback, or work on a project by requesting input from a large number of contributors.

cryptocurrency
Any digital currency, operating independently of a central bank, using encryption techniques to regulate the generation, verification, and transfer of funds. Using cryptography for regulation and security allows a decentralized system, meaning no central repository or administrator oversees the processes. Instead, it uses a blockchain. There are several kinds of cryptocurrency; three of the best known to date are bitcoin, ethereum, and ripple.

customer acquisition cost (CAC)
Measuring how much money a new customer has cost you.

D

dashboard
An interface, usually web-based, that organizes and displays information on a single screen.

database
A program that allows you to organize your information in an efficient manner on one platform.

dedication

Part of the front matter that dedicates a book to a specific person, place, or thing.

Demy Octavo

A very popular book format, which measures 216 x 138 mm.

developmental editing

See: content editing.

developmental editor

Person who deals with the overall organization of a manuscript rather than with detailed changes such as spelling and punctuation.

digital printing

A method of mass-production printing using toners on a press printing direct from a digital-based image. More suitable for shorter runs and most often used for print-on-demand books. *Compare:* offset printing.

digital wallet

Any electronic device or application that allows electronic transactions, using cryptocurrency or government-based currencies.

discounts

There are two kinds of discounts in publishing: retail discount, when books are offered at a reduced sale price to the reader; and publisher's discount, offered to wholesalers, distributors, and retailers.

discoverability

The process of making something discoverable for consumers.

disintermediation

The removal of intermediaries from a supply chain or cutting out the middleman in a transaction.

distributed ledger

A distributed ledger (also called shared ledger) is a consensus of replicated, shared, and synchronized digital data geographically spread across multiple sites, countries, or institutions where there is no central administrator or centralized data storage.

distributor

A service that makes books available for purchase by bricks-and-mortar or online retailers. *Compare:* aggregator.

DOC, DOCX
Microsoft Word file types.

domain name
A registered alias for an IP address; the most basic URL of a website, e.g. "selfpublishingadvice.org".

DPI (dots per inch)
A measure of the resolution of a graphic file, a computer monitor, or potential printing density.

Draft2Digital
A popular ebook aggregator and publishing service.

dust jacket
A detachable outer cover that protects the book, printed with the cover design. Usually for hardback/hardcover books.

E

ebook
An abbreviation of electronic (digital) book.

editorial review
A professional critic's opinion of a book published online or in a periodical. *See also:* review.

eID/electronic identity
Identity in a digital format. Often involves an identity card with embedded chip, certification, separate signatures for authentication and verification, etc. eID is legally binding and used to sign smart contracts in a number of countries.

email marketing
The promotion of products or services to list subscribers via email.

em dash and en dash
The en dash (longer than a **hyphen**) connects things that are related to each other by distance or range, as in the May–September issue of a magazine (also including June, July, and August). The em dash (longer than an en dash) is used to add an additional thought within a sentence, or to substitute for something missing. *See also:* hyphen.

encryption

The process of encoding messages. Encryption is vital to fintech, the blockchain, and anything else that needs to be secure. Data, like names and numbers, is turned into a code using algorithms (mathematical formulas). A key is required to turn that code back into useful data.

encumber

To license a right to another party, thereby creating restrictions on how that right may be used in the future.

end matter

See: back matter.

endorsement quotes

Short reviews of your book written by a well-known author, professional, or personality in your author niche.

epilogue

A section or chapter at the end of a book that comment on or draws conclusions about what has happened or been explained within the text.

EPUB

A common ebook file format.

epublishing

The publication of digital works such as ebooks.

ereader

A handheld device on which electronic versions of books, newspapers, magazines, etc. can be read.

etailer

An online retailer.

ether

The native cryptocurrency of the Ethereum platform, used to pay for computational services there.

Ethereum

A blockchain-based cryptocurrency platform that runs smart contracts, already in use by writers and artists.

Ethical Author

Alliance of Independent Authors campaign encouraging and educating authors in best practices in writing and publishing.

exclusivity
A publishing contract that binds you solely to one publisher. In self-publishing, being exclusive to one particular store or retailer.

F

Facebook ad
Advertising via Facebook that allows you to choose your target audience based on demographics, behavior, or contact information.

fintech
Financial technology that is allowing the disruption of traditional financial networks, facilitating innovation and the possibility of an author-centric financial model.

first rights
The exclusive right to publish a work for the first time.

font
A specific typeface of a certain size and style. *Compare:* typeface.

footnotes
Reference citations and supplementary information at the bottom of a page.

formatting
The process of designing a book for electronic distribution, with the desired layout, fonts, and appearance. *Compare:* typesetting.

forum
An online place where people with common interests or backgrounds come together to find and share information and discuss topics of interest.

front list
Traditional term for books in their first year of publication.

front matter
The sections of a book preceding the first chapter. *Also:* prelims. *Compare:* back matter.

full-service distribution
Wholesalers and distributors who perform a broad range of services,

such as stocking inventories, operating warehouses, supplying credit, and employing salespeople, as well as delivering goods.

G

galley copy
See: proof.

genre
A general category for a creative work, such as romance, science fiction, mystery.

ghostwriting
Writing all or part of a book on behalf of a collaborator whose name will be listed as the author.

go direct
To publish books to a retailer without the use of an intermediary service like an aggregator or distributor.

Goodreads
A social media site owned by Amazon, which is just for books. Readers connect with friends, get book recommendations, write reviews, and make reading lists.

Goodreads advertising
Pay-per-click advertising on Goodreads.

Goodreads giveaway
An online book giveaway that any Goodreads member can enter.

Google Adwords
Text-based ads that show up next to Google search results, graphic display ads that show up on websites or apps, or YouTube video ads that show up during videos.

Google Play
An ebook retailer which, although still in operation, has been closed to new authors for several years and is not expected to reopen.

Google Preview
Google Play's interface for viewing excerpts of an ebook before purchase. *Compare:* Look Inside the Book.

go wide
To sell books through a variety of retailers; the opposite of exclusivity, in which books are sold through one retailer.
greyscale
A color model that uses only shades of black. *See also:* CMYK, RGB.
guest blogging
Writing a post or short article for someone else's blog.

H

halftone
A method of representing an image with dots of varying sizes.
hardback/hardcover
A book with a hard rather than paper cover; or the cover itself.
hard return
Pressing the enter or return key to force a line break instead of allowing the text to flow naturally.
hashtag
A word or phrase immediately preceded by the # symbol. When you click a hashtag, you see other social media updates containing the same keyword or topic.
headshot
A professional-looking head-and-shoulders photograph used for promotional purposes.
hit
Accessing a web page or a file, image, or script on the page.
house ad
A self-promotional ad that you run on your own website to sell your own products.
hybrid author
An author who uses both trade and self-publishing services. (Not to be confused with hybrid publishing or partnership publishing.)
hybrid publishing
See: partnership publishing.

hyphen
Connects two things that are intimately related, usually words that work together as a single concept or joint modifier (e.g. self-publishing, two-thirds).

I

iBooks
The iBooks Store, an online publisher/retailer for ebooks. Also the application used to read books downloaded from the iBooks Store.
impression
A single display of an advertisement or web page.
imprint
A name used by a publisher to identify their books. Imprints are frequently genre-specific, and a single publisher may have multiple imprints.
inbound marketing
A model that relies on the initiative of customers to find and purchase a product, such as content marketing, social media marketing, and search engine optimization.
independent
Not involving the "Big Five" publishing corporations; self-published.
InDesign
Professional book formatting and design software produced by Adobe.
index
A list directing readers to specific subject matter in a book.
indie author
An author who acts as the creative director of their own books, whether through self-publishing, assisted self-publishing, or traditional publishing. *Compare:* self-publishing, traditional publishing.
Indie Author Fringe
Free online author conference organized three times a year by the

Alliance of Independent Authors, fringe to London Book Fair, Book Expo America, and Frankfurt Book Fair.

Ingram ipage
An online books search, order, and account management platform for bookstores.

IngramSpark
A large publisher and distributor of print-on-demand books and ebooks.

initial coin offering (ICO)
An unregulated means of crowdfunding by which money is raised for a new cryptocurrency, selling tokens in the currency to raise money.

Instafreebie
A streamlined way to send book copies to reviewers, beta readers, or bloggers by providing a link for people to download your book for free.

interior
All content within a book, except the covers. *Compare:* book block.

IPR License
Platform for authors, publishers, and agents to list and license publishing rights, providing access to a global marketplace. Owned by Frankfurt Book Fair with the Copyright Clearance Center.

ISBN (International Standard Book Number)
A unique, numeric identifier for a particular edition and format of a book.

J

jacket
See dust jacket.

joint venture
See: partnership publishing.

JPEG
A format for compressing image files; the most common image format used by digital cameras.

K

KDP Select
An optional program under Kindle Direct Publishing that requires exclusivity in exchange for promotional tools and enrollment in Kindle Unlimited and Kindle Owners' Lending Library.

keyword
A word or phrase used by search engines to identify matching subjects. For example, an edition of *Moby Dick* might have the keywords *whaling, revenge,* and *nautical themes.*

Kindle
Amazon's line of proprietary ebook readers.

Kindleboards
An online discussion forum dedicated to publishing on Amazon.

Kindle Direct Publishing (KDP)
Amazon's publishing and distribution platform for ebooks.

Kindle Owners' Lending Library (KOLL)
A program under Kindle Direct Publishing that allows Amazon Prime subscribers to read one free ebook per month. Enrollment in KOLL is mandatory for KDP Select authors. *See also:* Kindle Unlimited (KU).

Kindle Scout
An Amazon program in which readers nominate books for publication under the Kindle Press imprint. Winners receive a five-year contract, 50% royalties, and a $1,500 advance.

Kindle Singles
Amazon's digital, curated imprint for short works (primarily novellas, short fiction, and long-form journalism).

Kindle Unlimited (KU)
A program under Kindle Direct Publishing that allows subscribers to read ebooks in the KU catalog for free. Enrollment in KU is mandatory for KDP Select authors. *See also:* Kindle Owners' Lending Library.

Kindle Worlds
Amazon's digital publishing platform for fan fiction.

Kobo

A Toronto-based digital publishing platform, initially meant to service users of the Kobo e-reader.

L

launch party

Celebration of the publication of a book. Can be hosted at any suitable location, but popular spots include bookstores, libraries, coffee shops, or the author's home. You can also host a virtual book launch online.

LCCN (Library of Congress Control Number)

A unique identifier assigned to books by the US Library of Congress. *Compare:* ISBN.

legacy publishing

A somewhat derogatory term for trade-publishing.

license

Legal permission granted to someone other than the original holder of a right; for example, permitting a publisher to print a work for which you hold the copyright. *Compare:* copyright.

limited edition

A book printed in limited numbers, usually for special editions.

line editing

See: copyediting.

list price

The recommended retail price of a book. Set by the author or publisher and often referred to as the RRP.

literary agent

Person who acts as an intermediary for an author in transactions with the publisher.

litho printing (lithography)

A method of mass-production printing using wet ink and printing plates. More suitable for longer runs. *See also:* offset printing. *Compare:* digital printing.

Look Inside the Book

An Amazon feature that allows customers to view excerpts from an ebook or print book before buying. *Compare:* Google Preview.

M

makeready stage

Point in the printing process when a text is ready to be printed.

manuscript

Complete version of a book (often as an electronic text file) prepared by the author.

manuscript appraisal

See: content editing.

manuscript conversion

See: conversion.

marketing plan

A strategic plan that details all of the activities you need to deliver to promote yourself and your book.

mass-market paperback

Smaller, less expensive version of a book that is usually printed well after the hardcover and trade paperback versions have been made available.

media kit

A package of key information to send to media or journalists, retailers, book bloggers, event planners, editors, or anyone who plans on writing about you and your book. May include an author photo and bio, a book cover image, a full synopsis, a one-sentence description, book details, frequently asked questions, an excerpt, and reviews or media coverage.

media list

A collection of media outlets and contacts that you reach out to in order to increase awareness of your book.

media outlet

Any channel for disseminating news about your book, such as newspapers, magazines, radio shows, TV shows, online news sites, podcasts, or blogs.

metadata
The details of a book other than its actual text, such as author's name, publisher, book description, ISBN, and keywords.

micropayments
Financial transactions of very small sums of money.

MOBI
Amazon's digital format for Kindle ebooks.

N

NetGalley
An online book reviewing site. Book reviewers, librarians, booksellers, educators, and media professionals request complimentary ebooks in exchange for reviews.

networking
Using and expanding your social network or sphere of influence to promote your book.

newswire distribution
Circulation of news through a service intended for journalists and media outlets.

niche
A specialized target market characterized by a particular interest, topic, or subject.

Nielsen
The sole registrar for ISBNs in the UK and Ireland.

nonexclusive contract
Legal agreement in which the publisher does not exercise exclusive rights over the materials published in your book.

Nook
Barnes & Noble's line of e-readers and associated retailer.

O

offset printing
A method of mass-production printing in which the images on metal plates are transferred (offset) onto rubber blankets or rollers and thereby to paper. *Compare:* digital printing.

off-the-book-page attention
Mention made of a book outside the context of a book review, such as plugging a book on a talk show.

online bookseller/retailer
Internet-based bookstore.

online marketing
Using online methods to advertise, sell, or dispense products.

OUTIA (Open Up To Indie Authors)
Alliance of Independent Authors campaign encouraging bookstores, libraries, reviewing bodies, literary events, and prizes to find ways to include self-publishing writers in their programs. Uses the hashtag #PublishingOpenUp.

out of print (OOP)
Book no longer in a publisher's book inventory (and for which there is no reprint planned).

P

P2P lending
P2P means peer-to-peer, or person-to-person, and refers to anything decentralized and direct. P2P lending is loaning money to individuals without the systems and processes typically used by traditional financial institutions. Instead, it is often handled by digital platforms that use an algorithm to manage transactions between parties.

paperback
A book bound in stiff paper or flexible card. *See also:* mass-market paperback, trade paperback.

partnership publishing
A publishing arrangement in which the author and the publisher both contribute financially to the book's production, sharing risks and rewards. Sometimes used as a euphemism for vanity publishing. *See also:* joint venture, hybrid publishing, self-publishing services, shared publishing, subsidized publishing.

pay per click
See: cost per click

pay per impression
See: cost per impression

pbook
A physical, printed book generally constructed of a number of sheets of paper, bound in cardboard. *See also:* codex.

PDF (portable document format)
A file format popular for its cross-compatibility, particularly in keeping layout and fonts as intended. The preferred file format for print-on-demand and fixed layout ebooks.

perfect bound
An unsewn binding where glue/adhesive attaches the pages at the spine. Usually with a paper cover, hence the more common name paperback. *Compare:* hardback.

permafree
A book permanently available for free from online retailers; a strategy used to increase visibility and gain new readers by giving away a book, often the first in a series.

permission
Agreement from a copyright holder that permits the reproduction or publication of copyrighted material. Also the process of securing agreements from copyright holder.

permissioned blockchain
Blockchain with access restricted to a particular group. *Compare:* unpermissioned blockchain.

pitch emails
Emails targeting media contacts to get coverage for a book, which should include key points about the book and author.

plant costs
Initial costs incurred by a traditional printer in preparation for the first printing run of a given title.

platform
The computer hardware or online system used to run a program or digital tool.

plot
Flow or succession of actions in a story.

podcast
Online audio broadcast available on a website or to download.

prelims
Pages before a book properly begins. May include copyright page, table of contents, acknowledgments, and other publishing information. *Also:* front matter. *Compare:* back matter.

pre-order
A marketing tactic used by authors to offer readers the opportunity of reserving a copy of a book prior to its official release date.

press release
An official announcement that provides information about an event to reporters, bloggers, and other media outlets.

Prime Reading
A program that allows Amazon Prime subscribers to read free ebooks from a catalog of approximately 1,000 titles selected by Amazon.

print-on-demand (POD)
Printing in small quantities or as needed, usually by digital printing.

print ready
Used to describe the final layout file of a book, usually in PDF format, that is ready to go to the printer.

print run
The number of copies printed in a single order.

Pronoun
A now defunct ebook publisher and aggregator.

proof
A copy of a book printed for final inspection and correction of errors. *Also:* galley copy. *Compare:* advance review copy.

proofreading
The final step in the editing process, with a focus on essential corrections such as misspellings, the accuracy of captions, headings, page numbers, etc.

publication date
Official date when a book is to be released to the public.

publicist
Professional or press agent who promotes a book, often by generating free advertising.

publicity tour
Public circuit an author makes to publicize a book, either prior to or soon after the publication date.

PubMatch
Rights management platform that allows authors and publishers to trade publishing rights and permissions with publishers, agents, and other rights buyers. Owned by the London Book Fair.

Q

QR code
A machine-readable code that consists of black and white squares and is typically used for storing URLs.

R

region
A geographical area served by a retailer. For example, Amazon operates separate regional websites for the US, Canada, Mexico, the UK, India, France, Germany, China, Japan, Italy, Spain, the Netherlands, Australia, and Brazil. *Also:* territory.

remainder
A book returned to the publisher after not having sold, often offered for later sale at a discounted price.

return

A book returned to the publisher and refunded after failing to sell in a bookstore.

reversion

The process of reclaiming rights licensed to a publisher.

review

A customer's opinion of a book published on a retailer website or similar venue. *Compare:* editorial review.

RGB

A color model for digital and online use, using red, green, and blue. *See also:* CMYK, greyscale.

rights/publishing rights

The right to publish or produce a book, TV show, film, translation, or other format based on your material, in a particular medium or a particular territory. Granted to the publisher/producer by license.

ROI (return on investment)

The amount you spend versus how much money you earn.

royalties

A percentage of book sales paid to the author. Often used interchangeably with commission.

S

saddlestitch binding

Pages are bound along the fold with two staples.

sales funnel

A process that converts your website and social media visitors into paying readers by convincing them to purchase your books.

sales handle

A one-sentence call to action epitomizing your book, which is frequently used in online marketing.

sales rank

A ranking calculated by Amazon on the basis of daily sales and downloads of a book. *Also:* bestseller rank.

Scrivener
Popular editing and organizational software designed specifically for writers.

secondary rights
The right to resell a work after its first publication.

self-publishing
A form of publishing in which the author oversees the publishing process, retains control over creative decisions and disposition of publishing rights, and bears the costs of production.

self-publishing service
A company or freelancer commissioned by an author to provide any of the seven processes involved in publishing a book: editorial, design, production, distribution, marketing, promotion, or rights service. Some companies offer a full-service package. *Compare*: partnership publishing.

sell sheet
See: advance information sheet.

SEO (search engine optimization)
The process of making your web page more easily findable and indexed by search engines; or more relevant to particular topics in order to attract more visitors.

shared publishing
See: partnership publishing.

shelf life
The time an unsold book remains on the shelf of a retail store before being replaced by fresh or better-selling stock.

short discount
Smaller-than-typical discount on books purchased by retailers and wholesalers.

short-run print
Printing of a limited number of copies of a book in a single print run. Can now be as low as 300–400 copies. For fewer copies, digital printing is generally a better option.

slush pile
The unsolicited manuscripts submitted to a traditional publisher.

small press
Smaller publishing house that releases books often intended for specialized audiences.

smart contracts
Computer programs that automatically execute legally binding contracts. These automated and often blockchain-based computer protocols facilitate, verify, or enforce digital agreements, saving time and reducing costs in common legal and financial transactions and potentially replacing lawyers and banks.

Smashwords
A popular ebook publisher and aggregator.

special sales
Book sales through nonbookstore outlets such as restaurants, gift stores, and health spas.

spine width
Width of part of the book that is visible on a bookshelf. The spine connects the front and back covers.

spiral bound
A method of binding in which wire or plastic is wound through holes punched along the side of a book.

split A/B test
Comparing two versions of something to see which performs better (sometimes called split testing).

structural edit
See: developmental editing.

style sheet
Document prepared during copyediting that records consistency and style decisions, such as how numbers, abbreviations, word usage, and punctuation are to be handled.

subscript
A character (number, letter, or symbol) that is set slightly below the normal line of type. It is usually smaller than the rest of the text.

subsidiary right
The right to publish a work based on the original material but in a

different format (e.g. translations, audiobooks, film). *Also:* subright or sublease.

subsidized publishing
See: partnership publishing.

superscript
A character (number, letter, or symbol) that is set slightly above the normal line of type. It is usually smaller than the rest of the text.

synopsis
A summary introducing your main characters, the main conflict, and the basic emotional arc of your story.

T

table of contents
A list, usually in the front matter, of the book's chapters or main sections and their opening page numbers.

target audience
A specific audience that is most likely to buy your books and is usually based on demographic information or areas of interest.

termination clause
Section in a contractual agreement that specifies particular behavior, actions, or events that would result in nullification of the contract.

territory
See: region.

thumbnail
A small representation of a larger image, intended as a preview.

token
A type of security issued in digital form. For example, a READ token gives the owner the right to read an ebook.

trade paperback
A book bound with a paper or heavy stock cover, usually with a larger trim size than that of a mass-market paperback.

trade-publisher (traditional publisher)
A company that invests in publishing a manuscript, submitted by an

author, and controls most creative and marketing decisions. Trade-publishers bear the cost of production and promotion in exchange for a sizable percentage (typically 90%+) of the receipts from a book.

trim size
The dimensions of a print book, specifically the page size.

Tweep
Followers on the social media platform Twitter.

Twitter handle
The name, always preceded by @, that is used on the social media platform Twitter.

typeface
A set of letters, numbers, and characters that are all in the same style and that are used in printing. *Compare:* font.

typesetting
Professional preparation of a book for print with the desired layout, fonts, and appearance. *Compare:* formatting.

U

unit cost
The production or base cost of printing and putting together a book.

unique visitor (unique)
An individual who accesses a website. *Compare:* hit.

universal link
A link that allows you to simplify the process of author discoverability by directing your book customers to your preferred online retailer.

university press
Publishing house owned and operated by a university. Such presses typically issue academic material, often including works by their own academics.

unpermissioned blockchain
Blockchain open to all.

unsolicited manuscript
Manuscript sent to a publisher who did not request it.

URL (uniform resource locator)
The address of a web page.

V

vanity publishing (press)
A generally exploitative form of publishing in which the author pays to have their book published, with excessively high fees and substandard service. *Compare:* partnership publishing.

virtual book tour (VBT)
Advertisement strategy centered on publicizing a book on the internet, including ads on websites that the target audience frequents and book giveaways.

vlogging
A blog that contains video content. This growing segment of the blogosphere is sometimes referred to as the vlogosphere.

W

wholesaler
A company that sells books to retailers, often in bulk and at a discount.

word of mouth
Publicity through recommendations from friends, family, and associates.

ABOUT THE AUTHOR

Jim Giammatteo

Giacomo (Jim) Giammatteo is the author of gritty crime dramas about murder, mystery, and family. He also writes nonfiction books including the "No Mistakes" Careers series. He lives in Texas where he and his wife have an animal sanctuary with 45 loving "friends." His website is at giacomogiammatteo.com.

John Doppler

From the sunny California beaches where he washed ashore in 2008, John Doppler scrawls tales of science fiction, urban fantasy, and horror—and investigates self-publishing services as the Alliance of Independent Authors' Watchdog. John relishes helping authors turn new opportunities into their bread and butter and offers terrific resources for indie authors at Words on Words (johndopp.com/writers). He shares his lifelong passion for all things weird and wonderful on The John Doppler Effect (johndopp.com).

OTHER BOOKS FROM ALLI

ALLi Successful Self-Publishing Series

1: Creative Self-Publishing: How Indie Authors Publish for Pleasure and Profit by Orna Ross

3: How Authors Sell Publishing Rights by Helen Sedwick and Orna Ross

4: How to Get Your Self-Published Book into Bookstores by Debbie Young

ALLi Campaign Series

Opening Up to Indie Authors by Debbie Young and Dan Holloway

Blockchain for Books by Orna Ross and Sukhi Jutla

OUR ADVICE TO YOUR INBOX?

Sign up here for a weekly round-up from our self-publishing advice blog:

selfpublishingadvice.org/signup

REVIEW REQUEST

If you enjoyed this book, please consider leaving a brief review online at the retailers' site where you purchased it, on social media, and on your website, to help make it more discoverable for other authors.

76386468R00227

Made in the USA
San Bernardino, CA
11 May 2018